Contents

This offers a brief biography of Plath's life, which will introduce the reader to Plath's publishing history, taking into consideration her early publishing successes in journals and magazines, and also the post-humous publication of *Letters Home* and her journals. Initial reviews of *The Bell Jar* and her short stories are considered, before suggesting some recent critical studies for further interest. A brief survey of the critical reception of Plath's poetry introduces the central debates and critics.

1960s: Reviews of *The Colossus* and *Ariel*

This chapter offers some of Plath's insights into her work, primarily the 1962 essay, 'Context'. The critical reception of the first two collections of poetry, *The Colossus* published in 1960 and the posthumous publication of *Ariel* in 1965, will be illustrated by a selection of reviews mainly chosen from *Sylvia Plath: The Critical Heritage*, which highlight the dramatic contrast in response to the early and late work. Influential essays by A. Alvarez, M. L. Rosenthal, George Steiner and Robert Lowell begin to determine Plath's poetry as confessional, extremist and biographical.

1970s: Unifying Strategies and Early Feminist Readings

This chapter covers the decade following the publication of two further poetry collections, *Crossing the Water* and *Winter Trees* in 1971. Initially discussing the critical reception of these volumes, this chapter develops to consider the first full-length studies of Plath's poetry. Although the criticism develops in several directions, many critics share a desire for locating unifying strategies in Plath's poetry. We will consider several approaches, including early attempts at psychoanalytic readings such as

David Holbrook's *Sylvia Plath: Poetry and Existence* (1976), and readings concerned with defining the mythical structure of Plath's poetry such as Judith Kroll's *Chapters in a Mythology*. The debate over Plath's use of Holocaust imagery continues, with critics such as Irving Howe and Joyce Carol Oates accusing Plath of misappropriation and solipsism. The second half of the 1970s is dramatically defined by the emergence of feminist literary studies which, by adopting a largely biographical/cultural approach, begin to establish Plath at the centre of a feminist canon. Extracts from two central articles by Sandra Gilbert and Carole Ferrier illustrate the shift in emphasis towards defining Plath as a woman writer.

'Waist-Deep in History': Cultural and Historical Readings

The publication of Plath's *Collected Poems* in 1981 causes many critics to reconsider their earlier evaluations of Plath's poetry, leading to a wider understanding of the complexity and diversity of her work. This chapter considers an increasing interest in contextually based, historical and cultural interpretations of Plath's poetry throughout the 1980s. Stan Smith and James E. Young justify the historical references of Plath's work, in particular her so-called 'Holocaust poetry', suggesting that Plath's poetry reflects a postwar political consciousness. Brief extracts from Linda W. Wagner, Margaret Dickie and most recently Garry Leonard, argue for an awareness of Plath as a product of her culture, while also recognising her critique of the ideology of femininity. Finally, Pamela Annas's reading of the increasingly discussed 'Three Women' expands on the feminist interpretations of the previous decade, while Alan Sinfield's inclusion of Plath in *Literature, Politics and Culture in Postwar Britain* (1989) raises questions over nationality, and presents his persuasive 'case for extremism'.

Feminist and Psychoanalytic Strategies

This chapter focuses on the developments in psychoanalytic and feminist criticism throughout the 1980s and early 1990s. Although grounded in cultural studies, feminist analysis of the poetry begins to engage with the theories of *écriture féminine* in studies such as Alicia Ostriker's *Stealing the Language* (1986) and Liz Yorke's *Impertinent Voices* (1991), moving the critical attention towards poems that are concerned with issues of sexuality and selfhood. Steven Gould Axelrod (1990) and Toni Saldivar (1992) develop sophisticated psychoanalytic readings of Plath, although they disagree on the nature of Plath's subjectivity. The centrepiece of this chapter is Jacqueline Rose's impressive and stimulating book *The Haunting of Sylvia Plath*, a text that profoundly influences Plath studies. Concentrating on the chapters most concerned with textual readings, 'No Fantasy Without Protest' and centrally 'Daddy', this generous selection will provide the reader with an appreciation of the critical importance of Rose's argument.

New Directions

This chapter suggests possible new directions in Plath studies, offering extracts from recent articles, many of which are in some way a response to Jacqueline Rose. Anthony Easthope forcefully questions Rose's reading of 'Daddy', while Al Strangeways rejuvenates the discussion of mythic structure in Plath's poetry. Anna Tripp's impressive use of post-structuralist practices offers a revised feminist perspective of 'I Am Vertical', while Marilyn Manners further engages with *écriture féminine* in her comparison of Plath and Cixous. The recent publication of *Birthday Letters* may engender further discussion of the literary relationship between Plath and Ted Hughes and, here, Sarah Churchwell critiques Hughes's critical essays on Plath. We conclude with extracts from Tracy Brain's discussions of Plath in the light of ecofeminism, and her consideration of nationality and midatlanticism.

INTRODUCTION

■ Arrogant, I think I have written lines which qualify me to be The Poetess of America (as Ted will be The Poet of England and her dominions). Who rivals? Well, in history Sappho, Elizabeth Barrett Browning, Christina Rossetti, Amy Lowell, Emily Dickinson, Edna St. Vincent Millay – all dead. Now: Edith Sitwell and Marianne Moore, the aging giantesses, and poetic godmother Phyllis McGinley is out – light verse: she's sold herself. Rather: May Swenson, Isabella Gardner, and most close, Adrienne Cecile Rich – who will soon be eclipsed by these eight poems: I am eager, chafing, sure of my gift, wanting only to train and teach it – I'll count the magazines and money I break open by these eight best poems from now on. We'll see . . . □

Sylvia Plath, journal entry, March 1958[1]

In these confident, boastful, yet surely teasing, comparisons, Plath offers herself as the latest addition to the lineage of women's poetry. A young woman of twenty-five, Plath's confidence springs from her recently written cluster of poems inspired by the paintings of De Chirico and Rousseau, two of which, 'On the Decline of Oracles' and 'The Disquieting Muses', were to be included in her first collection of poetry, *The Colossus and Other Poems* (1960). Innocently raising questions of gender and nationality by identifying herself as the now redundant 'poetess', and foreshadowing Hughes's poet laureateship, these comments clearly show Plath's ambition and dedication to writing as she dismisses McGinley's 'light verse' in favour of a place among the literary nobility. That Plath has gained her place within the twentieth century is certain: her second volume of poetry, *Ariel*, published in 1965, is one of the defining texts of this period, and the eventual appearance of her *Collected Poems* in 1981 distinguished her as a major writer. Within the space of a few years, Plath's poetry has received considerable critical attention, often becoming the focus of critical and theoretical debates, particularly in relation to feminism. For the student new to Plath's poetry, the volume of criticism can often be daunting and confusing, Plath variously described as feminist and feminine, mythological and political, an English Romantic and an American Modernist. In the following discussion and selection of extracts, this guide will explore and explain these various responses within their critical context, considering the significant trends and identifying the influential critics on Plath's poetry. Rather than reductively arriving at a single, authoritative understanding of Plath's poetry, this guide will provide a critical tour of the poetry, placing the dominant critical positions into perspective by considering their impact and influence on Plath studies. This is not to suggest, however, a harmonious progression of opinion; there are disagreements and disputes, many crosscurrents and undercurrents of opinion, critical approaches that are complementary and oppositional. This guide, however, will map out the broad, shifting, critical demarcations in Plath studies. While the most influential and major extracts rightly dominate this guide, where space permits I have offered extracts from less well-known pieces, which often foreshadow later debates. This introduction begins with a short biography of Plath, focusing on her development as a writer. A novelist as well as a poet, we will briefly consider the critical reception of Plath's prose and offer some suggestions for further reading, before providing an overview of the critical developments in Plath studies.

From a very young age, Plath had aspirations to be a writer. Born in 1932, the oldest child of academic parents, Plath's childhood was spent in Winthrop, a seaside suburb of Boston, until, a couple of years after her father's death, the family moved inland to Wellesley, an experience which she explores in her 1962 essay 'Ocean 1212-W': 'And this is how it stiffens, my vision of that seaside childhood. My father died, we moved inland. Whereon those nine first years of my life sealed themselves off like a ship in a bottle – beautiful, inaccessible, obsolete, a fine, white flying myth.'[2] She regularly published poetry and stories in local newspapers and her school magazine until, in 1950, after nearly fifty rejections, the American teen magazine, *Seventeen*, accepted her short story 'And Summer Will Not Come Again'. The following year Plath entered Smith College, an exclusive women's college near Boston, with a part scholarship from the popular novelist Olive Higgins Prouty. A gifted student, Plath won a guest editorship for the college edition of *Mademoiselle* magazine in August 1953, an experience later shared by the feminist critic Sandra M. Gilbert who wittily describes the contest as 'the literary young woman's equivalent of being crowned Miss America.'[3] Although Plath's journalese does not compare to her later poetry in terms of accomplishment, many recent critics have explored the concerns and interests that this often formulaic work shares with the intensity of *Ariel*. On her return from New York and *Mademoiselle*, assumed to be suffering from emotional stress, Plath attempted suicide in the summer of 1953. Plath's life can fascinatingly be traced through text and print; while she was missing from her family home, unconscious in the basement after an overdose, the Boston press ran dramatic headlines appealing for her safety: 'Beautiful Smith Girl Missing at Wellesley', an experience with fame and notoriety that is reflected in Joan's hoarding of lurid suicide newspaper clippings in Plath's 1963 novel *The Bell Jar*.[4] At Olive Higgins Prouty's expense, Plath recovered in McLean hospital in Belmont, until she returned to Smith in January 1954. Graduating *summa cum laude* in 1955, Plath won a prestigious Fulbright scholarship to Cambridge University, entering Newnham College in October 1955.

Although over the next few years Plath was to struggle with career and emotional choices, she was certain of her need to be a writer. After marrying Ted Hughes in April 1956, they increasingly devoted their lives to writing. With Plath's encouragement, Hughes entered and won the New York Poetry Center competition with *Hawk in the Rain* in 1957, which subsequently established him as a major young poet, while Plath was regularly published in poetry journals, finally publishing *The Colossus* in 1960. While they were a professional literary couple, both promising and admired poets, Hughes was undoubtedly the literary star, photographed in 1960 with T.S. Eliot, Louis MacNiece, W.H. Auden and Stephen Spender, all five representing Three Generations of Faber Poets. In January 1959, while Plath and Hughes were living in Beacon Hill near Boston, *Mademoiselle* featured 'Four Young Poets', including this former guest editor's success story: returning from an English education with a handsome poet husband, Plath was the embodiment of *Mademoiselle*'s dreams and ambitions. Yet the accompanying photograph is rather telling; Hughes, darkly handsome and imposing, studies a book while Plath, crouched behind the chair, peers over his shoulder, appearing to be almost complementary.[5] As we will see, many feminist critics have returned to this dynamic, concerned with the difficulty of establishing oneself as a woman poet in the mid-century.

In 1960, Plath and Hughes settled in England, living in London before moving to Devon in late 1961. Now the parents of two small children, it was hoped Devon would provide a sanctuary for writing and family life, but the marriage deteriorated in 1962 and Hughes left the family home. Plath continued to live in Devon, writing many of the poems that would be collected in *Ariel*: '. . . writing like mad – have managed a poem a day before breakfast. All book poems. Terrific stuff, as if domesticity had choked me',[6] until in December 1962, she moved to London to live in what she felt was a fortuitous home, excitedly writing to her mother: 'it is *W.B. Yeats' house* – with a blue plaque over the door, saying he lived there!' (*LH*, pp. 477–8). Her novel *The Bell Jar* was published in January 1963 under Plath's chosen pseudonym Victoria Lucas. Plath, perhaps disingenuously, referred to it as a 'pot-boiler' (*LH*, p. 477), although it received admiring reviews welcoming 'Lucas' as a female Salinger. Despite the recognition of this work, Plath is believed to have suffered from emotional exhaustion and depression, taking her own life in February 1963. Although a published and hard-working writer, Plath was known in the gossipy London literary circles more for being the deserted wife of Ted Hughes than as a major poet of this century.

To return briefly to the opening quotation, Plath's identification of Adrienne Rich as her rival invites an early comparison. In 1958, the two seemed to have a lot in common; both women were of a similar age, graduates of exclusive American colleges, promising and talented poets producing precise, disciplined, accomplished poems, which pleased an academic readership. In her early publications, Rich's softening inclusion of 'Cecile', which almost appears to suggest that femininity is her middle name, seems to reflect the societal expectations of a woman poet in the mid-century. Yet Rich decisively challenged these expectations; the publication of her poetry collection *Diving Into the Wreck* (1976) is recognised as a feminist landmark, while her further contributions to feminist debates as a critic and theorist included her seminal *Of Woman Born: Motherhood as Experience and Institution* which briefly discusses Plath and her mother.[7] For critics, there is a sense of progression and development in Rich's work, a productive exchange between her critical writing and her own poetry.

In contrast, while the critic approaching Plath is presented with a fairly substantial body of writing, including her poetry, novel, and short stories, there are few of her own insights into the work. A couple of significant essays, 'Context' (1962) and 'A Comparison' (1962), a much quoted interview with Peter Orr for the British Council, *Letters Home*, which documents her correspondence with her mother, and a published journal which prematurely finishes in 1959, do offer limited reflections on her own work. In October 1962, Plath wrote to her mother, '. . . I am a genius of a writer; I have it in me. I am writing the best poems of my life; they will make my name.' (*LH*, p.468) While this is an acute realisation of her own talent, there is an unfortunate lack of critical perspective in Plath's commentary on her own writing. Subsequently, the initial reviews of *Ariel*, posthumously published in 1965, struggle to progress beyond the drama of her life. Plath's early death seems to lock her writing into a self-perpetuating, enclosed crisis of interpretation. The early critical obsession with Plath's life limits the readings, however incisive and insightful they may be, to problematic biographical interpretations, initially very concerned with debating the morality of Plath's writing. One of the major, if not crucial, developments in recent Plath studies has been the increasing critical distance placed between her personal life and her writing.

Although Plath is primarily considered a poet, there are also many critical studies of *The Bell Jar*, and of her short stories, some of which are collected in *Johnny Panic and the Bible of Dreams and other prose writings.*

The Bell Jar had been praised initially, but when it was reissued in Britain in 1966 under Plath's own name, critics largely compared it unfavourably to the poetry; C. B. Cox, for example, described it as 'a first attempt to express mental states which eventually found a more appropriate form in the poetry', although he does commend a 'notable honesty' and 'something of that fierce clarity so terrifying in the great poems of *Ariel*'.[8] When it was eventually published in the United States in 1971, American critics responded rather more enthusiastically, convinced by the 'American college girl of the fifties' who seemed to embody the tensions and paranoias of that era,[9] while Tony Tanner's influential *City of Words: American Fiction 1950–1970* (1971) did, however fleetingly, refer to *The Bell Jar*.[10] Many of the critics explored in this Guide also offer complementary readings of *The Bell Jar*, but for an entertaining yet intelligent consideration of the novel's context I would recommend Pat MacPherson's *Reflecting on The Bell Jar*.[11] The other significant critical debate surrounding *The Bell Jar* has been concerned with issues of women's writing and autobiography, and Linda Anderson's recent *Women and Autobiography in the 20th Century: Remembered Futures* contains an excellent chapter on Plath.[12] While *The Bell Jar* is established as an epochal American novel, Plath's short stories, mainly written for a magazine audience, disappointed critics on publication in 1977, reviewers finding them largely contrived and formulaic.[13] However, Margaret Atwood perceptively recognised *Johnny Panic* as:

■ . . . the record of an apprenticeship. It should bury forever the romantic notion of genius blossoming forth like flowers. Few writers of major stature can have worked so hard, for so long, with so little visible result. The breakthrough, when it came, had been laboriously earned many times over.[14] □

In recent years, Jacqueline Rose has argued most forcefully for the relevance of Plath's short stories to an appreciation of the poetry in her valuable consideration of high and low forms of art in Plath's writing.[15]

In 1975, the publication of *Letters Home: Correspondence 1950–1963*, containing a generous selection of letters that Plath wrote to her mother, seemed to critics dramatically to contradict the image of Plath found in her poetry, Jo Brans reviewing them as an exercise in 'bright insincerity'.[16] Marjorie Perloff locates an inverted prose version of the poems in the letters, suggesting that Plath carefully constructed a perfect daughter persona, 'Sivvy', in order to satisfy her mother while she revealed her true, antagonistic self through the poetry.[17] Along with the letters, the American publication of *The Journals of Sylvia Plath* in 1982 contributed to readings of Plath's poetry, as this Guide will show. However, the incompleteness of the journals, which end in 1959,[18] and the highly selective editing of the extracts have led to considerable discussion over authorial ownership and control, which often overshadows the contribution of the journals to an appreciation of the poetry. We will see the way in which critics such as Jacqueline Rose and Sarah Churchwell approach these problems in relation to the poetry, but for a critical analysis of the editing of the journals I would recommend Dee Horne's article 'Biography in Disguise: Sylvia Plath's Journals' where she compares the published journals with the original manuscripts, arguing that much of Plath's 'creativity and sensuality . . . her pain and anger' is edited from the text.[19] Fuller versions of the journals and Plath's letters, along with poetry manuscripts and other personal documents, are housed in two Plath collections: Smith College broadly contains material from Plath's marriage including the *Ariel* manuscripts, and Indiana University holds material from Plath's life in America, including the full manuscript of *Letters Home*.

The Plath Estate's notorious resistance to biographies has not successfully deterred their publication. To date, there are five biographies of Plath, several personal memoirs (the most notable of which is Nancy Hunter Steiner's *A Closer Look at Ariel*), and a recent metabiography, *The Silent Woman: Sylvia Plath and Ted Hughes* by Janet Malcolm, an investigative study into the genre of biography that takes Plath as its subject.[20] Anne Stevenson's finely written *Bitter Fame: A Life of Sylvia Plath* (1989) is the only biography to have received assistance from the Plath Estate, and is thus the most detailed, but it has come under severe criticism for being overly unsympathetic towards Plath.[21]

Chapter one of this Guide will consider the reviews of *The Colossus* (1960) and *Ariel* (1965), contrasting the earlier, considered response to *The Colossus*'s crafted, accomplished poems, with the critical shock that greeted *Ariel*. Plath's early death undoubtedly determines the critical response, with the contemporary opinion former, A. Alvarez, stressing the extremist nature of Plath's poetry, while the influential critic M.L. Rosenthal defines Plath as a confessional poet belonging to a school of American poetry; their two interpretations determine readings of her work for several years. Initially in chapter two, we will consider the publication of further collections of poetry in 1971, *Crossing the Water* and *Winter Trees*, which allow for the first full-length studies of the poetry to emerge, tentatively announced by Eileen M. Aird's biographically driven *Sylvia Plath: Her Life and Work* (1973). The 1970s become increasingly dominated by the totalising, mythic interpretations of Judith Kroll and Jon Rosenblatt, alongside the problematic psychoanalytical readings of David Holbrook. The second half of this decade is authoritatively defined by the emergence of a feminist literary criticism which concentrates on constructing an alternative canon of women's writing. Sandra M. Gilbert's essay on Plath, collected in the seminal study of women's poetry, *Shakespeare's Sisters*, is one of the first critical studies to define Plath primarily as a woman poet, powerfully arguing that she seeks a true female authorial voice through the restrictions of the masculine, lyrical 'I'.

The following two chapters are concerned with the impact of theoretical advances in literary criticism on discussion of Plath's poetry. Chapter three focuses on the emerging historical and political readings of her work, largely informed by Marxist criticism and often preoccupied with the debate surrounding Plath's so-called 'Holocaust' poetry. Critics such as Stan Smith and James E. Young define Plath as a politically aware poet, often reading her work as embodying the consciousness of an era. This chapter develops to consider increasingly cultural, gendered readings, principally Pamela Annas's reflections on the self and society in Plath's prose-play 'Three Women', and Alan Sinfield's consideration of the particular meaning of the Holocaust as metaphor for women writers. The following discussion of essentially feminist critics in chapter four is designed to illustrate the impact of *l'écriture féminine*, in particular the French feminist theorists' interest in 'the body', on Plath criticism, but it is important to stress that this is largely an adaptation of these ideas in order to complement a predominantly materialist, Anglo-American approach to feminism, evident in the negotiations of Alicia Ostriker, Susan Van Dyne and Liz Yorke. Chapter four concludes with extracts from biographical/psychoanalytic readings of Plath's poetry by Stephen Gould Axelrod and Toni Saldivar, before a detailed consideration of Jacqueline Rose's ground-breaking book *The Haunting of Sylvia Plath*.

Chapter five gives us an opportunity to anticipate possible new directions in Plath criticism, many of which are a response to Rose. Anna Tripp's use of post-structuralist strategies is an attempt to retrieve the authorial 'I' from restrictive biographical interpretations, while Marilyn Manners offers a further engagement with French feminism in her comparative reading of Plath and Hélène Cixous. We finish with two articles by Tracy Brain, which consider Plath's writing in the light of eco-feminism, further portraying her as a politically engaged writer, and the midatlantic nature of Plath's poetry, raising issues of nationality and alienation.

CHAPTER ONE

1960s: Reviews of *The Colossus* and *Ariel*

■ [. . .] the first British publisher I sent my new collection of poems to (almost one-third written at Yaddo;[1] 48 poems in all, after countless weedings and reweedings) wrote back within the week accepting them! Amaze of amaze. I was so hardened to rejections that I waited till I had actually signed the contract [. . .] before writing to you. □

Sylvia Plath to Aurelia Plath, February 11, 1960[2]

After struggling for over a year to find an American publisher for her first volume of poetry, and after much 'weedings and reweedings', Plath secured the British publisher Heinemann to publish the collection she now called *The Colossus and Other Poems*,[3] which appeared in October 1960, in the week of her twenty-eighth birthday.[4] Her delight in this success is evident from the above letter to her mother where she signs herself 'Your new authoress', a playful signature but one that reveals her dedication and determination to become a professional writer; and her favoured, yet disappointed, choice of the United States for initial publication reveals her desire to be recognised in her own country.[5] Heinemann did arrange Alfred Knopf as the American publisher, and the American edition appeared in May 1962, reduced to forty poems after much of 'Poem for a Birthday' was cut due to concerns that the series was too derivative of Theodore Roethke. On both sides of the Atlantic, *The Colossus* was favourably, if fairly quietly, received by the critics, and Plath subsequently became a successful, although minor, literary figure. While living in England, *Critical Quarterly* commissioned her to edit an American supplement, she recorded her own poetry for the BBC, and she was regularly asked to contribute reviews, essays and poetry to leading journals. However, it was not until the posthumous publication of *Ariel* in April 1965, followed by the American edition in 1966, that Plath became established, perhaps more accurately notorious, and the intense debate over her reputation as a poet began. This chapter will consider the initial reviews of both these volumes, selected from the standard source *Sylvia Plath: The Critical Heritage*,[6] alongside the critical reception of Plath's poetry in the 1960s, contrasting the calm, measured response to *The Colossus* to the critical shock that *Ariel* induced. We will also consider key extracts from Plath's own reflections on her poetry in her letters and essays.

Reviews of *The Colossus and Other Poems*

By the time Plath signed the contract for *The Colossus*, she had been a published writer for many years, confessing in an interview from October 1962: 'I wrote my first poem, my first published poem, when I was eight-and-a-half years old. It came out in *The Boston Traveller* and from then on, I suppose, I've been a bit of a professional.'[7]

After her early prize-winning successes and great promise, *The Colossus* temporarily rescued Plath from fears of stasis in her writing. Although her poetry regularly appeared in journals, and she had a 'first-reading' contract with the *New Yorker*, she desperately wanted her early achievements to be realised in a volume of poetry. The British critics responded well to *The Colossus*, particularly praising Plath's considerable achievements in clarity of form and language, admiring the careful precision and intelligence of her poetry. Bernard Bergonzi's review in the *Manchester Guardian* is typical of this approval, concentrating on Plath's impressive control of language:

■ Miss Sylvia Plath is [. . .] a young American poetess whose work is most immediately noticeable for the virtuoso qualities of its style. . . . She writes of people or natural objects in a detached yet sympathetic way, with a fastidious vocabulary and a delicate feeling for the placing of the individual word.[8] □

Critics responded enthusiastically to Plath's technical skill, variously enjoying her 'cleverness', 'complex but beautifully clear syntax'[9] and 'verbal precision'.[10] Welcomed as a poet of 'exceptional promise',[11] a gifted writer with admirable technique, this was generally agreed to be an assured first collection. These reviews of *The Colossus* now seem characteristic of the critical climate of the early 1960s, consistently adopting a slightly paternal tone, offering a measured, scholarly response to clever, intellectually stimulating poetry. John Wain's description of *The Colossus* as 'clever, vivacious poetry, which will be enjoyed most by intelligent people capable of having fun with poetry' is typical of an academic response.[12] A.E. Dyson's illuminating review in the *Critical Quarterly*, which concentrates on the themes of *The Colossus*, briefly compares Plath's poetry to Ted Hughes's, anticipating a line of inquiry that we will see developed in later chapters. In this short article, Dyson perceptively observes the distinction between their early writing: 'Ted Hughes is heroic and violent in his dominating mood, Sylvia Plath brooding and tentative.'

Also, at this early stage of Plath's career, Dyson almost intuitively enters into a debate that is to dominate Plath studies for many years by drawing attention to the possible latency of 'Mushrooms': 'The associations which the word 'mushroom' have for us since Hiroshima may enhance the effectiveness, which is not, however, dependent upon them.'[13] Any reservations about the effectiveness of the poetry are focused on a concern that Plath could be too derivative, articulated by Roy Fuller's criticism of her 'controlled and rather ventriloquial voice',[14] a concern later echoed by the American reviewers.

The most perceptive review of *The Colossus*, which most accurately defines the nature of Plath's developing talent, comes from the influential critic A. Alvarez, who was literary editor for the *Observer*. Published under the title 'The Poet and the Poetess', Alvarez's admiration and particularly incisive criticism established Plath on the literary scene in London, and led to a friendship developing between the poet and the critic.[15] Alvarez begins his review by dismissing conventional literary reservations, before enthusing over the effective combination of Plath's technical skill and concentrated intensity, especially in his famous reference to the dark, mysterious world lurking at the edge of her vision.

■ Sylvia Plath's *The Colossus* needs none of the usual throat-clearing qualifications, to wit: 'impressive, considering, of course, it is a first volume by a *young* (excuse me), *American* poetess.' Miss Plath neither asks excuses for her work nor offers them. She steers clear of feminine charm, deliciousness, gentility, supersensitivity and the act of being a poetess. She simply writes good poetry. And she does so with a seriousness that demands only that she be judged equally seriously. She makes this plain in the first stanza of her first poem ['The Manor Garden']:

> The fountains are dry and the roses are over.
> Incense of death. Your day approaches.
> The pears fatten like little buddhas.
> A blue mist is dragging the lake.

There is an admirable no-nonsense air about this; the language bare but vivid and precise, with a concentration that implies a great deal of disturbance with proportionately little fuss.

I think Miss Plath can allow herself this undemonstrativeness because most of her poems rest secure in a mass of experience that is never quite brought out into daylight:

> . . . the students stroll or sit,
> Hands laced, in a moony indolence of love –
> Black-gowned but unaware
> How in such mild air
> The owl shall stoop from his turret,
>   the rat cry out.

It is this sense of threat, as though she were continually menaced by something she could see only out of the corners of her eyes, that gives her work its distinction.

She is not, of course, unwaveringly good. At times her feeling weakens, the language goes off on its own and she lands in blaring rhetoric. At other times she hovers close to the whimsy of fairy stories. But here her tense and twisted language preserves her and she ends with something ominous, odd, like one of the original tales from Grimm. But it would be a strange first book that had no faults; *The Colossus* has more than enough excellent poems to compensate for them.[16] □

The Colossus was finally published in America in May 1962, and again critics, many of whom were familiar with Plath's writing, responded positively to her technical assurance. Mark Linenthal identified Plath as 'among the best poets of her generation', and in a decade in which Plath could be reviewed as Mrs Ted Hughes,[17] Linenthal praises her talent in fairly typical terms: 'Her poems are impressive because of their firm wedding of technique to statement and because her work is feminine, never effeminate.'[18] Yet amid these high critical commendations was a shared feeling among reviewers that Plath still had to discover that most elusive of literary qualifications: her true voice. While Nicholas King highly praises the 'objective language' of *The Colossus*, he suggests that this objectivity 'is still more of an attitude than a conviction'.[19] The poet and critic E. Lucas Myers, a close friend of Ted Hughes, came to know Plath when she was a young wife and mother, and in one of the first American responses to *The Colossus* identifies the strengths and weaknesses of the collection. Titled 'The Tranquilized Fifties', Myers's review incisively embodies the American response to *The Colossus* by sweetening negative criticism with admiration of her skill and confidence. He begins by surveying the state of American poetry in what he views as an increasingly bland, conformist, commercial decade:

■ The poets who first appeared during the fifties have some distinction: the best of them write with technical skill, intelligence, and resourcefulness. Yet a stack of their books, read through, leaves a sense of dissatisfaction, just as living through the decade did, [. . .]

What fails to emerge is a statement, in some measure coherent, of the experience of a decade, such as can be made out from the poetry of the twenties or the thirties. □

The Colossus, however, is welcomed into this sterile era for its boldness, and appropriateness of form. After praising the poetry's innovative subject matter, Myers concludes by admiring Plath's 'considerable objectivity', located in the skillful observer position, which she often adopts, while urging her to limit this feeling of restraint and discard the slightly clichéd poetic phrasing of some of her poetry:

■ There is not an imperfectly finished poem in Sylvia Plath's book. She is impressive for control of form and tone, appropriateness of rhythmic variation within the poem, and vocabulary and observation which are often surprising, and always accurate: 'The waves'/Spewed relics clicker masses in the wind,' or (the place is a laboratory), 'In their jars the snail-nosed babies moon and glow.' 'Poem for a Birthday', in seven parts,[20] concludes the volume, and catalogues the sensation of pregnancy in rich images altogether astonishing to the mere male, even though he may have heard described the parti-colored dreams of pregnant women. [. . .] I am struck, in reading a lot of her poems together, by her posture *vis-à-vis* her material, which is one of considerable objectivity, even when the material is her child-hood, her Muses, her pregnancy. The focus of the emotions, like the visual focus, is sharp and is found at medium distance or more, the perspective in which we see her spinster, her strumpet, her suicide, the perspective which, in the following from 'Blue Moles' is character-istically restored from the initial close-up by the words 'easy' and 'often': '[. . .] What happens between us/Happens in darkness, van-ishes/Easy and often as each breath.' Poems should be criticized as they are, not as the critic thinks they might have been, and these poems, as they are, merit anybody's reading; but I can not help won-dering what will happen if, in Miss Plath's second volume of poems, the emotional distance is shortened – no melting of the moulds her craftsmanship has created, I think, but a lesser frequency of phrases like, 'Now, this particular girl,' 'Mark, I cry,' 'gimcrack relics,' and more of the pressure of 'Lorelei,' of the close of 'The Colossus,' or of 'Departure,' which is an example of her finest writing.[21] □

Reviews of *The Colossus*, then, were scholarly, reserved if not even pater-nalistic, fairly conservative, and largely impressed by Plath's technical skill, while encouraging her to be less derivative or self-conscious. It is tempting to read these reviews as college report cards with Plath praised as the A grade student presenting accomplished, technically perfect poetry, offering a collection that aims to please the critics. Discussion of *The Colossus* is certainly overshadowed by the later poetry, but it does contain poems that remain central to an understanding of Plath's poetic development, placed in perspective with the publication of the *Collected Poems* in 1981.

In concluding these reviews, it is worthwhile briefly to consider the re-evaluation of *The Colossus* following Plath's death and the subsequent publication of *Ariel*. In a memorial broadcast from 1963, A. Alvarez reflects on the weaknesses of *The Colossus* in light of the emerging *Ariel* poems: '[. . .] certainly it's beautiful, but also peculiarly careful, held in check, a bit ornate and rhetorical.'[22] M.L. Rosenthal's review of the re-issue of *The Colossus* in 1967, two years after the British publication of *Ariel*, reflects accurately on the initial reaction to *The Colossus*:

■ Miss Plath's promise was quickly recognised, despite a general impression of academic precisionism. Except for a few poems whose bitter, concentrated force made them unlike the rest, her work seemed 'craft'-centred and a bit derivative. □

Rosenthal goes on to reconsider his own reading of *The Colossus* in the light of *Ariel*, revealing the impact of Plath's death on the process of rereading.[23]

■ After one has experienced *Ariel*, the poet's death obsession and its deep link with her fear of yielding to the impersonal processes of her body stand out in *The Colossus* with morbid emphasis. [. . .] the theme of suicide is seen to be more pervasive than was at first evident. [. . .] Familiarity with later poems like 'Lady Lazarus' and with the autobiographical novel *The Bell Jar* has sensitised me to the orientation of much *The Colossus*. [. . .] I do not mean that *The Colossus* is artistically on the same level as *Ariel*, but that it has become far more interesting than it was at first. □

The issues raised in this review concerning *Ariel* will be fully explored in the following section, but here it is important to note the shift in critical opinion revealed by the concern that some aspects of *The Colossus*, which were now self-evident, had been carelessly overlooked. Rosenthal concludes by chiding himself in an extremely revealing comment on the nature of reviewing poetry:

■ I feel rebuked not to have sensed all these meanings in the first place, for now they seem to call out from nearly every poem.[24] □

Reviews of *Ariel*

In an interview from 1962, Peter Orr asks Plath whether her poems are designed to be read aloud. Her reply is illuminating in terms of identifying the change in her style in the space of a few years:

■ [. . .] *The Colossus*, I can't read any of the poems aloud now, I didn't write them to be read aloud. They, in fact, quite privately, bore me. These ones that I have just read, the ones that are very recent, I've got to say them, I speak them to myself, and I think that this in my own writing development is quite a new thing with me [. . .][25] □

Plath's own evaluation of the prosodic shift in her writing towards poetry that is rhythmically designed to be spoken seems to welcome a new freedom and confidence in her expression, a relaxation of her tendency towards a mannered, academic style. Her 1962 essay 'Context', commissioned by the *London Magazine* and collected in *Johnny Panic and the Bible of Dreams* in 1977, is her most comprehensive statement on the nature of her late poetry, in which she suggests an almost osmotic relationship between her poetry and the tensions of the era:

■ The issues of our time which preoccupy me at the moment are the incalculable genetic effects of fallout and a documentary article on the terrifying, mad, omnipotent marriage of big business and the military in America – 'Juggernaut, The Warfare State,' by Fred J. Cook in a recent *Nation*. Does this influence the kind of poetry I write? Yes, but in a sidelong fashion. I am not gifted with the tongue of Jeremiah, though I may be sleepless enough before my vision of the apocalypse. My poems do not turn out to be about Hiroshima, but about a child forming itself finger by finger in the dark. They are not about the terrors of mass extinction, but about the bleakness of the moon over a yew tree in a neighboring graveyard. Not about the testaments of tortured Algerians, but about the night thoughts of a tired surgeon.

In a sense, these poems are deflections. I do not think they are an escape. For me, the real issues of our time are the issues of every time – the hurt and wonder of loving; making in all its forms – children, loaves of bread, paintings, buildings; and the conservation of life of all people in all places, the jeopardizing of which no abstract doubletalk of 'peace' or 'implacable foes' can excuse. [. . .]

Surely the great use of poetry is its pleasure – not its influence as religious or political propaganda. Certain poems and lines of poetry seem as solid and miraculous to me as church altars or the coronation of queens must seem to people who revere quite different images. I am not worried that poems reach relatively few people. As it is, they go surprisingly far – among strangers, around the world, even. **Farther than the words of a classroom teacher or the prescriptions of a doctor; if they are very lucky, farther than a lifetime.** □

JP, pp.92–3

The critics also respond to the maturation of Plath's poetry, but in a very different context: Plath's sudden and unexpected death in 1963 inevitably comes to determine the critical response of the 1960s.

In sharp contrast to *The Colossus*, the publication of *Ariel* in 1965 seems to stun, astound, shock and excite the critics in various measures. Not published until two years after Plath's death and hailed as a 'major literary event', it is difficult to overestimate the impact and significance of *Ariel* in establishing Plath's reputation, and her place within the literary canon. Although continuing to praise Plath's astonishing technical skill,[26] the intensive critical response is dominated by biographical readings primarily concerned with exploring the dangerous, problematic relationship between poetry and life that Plath's suicide seemed to confront. Many parallels are drawn with Keats as both poets are read as doomed, tragic yet brilliant figures whose artistic outbursts marked the almost inevitable end of their lives.[27] Stunned by Plath's suicide, many critics interpret the poems as highly personal and mysteriously powerful, seeming to conflate Plath with the personae of her poems, mythologising her in such archetypal terms as 'glamorous with misery [. . .] both murderer and victim, Sylvia Plath looms up as our infirm prophet', 'shrill, penetrating, visionary'.[28] These are terms of critical interpretation which really only begin to be challenged in the 1970s by the early feminist revisions of Plath's poetry and the myths surrounding it, a crucial debate we will see emerge in the following chapter. However, in the 1960s, the dominant critical response to *Ariel* is intense, mythicising, complex, seemingly struggling with a need to understand and comprehensively categorise these poems.

Prior to the publication of *Ariel*, several of Plath's most powerful poems, including 'Daddy' and 'Lady Lazarus', appeared in journals and literary reviews, and thus on news of her death, critics were able to offer a limited response to the startling development in Plath's writing, and initiate a swelling of literary anticipation. A. Alvarez remained an authority on Plath's work, and is the first critic to evaluate these astonishing poems in a memorial broadcast for the BBC's Third Programme in 1963. Intended both as a tribute and as a preliminary attempt to apprehend these few published poems, Alvarez begins by providing details of Plath's life, before accurately describing the rhythmic development of Plath's poetry as: 'the difference [. . .] between finger-count and ear-count'. Alvarez defines the progression in Plath's poetry by stating that she had 'discovered her own speaking voice; that is, her own identity' before exploring the way in which Plath relates the 'direct relevance of experience' through a reading of 'Ariel'. It is, however, Alvarez's reading of 'Daddy', the poem that dominates the critical response to *Ariel*, that introduces arguments and debates that remain at the heart of Plath studies for many years: the legitimacy of the Holocaust images, the appropriateness of psychoanalytic terms, and the relationship between poetry and death:

■ [In 'Daddy'] she goes right down to the deep spring of her sickness and describes it purely. What comes through most powerfully, I think, is the terrible unforgivingness of her verse, the continual sense not so much of violence – although there is a good deal of that – as of violent resentment that this should have been done to *her*. What she does in the poem is, with a weird detachment, to turn the violence against herself so as to show that she can equal her oppressors with her self-inflicted oppression. And this is the strategy of the concentration camps. When suffering is there whatever you do, by inflicting it upon yourself you achieve your identity, you set yourself free.

Yet the tone of the poem, like its psychological mechanisms, is not single or simple, and she uses a great deal of skill to keep it complex. Basically, her trick is to tell this horror story in a verse form insistently jaunty and ritualistic as a nursery rhyme. And this helps her to maintain towards all the protagonists – her father, her husband and herself – a note of hard and sardonic anger, as though he were almost amused that her own suffering should be so extreme, so grotesque. The technical psychoanalytic term for this kind insistent gaiety to protect you from what, if faced nakedly, would be insufferable, is 'manic defence'. But what, in a neurotic, is a means of avoiding reality can become, for an artist, a source of creative strength, a way of handling the unhandleable, and presenting the situation in all its fullness. When she first read me the poem a few days after she wrote it, she called it a piece of 'light verse'. It obviously isn't, yet equally obviously it also isn't the racking personal confession that a mere description or précis of it might make it sound.

Yet neither is it unchangingly vindictive or angry. The whole poem works on one single, returning note and rhyme, echoing from start to finish

> You do not do, you do not do [. . .]
> [. . .] I used to pray to recover you.
> Ach, du. [. . .]

There is a kind of cooing tenderness in this which complicates the other, more savage note of resentment. It brings in an element of pity, less for herself and her own suffering than for the person who made her suffer. Despite everything, 'Daddy' is a love poem.

[. . .] The achievement of her final style is to make poetry and death inseparable. The one could not exist without the other. And this is right. In a curious way, the poems read as though they were written posthumously. It needed not only great intelligence and insight to handle the material of them, it also took a kind of bravery. Poetry of this order is a murderous art.[29] □

Although Alvarez felt it necessary to clarify these final comments in a post-script in 1966, his suggestion of inevitability continued to be influential.[30]

Also prior to the publication of *Ariel*, C.B. Cox and A.R. Jones's 1964 essay 'After the Tranquilized Fifties, Notes on Sylvia Plath and James Baldwin' develops E. Lucas Myers's earlier review of *The Colossus*, by identifying Plath and Baldwin as the defining voices of their generation. Cox and Jones propose that Plath's writing mirrors the social chaos of the 1960s as powerfully as Eliot's *The Waste Land* shadows the turmoil of the 1920s.[31] Focusing on 'Daddy', they maintain that Plath's poetry moves beyond

■ [. . .] the expression of a personal and despairing grief. The poem is committed to the view that this ethos of love/brutality is the dominant historical ethos of the last thirty years. The tortured mind of the heroine reflects the tortured mind of our age. The heroine carefully associates herself and her suffering with historical events. For instance, she identifies herself with the Jews and the atrocities of 'Dachau, Auschwitz, Belsen' and her persecutors with Fascism and the cult of violence. The poem is more than a personal statement for, by extending itself through historical images, it defines the age as schizophrenic, torn between brutality and a love which in the end can only manifest itself, today, in images of violence. This love, tormented and perverse, is essentially life-denying: the only escape is into the purifying freedom of death.[32] □

While Cox and Jones appear to anticipate the much later historical approach of critics such as Stan Smith, and in some ways correspond with Plath's own understanding of her poetry as expressed in 'Context', it is Alvarez's seductive and dramatic argument on the almost inevitable nature of Plath's poetry and life which shapes the subsequent reviews on publication of *Ariel*.

On publication, *Ariel* was named 'Spring Choice' by the influential Poetry Book Society in February 1965, and was popular with the poetry reading public. Ted Hughes's brief article to accompany the choice is his earliest comment on the poetry, and is one of the early defining statements on Plath's work:

■ Behind these poems there is a fierce and uncompromising nature. There is also a child desperately infatuated with the world. And there is a strange muse, bald, white and wild [. . .] floating over a burningly luminous vision of a Paradise. A Paradise which is at the same time eerily frightening, an unalterably spot-lit vision of death.

[. . .] But the truly miraculous thing about [Plath] will remain the fact that in two years, while she was almost fully occupied with children and house-keeping, she underwent a poetic development that has hardly any equal on record, for suddenness and completeness. The birth of her first child seemed to start the process. All at once she could compose at top speed, and with her full weight. Her second child brought things a giant step forward. All the various voices of her gift came together [. . .]

Ariel is not easy poetry to criticise. It is not much like any other poetry. It is her. Everything she did was just like this, and this is just like her – but permanent.[33] □

Here, Hughes clearly suggests the link between maternity and creativity. Many recent critics, as we will see in later chapters, closely critique Hughes's editing and commentary on Plath, particularly his rearrangement of the *Ariel* manuscript,[34] but in this early statement, it is important to recognise the connection Hughes draws between Plath's text and her life, and also the implied inexplicable nature of Plath's poetry, as if the critical language to discuss her work does not exist.

In the months that followed, *Ariel* was reviewed by many prominent and respected critics. While praising the power of these poems, Stephen Spender does endorse the female poet as mystic, almost otherworldly, in excessive terms which become characteristic of *Ariel* reviews: 'Their power, their decisiveness, the positiveness and starkness of their outline, are decided not by an identifiable poetic personality expressing herself, but by the poet, a woman finding herself in a situation, out of which she produces these disconcerting, terrifying poems.'[35] One critic states that 'to be given over to poems like these is to stand at the poet's side frozen, but powerless to reach a hand out as she falls' while another, in contrast to Cox and Jones, finds *Ariel* 'filled with violence, but it is the violence of the disturbed mind rather than society'.[36] Other reviewers, while impressed and excited by the energy of Plath's poetry, are disturbed by their perceived triumphalism: 'The difficulty here is that death is seen in romantic terms, unsupported by expressed religious beliefs, as a purification, a peace, and in some ways a triumph.'[37]

Along with many other reviewers in 1965, Alvarez's 'Poetry in Extremis' considers *Ariel* alongside Robert Lowell's similarly epoch-making *For the Union Dead*. Alvarez credits Lowell's earlier work, 'Life Studies', as the origin of the extension of modernism he terms Extremist poetry, a style which he perceives Plath to be extending and embodying. Alvarez reflects on the time that had lapsed since his initial response, acknowledging the emergence of a seductive myth concerning Plath, which he appears to be fuelling:

■ It is over two years now since Sylvia Plath died suddenly at the age of 30, and in that time a myth has been gathering around her work. It has to do with her extraordinary outburst of creative energy in the months before her death, [. . .] All this last verse was intensely personal, nearly all was about dying. So when her death finally came it was prepared for and, in some degree, understood. However wanton it seemed, it was also, in a way, inevitable, even justified, like some final unwritten poem. □

Reiterating much of the argument of his memorial broadcast, Alvarez describes *Ariel* as containing 'that combination of exploratory invention, violent, threatened personal involvement and a quizzical edge of detachment. The poems are casual yet concentrated, slangy yet utterly unexpected. They are works of great artistic purity and, despite all the nihilism, great generosity.' Rejecting the term confessional – 'It is too concentrated and detached and ironic for "confessional" verse, with all that implies of self-indulgent cashing-in on misfortunes' – Alvarez concludes by specifying the nature of Plath's art as Extremist: 'Sylvia Plath learned a great deal from the extremist art – the perceptions pushed to the edge of breakdown – that Robert Lowell first handled in "Life Studies".'[38] His highly influential review sets the tone for many later reviewers and readers.

In his review 'Poets of the Dangerous Way', M.L. Rosenthal shares Alvarez's need to categorise but disagrees on the denomination, suggesting that Plath possessed an 'almost demonically intense commitment [. . .] to the confessional mode'. Again outlining the details of Plath's biography, Rosenthal highlights the dangerous nature of this poetry:

■ [. . .] she threw herself into that last passionate burst of writing that culminated in *Ariel* and in her death, now forever inseparable. We shall never be able to sort out clearly the unresolved, unbearably exposed suggestibility and agitation of these poems from the purely aesthetic energy that shaped the best of them. [. . .] Sometimes Sylvia Plath could not distinguish between herself and the facts of, say, Auschwitz or Hiroshima. She was victim, killer, and the place and process of horror all at once.

This is not the whole picture. Though Sylvia Plath may become a legend, we ought not to indulge in over-simplification. There are some lovely poems in the book ('Poppies in October,' for instance) that are

cries of joy despite a grim note or two. There is rhythmic experimenta-
tion looking to the future, in particular with an adaptation of
Whitman's characteristic line; and beyond that, the sheer wild leap
into absolute mastery of phrasing and the dynamics of poetic movement in the title-poem alone, despite its tragic dimension, cannot but
be considered an important kind of affirmation. But there are poems
too that are hard to penetrate in their morbid secretiveness, or that
make a weirdly incantatory black magic against unspecified persons
and situations, and these often seem to call for biographical rather
than poetic explanation.

Under all other motifs, however, is the confusion of terror at death
with fascination by it. The visions of the speaker as already dead are
so vivid that they become yearnings toward that condition. 'Death &
Co.' is one of several nearly perfect embodiments of this deeply compulsive motif. It moves from a revolted imagery of death as a
condor-like predator, a connoisseur of the beauty of dead babies, to a
disgusted yet erotic picture of him as would-be lover, and at last to a
vision of the speaker's own death such as I have mentioned:

> I do not stir.
> The frost makes a flower,
> The dew makes a star,
> The dead bell,
> The dead bell.
>
> Somebody's done for.

Thinking of this pitifully brief career, it is hard not to ask whether the
cultivation of sensibility is after all worth the candle. The answer is
yes, for reasons that I hope we all know – yet it seems important to
raise the questions anyway.[39] □

Rosenthal expands this argument and clarifies his position on Plath as
belonging to a 'confessional' school of poetry in his 1967 revised edition
of *The New Poets*. Qualifying 'Lady Lazarus' and Robert Lowell's 'Skunk
Hour' as true examples of confessional poetry, Rosenthal explains this
label in the following terms:

■ [. . .] they put the speaker himself at the center of the poem in such
a way as to make his psychological vulnerability and shame an
embodiment of his civilization [. . .] Sylvia Plath's poem presents the
author in the midst of what proved to be her final, and finally successful, suicide attempt. She sees herself as a skilled suicide-artist whose
self-loathing the sadistic and voyeuristic audience, easily envisioned

as the Nazi-tending aspects of the civilization, appreciates all too well.[40] □

A highly influential study, *The New Poets* placed Plath within a recognisable literary movement, or group, and although the term 'confessional' came under criticism for being inaccurate and vague, it effectively defined Plath's work for many years.

Many critics take their cue from Alvarez and Rosenthal, concentrating on the perceived intense subjectivity of the poetry, describing it as 'condensed, elliptical, and autobiographical'.[41] Critical opinion is further influenced by Robert Lowell's foreword to the 1966 American edition of *Ariel*. It is a much quoted and referred to essay, both by early reviewers concurring with his image of Plath, and later feminist critics deconstructing what is viewed as male literary chauvinism, as we will see in later chapters. Lowell principally provides the rhetoric for imaginatively figuring Plath while offering an insightful reading of the audacity and power of *Ariel* from a fellow poet:

■ In these poems, written in the last months of her life and often rushed out at the rate of two or three a day, Sylvia Plath becomes herself, becomes something imaginary, newly, wildly and subtly created – hardly a person at all, or a woman, certainly not another 'poetess,' but one of those super-real, hypnotic, great classical heroines. This character is feminine, rather than female, though almost everything we customarily think of as feminine is turned on its head. The voice is now coolly amused, witty, now sour, now fanciful, girlish, charming, now sinking to the strident rasp of the vampire – a Dido, Phaedra, or Medea, who can laugh at herself as 'cow-heavy and floral in my Victorian nightgown.' [. . .]

Everything in these poems is personal, confessional, felt, but the manner of feeling is controlled hallucination, the autobiography of a fever. She burns to be on the move, a walk, a ride, a journey, the flight of the queen bee. She is driven forward by the pounding pistons of her heart. [. . .] What is most heroic in her, though, is not her force, but the desperate practicality of her control, her hand of metal with its modest, womanish touch. Almost pure motion, she can endure 'God, the great stasis in his vacuous night,' hospitals, fever, paralysis, the iron lung, being stripped like a girl in the booth of a circus sideshow, dressed like a mannequin, tied down like Gulliver by the Lilliputians [. . .] apartments, babies, prim English landscapes, beehives, yew trees, gardens, the moon, hooks, the black boot, wounds, flowers with mouths like wounds, Belsen's lampshades made of human skin, Hitler's homicidal iron tanks clanking over Russia. Suicide, father-hatred, self-loathing – nothing is too much for the macabre gaiety of her control. Yet it is too much; her art's immortality is life's disintegration. The surprise, the shimmering, unwrapped birthday present, the transcendence 'into the red eye, the cauldron of morning,' and the lover, who are always waiting for her, Death, her own abrupt and defiant death. [. . .]

There is a peculiar, haunting challenge to these poems. [. . .] These poems are playing Russian roulette with six cartridges in the cylinder, a game of 'chicken,' the wheels of both cars locked and unable to swerve. [. . .] And yet Sylvia Plath's poems are not the celebration of some savage and debauched existence, that of the 'damned' poet, glad to burn out his body for a few years of continuous intensity. This poetry and life are not a career; they tell that life, even when disciplined, is simply not worth it. [. . .][42] □

P. N. Furbank's review introduces psychiatric terms to describe both the poems and Plath, stating that the last poems 'are an attempt to give words to what the psychiatrists call 'the non-me',[43] while Richard Tillinghurst offers the conjectural claim that these are 'poems of schizophrenia, or rather poems by a schizophrenic who had painstakingly, over a period of years, mastered the craft of poetry'.[44] This is a diagnosis that is to gain some currency in the 1970s and which finds its apotheosis in David Holbrook's *Sylvia Plath: Poetry and Existence* (1976).[45] Hugh Kenner's review 'Arts and the Age, on *Ariel*', however, introduces a stern voice of reason, encouraging critics to recognise and appreciate the control and skill of these poems, which seem to be firing the critics' imaginations:

■ There's a lot of nonsense being talked about these poems, as if, for instance, they were unmediated shrieks from the heart of the fire. [. . .] But like Villion, whom legend has writing *Le Testament* under the shadow of the hangman, Sylvia Plath was counting her lines and governing her rhetoric. [. . .] The resulting control, sometimes *look* of control, is a rhetoric, as cunning in its power over our nerves as the stream of repulsions. [. . .] On the death poems, [. . .] fingerprints of contrivance don't show, and I'd point to her mustering of the craft that was necessary in that harrowing time as the victory for which she deserves to be celebrated: that, and not the shrieking 'sincerity.'[46] □

Similarly, in a review that briefly compares Plath to Emily Dickinson, John Malcolm Brinnin contends: '[. . .] what we have here is not, as some bewildered critics have claimed, the death rattle of a sick girl, but the defiantly fulfilling measures of a poet', and tellingly concludes: 'Taken in small – one is almost forced to say, medicinal – doses, she is a marvel.'[47]

The 1960s also sees the publication of several essays that begin attempts to assess Plath as a poet. We will finish this chapter with short extracts from two of the most notable essays. Alicia Ostriker's 'The Americanization of Sylvia Plath' (1968) is the first considered analysis of nationality in Plath's writing, which Ostriker identifies as determinedly American. Plath is identified as belonging to an 'American grain [. . .] which, since the nineteenth century, has been deliberately antibelletristic, deliberately naïve, programmatically occupied with climbing over the enclosures of established forms, and perpetually re-insisting that the true function of the writer is the documentation of physical and emotional facts, in a fashion as close to journalism as possible'.[48] Listing both 'major and minor' American writers, all incidentally male, Ostriker suggests that 'the native American tradition continually produces writers who write as if art were literally supposed to represent life without falsification [. . .]', an attitude arising from a Western tradition that encourages 'individualism and the cult of experience [. . .]'.

Ostriker concludes with a comparison between Plath and Emily Dickinson in which she defines the nature of American poetry:

■ I remember another poem of Emily Dickinson's, one which begins 'The heart asks pleasure first' and concludes with 'the liberty to die.' In that nutshell rests the connection between American narcissism and American self-destructiveness. We are 'free' to slide from one to the other. It is true for us that the blood jet is poetry and that there is no stopping it. Sylvia Plath's poetry is a withering into the truth of a national predicament.[49] □

The final commentary in this chapter is George Steiner's influential review of *Ariel*, 'Dying is an Art', which, by considering work from both volumes, offers the first major assessment of Plath's career. Although this article is mainly known for Steiner's comments on the Holocaust poetry, which we will turn to shortly, it is worth noting his occasional perceptive comments on the poetry's fascination with the physical body, which pre-empt later critical discussions on physicality. Although undoubtedly written in misogynist terms, Steiner does recognise a concern with the experience of a woman's body:

■ Undoubtedly, the success of ['Poem for a Birthday'] arises from the fact that Sylvia Plath had mastered her essential theme, [. . .] the infirm or rent body, and the imperfect, painful resurrection of the psyche, pulled back, unwilling, to the hypocrisies of health. [. . .]

[. . .] so sharply feminine and contemporary [. . .] This new frankness of women about the specific hurts and tangles of their nervous-physiological makeup is as vital to the poetry of Sylvia Plath as it is to the tracts of Simone de Beauvoir or to the novels of Edna O'Brien and Brigid Brophy. Women speak out as never before:

> The womb
> Rattles its pod, the moon
> Discharges itself from the tree with nowhere to go.
> ('Childless Woman')

> They have swabbed me clear of my loving associations.
> Scared and bare on the green plastic-pillowed trolley
> ('Tulips')

[. . .] It is the need of a superbly intelligent, highly literate young woman to cry out about her especial being, about the tyrannies of blood and gland, of nervous spasm and sweating skin, the rankness of sex and childbirth in which a woman is still compelled to be wholly of her organic condition. Where Emily Dickinson could – indeed was obliged to – shut the door on the riot and humiliations of the flesh, thus achieving her particular dry lightness, Sylvia Plath 'fully assumed her own condition'. [. . .][50] □

Identifying the 'vivid and disturbing' impact of *Ariel* on both critics and readers, Steiner's closing comments on the so-called 'Holocaust' poetry, particularly his analogy with Picasso, were to stoke the controversy concerning the legitimacy of Plath's metaphors. His defence that the Holocaust has 'stepped outside the real', raising questions over the limits of representation, is an argument that we will see developed by such later critics as James E. Young and Jacqueline Rose. Steiner's famous parallel between 'Daddy' and Picasso's *Guernica* suggests that both speak directly to the trauma of their generation, yet, even with this qualification, Steiner fears the ethical risk of these images:

■ Sylvia Plath had no personal, immediate contact with the world of the concentration camps. [. . .] But her last, greatest poems culminate in an act of identification, of total communion with those tortured and massacred. [. . .]

Sylvia Plath is only one of a number of young contemporary poets, novelists and playwrights, themselves in no way implicated in the actual holocaust, who have done most to counter the general inclination to forget the death camps. Perhaps it is only those who had no part in the events who *can* focus on them rationally and imaginatively; to those who experienced the thing, it has lost the hard edges of possibility, it has stepped outside the real.

Committing the whole of her poetic and formal authority to the metaphor, to the mask of language, Sylvia Plath *became* a woman being transported to Auschwitz on the death trains. The notorious shards of massacre seemed to enter into her own being:

> A cake of soap,
> A wedding ring,
> A gold filling.
> ['Lady Lazarus']

In 'Daddy' she wrote one of the very few poems I know of in any language to come near the last horror. It achieves the classic act of generalization, translating a private, obviously intolerable hurt into a code of plain statement, of instantaneously public images which concern us all. It is the 'Guernica' of modern poetry. And it is both histrionic and, in some ways, 'arty' as is Picasso's outery.

Are these final poems entirely legitimate? In what sense does anyone, themselves uninvolved and long after the event, commit a subtle larceny when they invoke the echoes and trappings of Auschwitz and appropriate an enormity of ready emotion to their own private design? Was there latent in Sylvia Plath's sensibility, as in that of many of us who remember only by fiat of imagination, a fearful envy, a dim resentment at not having been there, of having missed the rendezvous with hell? In 'Lady Lazarus' and 'Daddy' the realization seems to me so complete, the sheer rawness and control so great, that only irresistible need could have brought it off. These poems take tremendous risks, extending Sylvia Plath's essentially austere manner to the very limit. They are a bitter triumph, proof of the capacity of poetry to give to reality the greater permanence of the imagined. She could not return from them.[51] □

Throughout the 1960s Plath is increasingly recognised as a significant, if not yet major, writer, but critics seem to experience difficulty in interpreting the work, often resorting to excessive language and description. Mary Kinzie accurately defines this initial reaction: '[. . .] they sense her importance, but they cannot verbalize it.'[52] While often recognising the uncomfortableness of assigning her to the 'confessional' school, critics could see no other alternative, and tended on the whole to view her talent as rather singular. An early attempt at inclusiveness which places Plath within an alternative canon is the classic 1968 study *Thinking About Women* by Mary Ellman, one of the first feminist critics to discuss Plath's work. Ellman draws attention to Plath's depiction of the body, but it is a discussion which has shifted from the inherent self-revulsion identified by Steiner to assertive violation: 'Menstruation [. . .] is now socially so concealed as to seem more denied than before. It is perhaps this sense of reconstituted taboo that has prompted Doris Lessing, Sylvia Plath and Anne Sexton to violate it.' Although lacking in textual analysis of Plath's poetry, Ellman's witty study does anticipate the challenging feminist interpretations of the 1970s, and, like much later criticism, it takes issue with the critics' fantasies of Plath, especially Lowell's configuring of the 'poetess':

■ A little cloudburst, a short heavy rain of sexual references. The word *poetess*, whose gender killed it long ago, is exhumed – to be denied. [. . .] But poetess is only part of the general pelting away at the single fact that Sylvia Plath belonged to a sex (that inescapable membership) and that her sex was not male – *woman, heroines, feminine, female, girlish, fanciful, charming, Dido, Phaedra, Medea, Vampire,* too.[53] □

As Ellman's belligerency reveals, on the eve of the 1970s the social and literary climate was certainly changing from that of the era when Plath imagined herself 'The Poetess of America'.

CHAPTER TWO

1970s: Unifying Strategies and Early Feminist Readings

THE 1970s is an exciting and productive period for Plath criticism. This decade sees the American publication of *The Bell Jar* along with the publication of Plath's letters to her mother, *Letters Home: Correspondence 1950–1963* in 1975, and a collection of her short prose pieces, *Johnny Panic and the Bible of Dreams and other prose writings* in 1977. With the publication of two further volumes of poetry in 1971, *Crossing the Water* and *Winter Trees*, critics are able to form more complex responses to Plath's work, often rejecting the limitations of 'extremist' or 'confessional' to become more interested in highlighting the differences rather than similarities between Lowell and Plath.[1] Yet they do remain heavily influenced by a biographically driven approach, encouraged and informed by A. Alvarez's *The Savage God: A Study of Suicide* in 1971 and Edward Butscher's biography, *Sylvia Plath: Method and Madness* in 1976. However, during the decade, critics read Plath's poetry less as a symptom of a personal psychosis, and increasingly in relation to universal mythic and patriarchal structures. In particular, feminism offers an empathetic reading of Plath and her poetry, often countering the confusion that had greeted *Ariel*.

The first half of the 1970s is largely concerned with reviews of the emerging poetry and initial, even tentative, full-length studies such as Eileen M. Aird's *Sylvia Plath: The Woman and Her Work*. Also, 1970 sees the appearance of the first collection of essays and reviews, *The Art of Sylvia Plath*, which includes Anne Sexton's memoir 'The Barfly Ought to Sing'. In the second half of the 1970s, the volume of critical debate increases with the appearance of several book-length studies and the publication of two further collections of essays. *Sylvia Plath: The Woman and the Work*, edited by Butscher, retains a biographical direction while offering a fairly contentious collection of essays, followed by *Sylvia Plath, New Views on the Poetry* (1979), a well-organised collection of

predominantly commissioned essays, many of which intelligently foreshadow the work of the following decade. Throughout the 1970s, critics
reveal an increasingly holistic approach to Plath's ouevre, impelled by
the desire to identify an encompassing factor in Plath's writing often
through the application of a mythological, psychoanalytic or thematic
approach. Poems such as 'Daddy' are increasingly viewed as part of a
complex personal narrative, either psychic or mythic, rather than the
political analogies suggested by some earlier commentators. Whatever
their approach, critics became increasingly interested in issues of duality
and conflict in the poetry, influenced by such recently published poems
as 'In Plaster'.[2] The publication of *Letters Home*, which many reviewers
read as Plath's struggle to conceal the creative inner self under a conformist veil of 'bright insincerity',[3] seemed to embody the emerging
notions of the divided self.

Towards the end of the 1970s, the publication of several essential
feminist studies, such as Elaine Showalter's *A Literature of Their Own*,
Ellen Moer's *Literary Women*, and, significantly for Plath studies,
Shakespeare's Sisters: Feminist Essays on Women Poets edited by Sandra M.
Gilbert and Susan Gubar in 1979, define what is broadly recognised as an
Anglo-American feminist approach to literature. Initially concerned with
challenging the male-dominated canon of English literature, these critics
wished to establish and explore an alternative tradition, one that
accepted the canon's literary privileging of writers such as Jane Austen
and Virginia Woolf, but, crucially, reconsidered the critical figuring of the
'woman writer' and attempted to place their work within a continuum
of women's writing. Out of this basic premise, many debates began that
continue into the following decade, with Plath situated at the heart of
many of these discussions, Ellen Moers stating 'No writer has meant
more to the current feminist movement . . .'.[4] Through attentive textual
analysis, critics in the 1970s begin tentative attempts to read Plath's
poetry beyond the facts of a suicide.

This chapter will briefly consider the critical reception of *Crossing the
Water* and *Winter Trees*, and offer extracts from the major, defining works
of this period. We will consider the critical works in two sections: the
early 1970s followed by the late 1970s.

The decade begins with critics welcoming the publication of two further volumes of Plath's poetry, *Crossing the Water* and *Winter Trees*.[5]
Although expensive, limited edition collections of Plath's poetry were
available,[6] the affordability and accessibility of these two volumes, both
edited by Ted Hughes, enabled critics to form a fuller appreciation of
Plath's poetic development, and subsequently produce the first full-
length critical studies. Reviews were positive and generally less
hyperbolic than the reaction to *Ariel*, one critic welcoming *Crossing the
Water* as 'perfectly satisfying in the way only major poetry can be', while

another suggests that the poetry of *Winter Trees* 'on the whole, represents Sylvia Plath at her best'.[7] This praise continues in Linda Ray Pratt's review of both volumes: 'Plath's images combine the stunning intensity and originality of her best poems with an occasional grace of tenderness and melancholy that is lacking in the near hysterical poems of *Ariel*.'[8] On the other hand, Robin Skelton's review continued the perception of Plath's work as embodying 'dangerous distortions', containing evidence of 'neurotic self-absorption'.[9]

Crossing the Water's preliminary note indicating that 'with a few exceptions, the poems in this volume were written in 1960 and 1961', led many critics to interpret the suggested 'transitional' nature of these poems as an explanation for the dramatic poetic breakthrough that seemed to occur suddenly between *The Colossus* and *Ariel*. 'Billed as "transitional poems" they help to bridge the gap between the sober, workmanlike verses of *The Colossus* and the wild, expressionistic outcries of *Ariel*.'[10] Reviewers emphasise an increasing sense of unity within Plath's oeuvre, often illustrated by affinities with both the late and early poetry. Eileen M. Aird recognises that:

■ A poem like 'Wuthering Heights' has very close affinities with some of the earlier poems, particularly 'Hardcastle Crags'. Both poems are about the same area of West Yorkshire, both reject the Romantic celebration of unity with Nature in favour of an uncompromising delineation of a stony force striving to subdue man into its own bleak pattern [. . .] However the poem also has affinities with poems in *Ariel*. [. . .] This sense of oneself as inanimate and without identity is a recurrent element in *Ariel*, notably in 'Tulips' where the depression and lethargy which follows illness is conveyed in the poet's description of herself as a 'cut-paper shadow', a phrase which also occurs in the title poem of *Crossing the Water*.[11] □

Helen Vendler's review of *Crossing the Water* in the *New York Times Book Review* dismisses the fashionable tendency of applying psychiatric terms to the poetry, sensibly stating that: 'Some critics have invoked the word "schizophrenic" in talking about these poems, but Plath's sense of being several people at once never here goes beyond what everyone must at some time feel',[12] before offering an insightful reading of 'split selves' in 'Two Sisters of Persephone' and 'In Plaster'. Vendler proceeds to suggest that Plath reveals a solipsistic relationship with nature:

■ Plath would like, in distrust of mind, to trust nature, and yet she ends, in this volume, by refusing nature any honorable estate of its own. [. . .] The poet's eye bounds the limits of her world, and all of nature exists only as a vehicle for her sensibility. The wind stops her breath 'like a bandage'; the sky exists as her 'ceiling' with an 'old star-map' on it; the night sky is 'only a sort of carbon paper' poked through with holes; the new moon looks like 'the skin seaming a scar.' Some such scrim-curtain of pain veils all images of the natural world in reductive metaphors, till we ask whether there ever was, in Sylvia Plath at this time, a genuine sense of something existing that was not herself. [. . .] Too often in this volume a metaphor is chosen and used without any full sense of its own unalterable solidity apart from the poet's use of it. □

This is a point with which other critics concur, reading Plath as isolated and removed from nature, and it is useful to compare this approach with the recent argument for reading Plath in the light of ecofeminism, which we will consider in the final chapter. Although hostile, Vendler does accept Plath's own self-criticism of these transitional poems, recognising them as 'pointing to a depth opening towards *Ariel*'.[13] Robert Boyers, however, takes issue with Vendler's criticism of Plath's solipsism, urging the reader to

■ [. . .] go back to the poems themselves, and study them even as the *Ariel* poems resound in the inner ear, and consider again whether the former work upon you exactly as do the latter. That the Plath of the present volume would like to trust nature and cannot, we do not deny, but that she permits it some authentic and uncompelled expression in the dozen best poems is a certainty.[14] □

Winter Trees is a similarly slim volume of Plath's poetry yet its impact is crucial: a much admired volume of mature poetry, it is seen to clarify the domestically contextualised tensions within Plath's poetry, and, with the inclusion of 'The Swarm', completes the series of poems recognised as the 'bee sequence'.[15] Ted Hughes again provides a note on publication, stating that these poems were written in 'the last nine months of Sylvia Plath's life' excepting the verse-play commissioned for radio, 'Three Women', initially broadcast by the BBC on 13 September 1962.[16] In a decade in which Plath is depicted as being in thrall to Alvarez's savage god of suicide, and accused by Butscher of embodying the spirit of the mythic 'bitch-goddess', critics are in some ways surprised by *Winter Trees*. Many of these poems are situated within a domestic world, concerned with exploring the experience of being a mother. This is a largely un-expected view of Plath – although complemented by Barbara Hardy's earlier essay 'The Poetry of Sylvia Plath: Enlargement or Derangement', which includes a sympathetic and incisive reading of the *Ariel* poem 'Nick and the Candlestick'.[17] Along with several other reviewers, Raymond Smith recognises the centrality of 'Three Women' and offers a sympathetic reading of the diversity of experience in Plath's portrayal of motherhood and maternity:

■ *Three Women* is probably the most interesting item in the new collection. Childbirth is the subject of this poem, and it is approached from three different points of view. [. . .] The poem explores with great sensitivity a wide range of feelings associated with this central factor of womanhood. 'I cannot help smiling at what it is I know,' confesses the happily pregnant woman. 'There is this cessation,' mourns a second woman after a miscarriage. 'There is this cessation of everything.' [. . .]

Most of the other poems, written some time after *Three Women*, are related to that work insofar as they focus on the woman in her roles as mother and wife. Closely related to the earlier work is the bitter 'Childless Woman', which could almost have been part of the secretary's monologue. Other aspects of motherhood are evoked in the disturbing 'Thalidomide', [. . .] and in the mournful 'Child', where the mother's wishes for her baby are so woefully frustrated . [. . .][18] □

A perceptive reviewer, Smith goes on to discuss the absent father and husband, suggesting a 'fatal discord in the relationship between the sexes', which he illustrates by short readings of 'The Rabbit Catcher', 'Gigolo' and 'By Candlelight'.

Several critics also detect in *Winter Trees* a sense of self which, in marked contrast to the assertion and confidence of *Ariel*, is amorphous, even nebulous. Joyce Carol Oates describes *Winter Trees* as 'fascinating in its preoccupation with formlessness, with dissolving, with a kind of premature posthumous disappearance of the poet's personality',[19] while in a review of *Crossing the Water*, Terry Eagleton identifies a similar sense of self which is in tension with concrete fixed images, concluding with an echo of Vendler's earlier criticism:

■ Throughout this volume, as in much of Plath's work, run two uneasily conflicting trends of imagery. On the one hand, the perceived world of the poems is hard, blank and static: a world of round, flat, bald, faceless surfaces without depth and solidity, whose apparent dynamism is merely the glitter of tin, the crinkling of paper or the smooth polish of stone. ('Moon' and 'star' are recurrent images, combining as they do a static sparkle with a flat two-dimensional expressionlessness.) Yet at another level there is movement beneath these fixed synthetic surfaces: a movement of draining, flaking, melting and emptying, a sticky, protoplasmic dripping, pumping or oozing, a steady dissolution into blackness and absence. [. . .] ['Wuthering Heights'] while appearing to domesticate Nature, in fact transmutes it to a commodity, trivializing and distancing it in the act of seeming to appropriate it to human concerns.[20] □

Plath's poetry is clearly reassessed in the reviews of these two volumes: in contrast to the reviews of the 1960s, very little reference is made to Plath's biography, and a greater concentration is placed on detailed textual readings which attempt to define Plath's oeuvre. Critics remained interested in 'the Plath myth', but they adopted a much more critical view towards the mystique of reading Plath's poetry, often criticising the rhetoric of the *Ariel* reviewers in the process. Many critics, however, still felt restricted by the limited, even piecemeal, publication of Plath's work, and the demand for a collected volume of poems grew larger, expressed most articulately by Eric Homberger's detailed criticism of Plath's literary executors, 'The Uncollected Plath'.[21]

With a substantial body of Plath's writing to work with, the first full-length studies of the poetry began to appear in the early 1970s, many developed from previous essays and reviews. Critics in this decade often appear to adopt the position of detective, attempting to provide a key which would unlock the meanings of Plath's poetry. This is reflected in the essays collected in *The Art of Sylvia Plath*, which includes John Fredrick Nims's technical analysis of the poetry, a structuralist analysis by Annette Lavers which claims to reveal an 'underlying code', and Richard Howard's description of Plath's poetry as espousing 'Nietzschean Joy', all attempts at identifying recurring symbols which allow the critic to arrive at a totalising view of the poetry.[22] Published in 1972, Ingrid Melander's *The Poetry of Sylvia Plath: A Study of Themes*, offered the first full-length study. Melander identifies with Spender's understanding of Plath as a visionary poet, an argument she illustrates with biographical material. While offering some attentive interpretations of the poetry, Melander is restricted by a biographical understanding of Plath's poetry, simplistically relating the purifying and renewing images of death to Plath's suicide, and comparing the complex portrayal of fathers to Plath's own relationship with her father. In chapter two, however, Melander offers a most informative and reflective discussion of poems which are inspired by art, illuminating Plath's 'belief in art and in the artist's ability and right to create a world of his own.'[23] Melander discusses the obvious influence of Rousseau and De Chirico, but also suggests the influence of Jackson Pollock on 'Full Fathom Five', a discussion that goes some way towards advancing the perception of Plath as an involved, culturally receptive writer.[24]

Eileen Aird's 1973 book *Sylvia Plath: The Woman and Her Work* is the first study to take full advantage of the recently published material, offering chapters on each volume of poetry, and *The Bell Jar*. In a well-written, accessible study that again adopts a largely biographical approach, Aird manages to suggest a reasoned relationship between Plath's life and work, and offers an early cultural discussion of the poetry. Through substantial close readings of the work, Aird discusses the main themes and concerns of the poetry and attempts to trace Plath's poetic development (although this is an attempt that is perhaps undermined by the careful dating of Plath's poems in the eventual publication of the *Collected Poems* in 1981, which upsets many of the previously accepted divisions of early, transitional and late).

The introduction offers a short biography of Plath that is perceptive and balanced, focused on interpreting Plath's life through her publishing attempts and successes. Aird outlines Plath's early publishing interests and suggests the possible influence of *Mademoiselle*:

■ This magazine is [. . .] important as being the source of one of her earlier poems, 'A Mad Girl's Love Song', and her literary versatility is illustrated by the fashion and gossip column which she wrote under the heading '*Mademoiselle*'s Last Word on College 1953'. Its easy flippancy is a far cry from the tortured poetry of *Ariel* but the maintained astronomical imagery perhaps indicates a more developed literary talent than is usually found in fashion columnists.[25] □

Although recognising the mystical elements of the poetry, Aird essentially finds the despair of Plath's later poems to be grounded in domestic tensions, and is most perceptive when discussing Plath's work within a domestic context, drawing attention to the object, material world of the poetry:

■ Her originality, however, lies in her insistence that what has been traditionally regarded as a woman's world of domesticity, childbearing, marriage, is also a world which can contain the tragic. She draws from this female world themes which are visionary and supernatural; although it is a world which is eventually destroyed by death, her work is far from depressing because of the artistry with which she delineates her vision.[26] □

Interpreting the opening paragraph of 'Context' as Plath's statement that 'hers was an art in which image and symbol are often related to preoccupations beyond the specific areas of the poem',[27] Aird shares Barbara Hardy's concept of enlargement. Aird proceeds to enter into the continuing controversy over the appropriateness of historical images, in light of this interpretation:

■ To describe Sylvia Plath's subject as 'domestic' is not to diminish it in any way, for as in *Ariel*, these poems [*Winter Trees*] move from a limited private world to a limitless public one. The best example of this width of reference undoubtedly appears in 'Mary's Song' . . . Mary, Christ, God are frequently referred to in *Winter Trees*, although as has already been noted in relation to 'Three Women' Sylvia Plath's intention was never doctrinal; she uses Christianity as one element in the drama of her own poetic world, but gives equal value to the mythological and classical figures who still move through this world [. . .] 'Mary's Song' is strangely named for the poem emerges as a lamentation rather than a celebration. It begins calmly, domestically, with the Sunday joint cooking in the oven – three of the most anguished poems, 'Lesbos', 'Mary's Song' and 'A Birthday Present', begin in the unremarkable and unlikely setting of a kitchen. But the first line of the poem imme-diately conducts us into a world of religious persecution and sacrifice where heretics are burnt at the stake and the smoke from the gas oven of the twentieth century floats over Europe. For Mary the suffering is personal for the repeated 'holocaust' of history is contained in her heart as she contemplates the baby whose sacrifice will not prevent suffering, indeed it will engender a new form of persecution. . . . It even has its own strange beauty, the smoke clouds of the ovens hang-ing over Germany and Poland have the melancholy beauty of utter desolation: 'Gray birds obsess my heart,/Mouth-ash, ash of eye.' 'Mary's Song' belongs to the group of political poems collected in *Ariel* – 'Daddy', 'Lady Lazarus', 'Fever 103°' [. . .]28 □

The second half of the 1970s sees the publication of increasingly ambi-tious studies as critics began to adopt critical positions from which to consider the poetry. The publication of two major Plath studies in 1976 initiated debate and discussion that advanced the understanding of Plath's poetry into new areas. David Holbrook's *Sylvia Plath: Poetry and Existence* divides the opinion of critics; although it is fair to say that many critics are dissatisfied with his attempt at a psychoanalytic reading of Plath's poetry, others, while holding reservations about his diagnosis of Plath as revealing a schizoid condition, credit Holbrook with occasional insights into the poetry.29 Developed from earlier published essays, *Poetry and Existence* is an attempt at relating 'two languages: that of literary crit-icism and that of those disciplines which investigate the meanings of consciousness'.30 Holbrook certainly sees Plath as an extremist writer but strongly disagrees with what he understands to be Alvarez's endorse-ment of this: 'A. Alvarez's admiration for the "creative destruction" is an endorsement of this schizoid delusion.'31 A highly problematic study, which is preoccupied with proving the false logic and corruptibility of Plath's poetry, portraying her as a dangerously influential, even patho-logical, writer, Holbrook's moral imperative underwrites the study's value as literary criticism.32 Holbrook's heavy reliance on the theories of

R.D. Laing, Melanie Klein and D.W. Winnicott, in order to explore the schizoid nature of Plath's writing, and more objectionably, Plath herself, is also problematic, yet Holbrook's reductive study can be seen as a forerunner of later, much more sophisticated psychoanalytic readings of Plath's poetry.

While psychoanalysis introduced a new area of discussion in Plath studies, Judith Kroll's *Chapters in a Mythology: The Poetry of Sylvia Plath* (1976), offers an alternative, mythic key to the interpretation of Plath's poetry. Crediting Annette Lavers's structuralist analysis with 'noting certain recurrent patterns of association', with recognising some kind of 'code', Kroll claims that 'beyond that there is a mythic system that is encoded, in which virtually every image in the late poems participates'.[33] Taking her cue from what she describes as the 'germinal and somewhat cryptic statement' of Hughes's 1966 essay 'Notes on the Chronological Order of Sylvia Plath's Poems', Kroll expands on his highly influential proposition that: 'The poems are chapters in a mythology where the plot, seen as a whole and in retrospect, is strong and clear – even if the origins of it and the dramatis personae, are at bottom enigmatic . . .'[34] The initial chapter, 'The Mythic Nature of the Poetry', outlines her own understanding of these comments and the rationale behind her argument, which suggests a fusion between autobiography and universal myth. Significantly, she describes Plath's poetic development as 'logically and consistently progressing' towards a final realisation, underlining the sense of unification she identifies:

■ [Plath's] poetry is not primarily literal and confessional. It is, rather, the articulation of a mythic system which integrates all aspects of her work, and into which autobiographical or confessional details are shaped and absorbed, [. . .] 'Confessional' poetry usually comprises a plurality of concerns – politics, the writing of poetry, marriage, aging, fame, and so on – that remain relatively independent. But in Plath's poetry there is one overriding concern: the problem of rebirth or transcendence; and nearly everything in her poetry contributes either to the statement or to the envisioned resolution of this problem. [. . .] She has a vision which is complete, self-contained, and whole, a vision of mythic totality, which such poets as Lowell and Sexton do not have [. . .]

If her poetry is understood as constituting a system of symbols that expresses a unified mythic vision, her images may be seen to be emblems of that myth. Red, white, and black, for example, the characteristic colors in her late poetry, function as mythic emblems of her state of being much as they do in the mythologies which she drew upon. A great many other particulars of her poetry are similarly determined by her system, and personal and historical details as well are subordinate to it. [. . .]

To deal with the structure of Plath's poetry is primarily to deal with the voices, landscape, characters, images, emblems, and motifs which articulate a mythic drama having something of the eternal necessity of Greek tragedy. The myth has its basis in her biography, but it in turn exercises a selective function on her biography and determines within it an increasingly restricted context of relevance as her work becomes more symbolic and archetypal. [. . .]

If one first grasps the plot of the myth and the dynamics of the mythic motifs and then returns to the late poems, it becomes immediately apparent that they constitute a unified body of work, and that the early poems logically and consistently progress towards the final formation of the myth and its subsidiary motifs. All of Sylvia Plath's late poems, including even the few that seem to be out of the mainstream, can best be understood in terms of her underlying system, as can her characteristic and effortless skills – the arrestingly exact images; the language that is at once colloquial and charged with extraordinary intensity; the ritualistic and prophetic tone; the shifting perspectives, masks, and other devices – these all evolve from the basic concerns and necessities.[35] □

Kroll identifies Frazer's *The Golden Bough* and particularly Graves's *The White Goddess* as 'crucial in revealing [Plath's] artistic purposes', claiming that Plath felt a deep identification with these mythic texts. In her chapter establishing the moon as a central symbol in Plath's personal mythology, Kroll specifies Plath's commitment to the White Goddess:

■ The mythological explanations of her private history with which the White Goddess myths provided her, and the connections between poetry and the White Goddess, must have made it irresistible to her to immerse herself in the White Goddess 'cult.' The myths gave her a map on which she could, consciously or unconsciously, chart and locate her past (the relationship with her dead father), her present (herself as heroine, her husband as renewed 'god,' replacing the old dead one), and, even more surprisingly, it was a map into which major future events would also fit, for the White Goddess myths would also accommodate her estrangement from her husband (a new phase of the old cycle of union and separation), and the character of the 'rival' responsible for it. All this gave Plath license and encouragement to cast herself as a mythic heroine within the drama the Moon-goddess superintends and symbolizes.[36] □

The concept of Plath's poetry containing a personal, internal mythic system is continued in Jon Rosenblatt's 1979 study *Sylvia Plath: The Poetry of Initiation*. In the Preface, Rosenblatt states his objective as 'a desire to understand the relationship between two aspects of [Plath's] work: its powerful images and rhythms and its ritual or quasi-ritual patterns'. Outlining his argument for the recognition of the mythic cohesiveness of Plath's poetry, he claims that Plath 'linked private images and motifs into sequences that formed part of a coherent drama, a symbolic enactment', conceiving her work as 'a poetry of personal process in which the central development was an initiation, a transformation of the self from a state of symbolic death to one of rebirth'.[37] While acknowledging that Kroll's study of Plath's mythological sources 'fills gaps in our knowledge' Rosenblatt accuses Kroll of 'imposing an extremely misleading system on the poetry' by focusing on Graves's *The White Goddess*, claiming that 'Kroll's systematic interpretation of every color, object and figure in the poems falsifies the character of Plath's work [. . .]'.[38] In the opening chapter 'Misconceptions', which discusses the 'misinterpretation and distortion' of previous critics, Rosenblatt questions the critical debate on Plath so far, claiming, in a sentence which seems to prefigure Jacqueline Rose's later complex insights into the relationship between critic and poet, that: 'We continue to brood about Sylvia Plath in ways that have more to do with our own obsessions than with hers.'[39]

Rosenblatt argues that Plath arrives at 'a coherent strategy' through lived experience, and in the closing chapter asserts that in her final 'brilliant, though sometimes chaotic poems, Plath continually dramatises her encounter with death. Writing out of her dual obsession with annihilation and salvation, she converts the various subjects of her poetry into instances of the death-and-rebirth pattern.'[40] Rosenblatt's reading of the often oblique, difficult poem 'The Couriers' illustrates his approach:

■ 'The Couriers' is, like most of the late work, 'personal poetry.' Its hermetic images constitute a private language of the psyche that at first seems opaque and impenetrable. Yet its rapid association of images and its manipulation of condensed symbolic elements reveals, more accurately than any other technique could, the personal world of conflict and process that the poet experiences. On second and third readings, the poem's metaphors, opposed image sequences, and elliptical development seem the appropriate and natural methods of conveying the tense, deep contradictions involved in marriage and love. The dominant metaphor of the poem – poetry as a courier for 'imagistic messages' – indicates that Plath's late poetry is not self-enclosed but is open to the reader as a recipient of its message.

[. . .] In 'The Couriers', the poetic voice is clipped and somewhat muted; in 'Ariel', it is fluent and energetic; in 'Lady Lazarus', it turns shrill and hysterical; and in 'Fever 103°,' it becomes meditative and whimsical. We may, of course, link all the speakers to Plath herself and view the various dramas as autobiographical reflections, but this is hardly necessary. The poems embody an objective pattern: the movement from the familiar world of stasis and death to a new universe of life and energy.[41] □

Recognising Plath's achievement as the creation of an 'initiatory drama of life and death', Rosenblatt's identification of a death-and-rebirth pattern which, he suggests, becomes increasingly ritualised as the poetry develops, enables him to resolve the difficulties and disparities of Plath's poetry, and offer a cohesive reading.

Margaret Dickie Uroff's influential study, *Sylvia Plath and Ted Hughes*, explores in detail the creative relationship between the two poets, offering particularly perceptive insights into Plath's later poetry. Uroff also provides an early consideration of the impact of Plath's legacy on Hughes's later poetry. Although recognising that much of her book is 'speculative', Uroff asserts that it is 'speculation based on a careful reading of the poems and a certain knowledge that the two poets knew each other's work intimately'.[42] Questioning previously held assumptions about the influences evident in Plath's work, Uroff interprets Hughes's creative influence as superseding the conventional influence of 'confessional' poetry:

■ Even as they swerved away from each other in their choice of subjects, Plath and Hughes profited from a creative association which remained central, despite other influences. [. . .] In its ritualistic quality, and especially in its ritual of creation and destruction, her late poetry is closer to Hughes's than to Lowell's and Sexton's [. . .] the speakers of 'Lady Lazarus' and certainly of 'Daddy' owe more to the defiant tone and incantatory rhythm of Hughes's 'Hawk Roosting' than to the melancholic analysis of the man in Lowell's 'Skunk Hour.' To be sure, the rage of the killer woman in Plath's poems stems from a complex psychological situation that Hughes would claim has no counterpart in the hawk's mindless murderousness, however much the quality of that mindlessness must reflect the psyche of its creator. But she has been so brutalized by her experience that she is reduced almost to the level of the hawk. The violent energy that drives her wipes out her analytic powers, her humanistic scruples, until she rises at the end to the kill with the same instinctive fury that propels the hawk. To make this connection is not to claim that Plath modeled her women after Hughes's predatory animals, but only to suggest that, in addition to the psychological sources of the poem, literary sources should be considered. In creating the myth of the vengeful female who rises against her oppressors, Plath has available as an aid Hughes's own myth of enraged and captive energies, and his own image of the creative-destructive female.[43] □

In concluding her incisive consideration of the relationship of influence and encouragement to be found between Plath's and Hughes's poetry, Uroff summarises Plath's development while she was writing the poems which would form *The Colossus*, the creative period Uroff earlier identifies as being heavily informed by Hughes.[44] The contextual nature of Uroff's understanding of the poets' shared influences allows her to be more generous than Rosenblatt in her summation of Kroll's proposition:

■ As she continued to write the poems that eventually formed *The Colossus*, Plath developed on two fronts. Responding to Hughes's advice and example, she moved inward and began to explore her own background and its mythic associations, and at the same time turned outward to describe the natural world. Her interest in her own background [. . .] this search for what she called 'the foundation of my consciousness' was narrowly focused on herself and on what her psyche had absorbed of roots and family. It was encouraged, no doubt, by her early psychotherapy, as well as by her thesis reading of Freud and Jung and Frazer while she was a student at Smith, but it surfaced when she and Hughes were trying to elicit subjects for poems by meditating over the Ouija board. [. . .] She began to see her own story not as peculiar and private, but as universal. Judith Kroll has surveyed this important aspect of Plath's work, emphasizing the unified mythic vision of her poetry and underscoring debts to Frazer and Graves particularly. Here it is necessary to remember that Hughes also was heavily influenced by Frazer and Graves and that through them he directed Plath's attention to the archetypal quality of her experience.[45] □

While *Sylvia Plath and Ted Hughes* remains the most in-depth consideration of mutual influence and exchange in both poets' work, more recent critics, such as Alan Sinfield, have advanced this connection in increasingly cultural, even archetypal terms, as we shall see in later chapters.[46]

Although the 1970s is an era defined by attempts to decipher and decode Plath's poetry, several studies do challenge her increasing stature as a poet, often questioning the intense subjectivity of her poetry. While Calvin Bedient admiringly describes Plath's poetic as 'Poundian-romantic', and locates Plath's intensity in her subjective dramas, he does express concern and reserve over the endorsement of Plath's mythic and historical sources: 'Plath uses the historical and mythical as a vanity mirror. When she writes as if she were abused as a Nazi victim she climbs to self-importance over the bodies of the dead. She enters a moral sphere that her amoral personal imagination cannot apprehend.'[47] Hugh Kenner's essay 'Sincerity Kills' develops his objections to *Ariel*'s 'bogus spirituality',[48] while the poet David Shapiro patronisingly decries Plath's work for being melodramatic and exaggerated.[49]

In her essay 'The Death Throes of Romanticism: The Poetry of Sylvia Plath', Joyce Carol Oates joins the dissenting critics. By identifying the romantic dialectic of Plath's poetry as the 'opposition between self and object, "I" and "non-I", man and nature', Oates argues that Plath cultivates a romantic subjectivity that is solipsistic and egotistical, a criticism she levels problematically at both the poetry and the poet. Positioning Plath 'at the end of a once-energetic tradition' of lyric poetry, Oates insists that 'Plath must be diagnosed as one of the last romantics; and already her poetry seems to us a poetry of the past, swiftly receding into history'. The absoluteness of Plath's 'solitary ego' is delineated as the acting out of: 'the deathliness of an old consciousness, the old corrupting hell of the Renaissance ideal and its "I"-ness, separate and distinct from all other fields of consciousness, which exist only to be conquered or to inflict pain upon the "I"'. Oates decries this as a condition of modern poetry which leads to an almost inevitable stasis and ultimate silence. She concludes by locating the danger of this solipsism in Plath's Holocaust poetry, an area which continued to generate the fiercest of debates:

■ 'Lady Lazarus,' risen once again from the dead, does not expect a sympathetic response from the mob of spectators that crowd in to view her, a mock-phoenix rising from another failed suicide attempt: to Plath there cannot be any connection between people, between the 'I' who performs and the crowd that stares. All deaths are separate, and do not evoke human responses. To be really safe, one must be like the young man of 'Gigolo,' who has eluded the 'bright fish hooks, the smiles of women,' and who will never age because – like Plath's ideal self – he is a perfect narcissus, self-gratified. He has successfully dehumanized himself.

The cosmos is indeed lost to Plath and her era, and even a tentative exploration of a possible 'God' is viewed in the old terms, in the old images of dread and terror. 'Mystic' is an interesting poem, on a subject rare indeed to Plath, and seems to indicate that her uneasiness with the 'mill of hooks' of the air – 'questions without answer' – had led her briefly to thoughts of God. Yet whoever this 'God' is, no comfort is possible because the ego cannot experience any interest or desire without being engulfed:

Once one has seen God, what is the remedy?
Once one has been seized up

Without a part left over,
Not a toe, not a finger, and used,
Used utterly . . .
What is the remedy?

Used: the mystic will be exploited, victimized, hurt. He can expect no liberation or joy from God, but only another form of dehumanizing brutality. Plath has made beautiful poetry out of the paranoia sometimes expressed by a certain kind of emotionally disturbed person who imagines that any relationship with anyone will overwhelm him, engulf and destroy his soul. [. . .]

The dread of being possessed by the Other results in the individual's failure to distinguish between real and illusory enemies. What must be in the human species a talent for discerning legitimate threats to personal survival evidently never developed in Plath – this helps to explain why she could so gracefully fuse the 'evil' of her father with the historical outrages of the Nazis, unashamedly declare herself a 'Jew' because the memory of her father persecuted her. In other vivid poems, she senses enemies in tulips (oxygen-sucking tulips? – surely they are human!) or sheep (which possess the unsheeplike power of murdering a human being) or in the true blankness of a mirror, which cannot be seen as recording the natural maturation process of a young woman but must be reinterpreted as drawing the woman toward the 'terrible fish' of her future self.[50] □

In her 1979 essay, 'Sylvia Plath's "Sivvy Poems": A Portrait of the Poet as Daughter', Marjorie Perloff reconsiders her earlier endorsement of Plath's affinity with nature. In light of the recently published poetry, and *Letters Home*, Perloff now argues that the connection between Plath and such oracular nature poets as Roethke and Lawrence is 'more apparent than real, [and] that Plath did not and could not "identify imaginatively with the life of animals and plants" (see "Angst and Animism," p. 57)'.[51] Echoing Oates's argument, Perloff asserts that Plath is the single subject of her work, suggesting that 'her identification with the Jews who suffered at Auschwitz has a hollow ring, just as her violent rejection of Christianity is no more than a rejection of herself'.[52]

Irving Howe similarly questions Plath's increasing reputation in 'The Plath Celebration: A Partial Dissent'. In comparing Plath with Lowell, Howe questions the quality and sustainability of Plath's 'confessional' poetry, rejecting 'Lady Lazarus' as 'sentimental violence'. But it is Howe's discussion of Plath's Holocaust imagery and his argument that the comparisons are 'utterly disproportionate', which takes issue with Steiner's earlier praise and longs for a return to the impersonality of New Criticism:

■ In the poem ['Daddy'] Sylvia Plath identifies the father (we recall his German birth) with the Nazis ('Panzer-man, panzer-man, O You') and flares out with assaults for which nothing in the poem (nor, so far as we know, in Sylvia Plath's own life) offers any warrant: [. . .]

What we have here is a revenge fantasy, feeding upon filial love-hatred, and thereby mostly of clinical interest. But seemingly aware that the merely clinical can't provide the materials for a satisfying poem, Sylvia Plath tries to enlarge upon the personal plight, give meaning to the personal outcry, by fancying the girl as victim of a Nazi father [. . .]

The more sophisticated admirers of this poem may say that I fail to see it as a dramatic presentation, a monologue spoken by a disturbed girl not necessarily to be identified with Sylvia Plath, despite the similarities of detail between the events of the poem and the events of her life. I cannot accept this view. The personal-confessional element, strident and undisciplined, is simply too obtrusive to suppose the poem no more than a dramatic picture of a certain style of disturbance. If, however, we did accept such a reading of 'Daddy', we would fatally narrow its claim to emotional or moral significance, for we would be confining it to a mere vivid imagining of a pathological state. That, surely, is not how its admirers really take the poem.

It is clearly not how the critic George Steiner takes the poem when he calls it 'the "Guernica" of modern poetry.' But then, in an astonishing turn, he asks: 'In what sense does anyone, himself uninvolved and long after the event, commit a subtle larceny when he invokes the echoes and trappings of Auschwitz and appropriates an enormity of ready emotion to his own private design?' The question is devastating to his early comparison with 'Guernica.' Picasso's painting objectifies the horrors of Guernica, through the distancing of art; no one can suppose that he shares or participates in them. Plath's poem aggrandizes on the 'enormity of ready emotion' invoked by references to the concentration camps, in behalf of an ill-controlled if occasionally brilliant outburst. There is something monstrous, utterly disproportionate, when tangled emotions about one's father are deliberately compared with the historical fate of the European Jews; something sad, if the comparison is made spontaneously. 'Daddy' persuades once again, through the force of negative example, of how accurate T. S. Eliot was in saying, 'The more perfect the artist, the more completely separate in him will be the man who suffers and the mind which creates.'[53] □

The second half of the 1970s is perhaps most spectacularly defined by the development of a feminist approach to literary studies, an approach which often places Plath at the centre of the debates. Emerging from the political and social basis of the women's movement, informed by such ground-breaking studies as Germaine Greer's *The Female Eunuch* (1970) and Kate Millet's *Sexual Politics* (1969), feminist literary criticism began by revising, questioning, and even interrogating, the existing power relationships embedded in masculinist criticism, which marginalised women writers. Sexual identity is placed at the heart of the debate, and while this does not always result in a unified approach, since feminist criticism itself generates arguments and disagreements, it does significantly revise the conditions of evaluation for the woman writer. Although the following critical texts can all be described as 'women-centred', primarily concerned with recovering neglected texts and exploring their value within a patriarchal society, they also highlight one of the central debates within feminist thinking over the definition of a distinctive female imagination.

In light of Mary Ellman's early consideration of the female imagination and the work of Patricia Meyer Sparks,[54] Sandra M. Gilbert and Susan Gubar's 1979 central text of feminist criticism, *The Madwoman in the Attic: The Woman Writer and the Nineteenth-Century Literary Imagination*, suggests that there is difference in women's writing which can be located at a textual and psychological level. While concerned with recovering women writers and questioning a male dominated canon, this study is centrally concerned with defining a particularly female imagination. Developing Harold Bloom's influential theory of 'anxiety of influence', Gilbert and Gubar suggest that women's writing further betrays an 'anxiety of authorship',[55] an idea they develop in their understanding of the particular, often viewed as peculiar, role of the woman poet, as we shall see.

In a slightly different direction, Ellen Moers's *Literary Women* (1976) adopts a culturally determined view of women's writing, and attempts to achieve the establishment of a female tradition by unearthing and re-interpreting texts by forgotten women writers. Similarly, Elaine Showalter's *A Literature of Their Own: British Women Novelists From Brontë to Lessing* (1977) establishes a lineage of tradition and influence in women's writing, while outlining concerns over a possibly essentialist 'female imagination': 'I am . . . uncomfortable with the notion of a "female imagination". The theory of a female sensibility revealing itself in an imagery and form specific to women always runs dangerously close to reiterating familiar stereotypes. It also suggests permanence, a deep, basic, and inevitable difference between male and female ways of perceiving the world.'[56] Showalter develops this argument in her seminal essay 'Towards a Feminist Poetics', where she exposes universal interpretations of literature to be essentially masculine.[57] Although Plath does not feature centrally in these leading feminist texts, preoccupied as they are with fiction, they do impact onto slightly later considerations of women's poetry, as we shall see in Sandra M. Gilbert's essay that establishes Plath as a major poet of interest to feminist critics by redefining and reassessing her as a women writer. Gilbert's analysis of Plath's poetry shifts the critical focus by giving prominence to the bee sequence, the verse-play 'Three Women', and poems that explore the maternal role, concerns highlighted by the publication of *Letters Home* in 1975.

It is interesting to note briefly the resistance, even antagonism, towards feminist interpretations of Plath's writing from a variety of commentators. This ranges from Douglas Dunn's insightful yet condescending view of domesticity in Plath's poetry – 'She mocks the masculine world with flurries of domestic detail. The irritation and peevishness of this is profoundly miles beyond the fashionable nonsense of Women's Lib . . .' – to David Holbrook's derision of Plath as 'sadly pseudo-male, like many of her cultists'.[58] As if in reply to these comments, critics such as Cora Kaplan in her introduction to an impressive collection, *Salt and Bitter and Good: Three Centuries of English and American Women Poets* (1975), Gilbert and Gubar in their introduction to *Shakespeare's Sisters*, and Alicia Ostriker in her later *Stealing the Language*, all begin their consideration of women's poetry by examining the often sexual and derogatory terms in which women's writing is reviewed and evaluated; Theodore Roethke's particularly disparaging 1961 review of the poet Louise Brogan, and Lowell and Alvarez's peculiarly sexualised commentary on Plath, are prime examples. As Mary Ellman previously noted, women writers are often written about in such disparaging terms as 'shrill', and 'hysterical', both terms applied to Plath, while Kaplan, in a collection of poetry that attempts to readdress the gender balance of anthologies by emphasising the poets' gender, recognises the temptation 'for male critics to admire the aesthetic contours of Plath's poetry while describing its inspiration as the special and sexless pathology of the potential suicide'.[59] Tillie Olsen's radical, decentering study *Silences* (1978) explores the social silencing of women writers, both in the domestic restrictions of their own lives, and their place within the literary canon.[60] Suzanne Juhasz is one of the first feminists to consider the tradition of women's poetry in her 1976 study *Naked and Fiery Forms: Modern American Poetry by Women*, a central text in the development of a theoretical feminist approach. Juhasz identifies the 'double bind' suffered by women writers who are either derided as aggressively intellectual 'bluestockings' or dismissed as sentimental, feminine writers.[61] Seemingly unable to escape societal expectations of female creativity, the woman writer is seen to devise literary strategies which often subvert or exploit expectations of femininity. Thus, feminism began to interpret metaphors of division as reflective of the woman writer's socially acceptable self and repressed creative self; the duality that is often interpreted as an indicative of a 'split personality' is increasingly read in explicitly feminist terms.

Shakespeare's Sisters, taking its title from Virginia Woolf's feminist fantasy of Judith Shakespeare, is an impressive collection of essays by emerging feminist critics, with an excellent introduction by the editors Sandra M. Gilbert and Susan Gubar. They specifically explore the position of the woman poet, expanding on Suzanne Juhasz's influential theory of the 'double-bind' by recognising the additional difficulties for the woman writer who identifies herself as a poet:

■ [. . .] while the woman novelist, safely shut in prose, may fantasize about freedom with a certain impunity (since she constructs purely fictional alternatives to the difficult reality she inhabits), it appears that the woman poet must in some sense become her own heroine, and that in enacting the diabolical role of witch or wise woman she literally or figuratively risks a melodramatic death at the crossroads of tradition and genre, society and art. [. . .] Suzanne Juhasz has recently and persuasively spoken of the 'double bind' of the woman poet, but it seems almost as if there is a sort of triple bind [in addition to the denigration of 'bluestockings' and ignorant sentimentality] . . . whatever alternative tradition the woman poet attempts to substitute for ancient rules is subtly devalued. [. . .] Finally, and perhaps most crucially, where the novel allows – even encourages – just the self-effacing withdrawal society had traditionally fostered in women, the lyric poem is in some sense the utterance of a strong and assertive 'I'. Artists from Shakespeare to Dickinson, Yeats, and T. S. Eliot have of course qualified this 'I,' emphasizing, as Eliot does, the 'extinction of personality' involved in a poet's construction of an artful, masklike persona, or insisting, as Dickinson did, that the speaker of the poems is a 'supposed person.' But, nevertheless, the central self that speaks or sings a poem must be forcefully defined, whether 'she'/'he' is real or imaginary. If the novelist, therefore, inevitably sees herself from the outside, [. . .] as an object, a character, a small figure in a large pattern, the lyric poet must be continually aware of herself from the inside, as a subject, a speaker: she must be, that is, assertive, authoritative, radiant with powerful feelings while at the same time absorbed in her own consciousness – and hence, by definition, profoundly 'unwomanly', even freakish. For the woman poet, in other words, the contradictions between her vocation and her gender might well become insupportable, impelling her to deny one or the other, even (as in the case of 'Judith Shakespeare') driving her to suicide.[62] □

Collecting major essays on women's poetry by feminist critics into an intelligent, academically acknowledged and admired volume significantly advances the understanding and appreciation of Plath's poetry, by enabling it to be seen more as part of a tradition of women's writing, and less as a sparkling exception. Barbara Charlesworth Gelpi's essay 'A Common Language: The American Woman Poet' adapts theories of Margaret Atwood and Arnold Rampersad in an attempt to classify the subjectivity of women poets. She includes a reading of Plath's 'The Disquieting Muses', which reflects the shift from viewing Plath as an 'extremist writer' to considering her as a woman writer: 'These poems which explore her ambivalence towards images of mother figures may actually be more central to an understanding of her work than are "Daddy" and "Lady Lazarus."'[63] But it is Sandra M. Gilbert's essay 'A Fine White Flying Myth: The Life/Work of Sylvia Plath' that establishes Plath as a major poet within this volume. Adopting a feminist, biographically informed approach, Gilbert's essay opens with her own personal memoir of Plath which stresses the similarities between Plath and other women, which is then expertly subverted into a consideration of the patriarchal myths that women contend with in order to define themselves as writers:

■ Though I never met Sylvia Plath, I can honestly say that I have known her most of my life. To begin with, when I was twelve or thirteen I read an extraordinary story of hers in . . . *Seventeen*. It was called 'Den of Lions,' and though the plot was fairly conventional, something about the piece affected me in inexplicable, almost 'mythic' ways – ways in which I wouldn't have thought I could be affected by a *Seventeen* reader's story. [. . .]

Plath next surfaced, of course, as guest editor of *Mademoiselle* and as a winner of that magazine's College Fiction contest – the literary equivalent of being crowned Miss America. And when I myself became a guest editor, four years after she did, I found myself assigned to the same staff editor she had worked for. Now our likenesses, our common problems, as well as our divergences, begin to clarify. What I had unconsciously responded to in 'Den of Lions,' what had made me uneasy about it, was probably that it was a story of female initiation, an account of how one girl learns to see herself as intelligent meat-victim and manipulator of men, costumes, drinks, cigarettes – flesh and artifice together. But what I much more consciously knew about the *Mademoiselle* experience was that for me, as for Sylvia and all the other guest editors, it was a kind of initiation ritual, a dramatic induction into that glittery Women's House of fashion and domesticity outside whose windows most of us had spent much of our lives, noses pressed to the glass, [. . .]

The next I heard of Sylvia Plath was in the early sixties. She was publishing careful, elegantly crafted poems in places like *The Atlantic* and *The New Yorker*, poems that bore out Robert Lowell's later remarks about her 'checks and courtesies,' her 'maddening docility.' Then one day a friend who worked at *The New Yorker* called to say 'Imagine, Sylvia Plath is dead.' And three days later 'Poppies in July,' 'Edge,' 'Contusion,' and 'Kindness' appeared in *TLS*. Astonishingly undocile poems. Poems of despair and death. Poems with their heads in ovens (although the rumor was at first that Plath had died of the flu or pneumonia). Finally the violence seeped in as if leaking from the poems into the life, or, rather, the death. She had been killed, had killed herself, had murdered her children, a modern Medea. And at last it was really told, the story everyone knows already, and the outline of history began to thicken to myth. All of us who had read her traced our own journey in hers: from the flashy Women's House of *Mademoiselle* to the dull oven of Madame, from college to villanelles to babies to the scary skeletons of poems we began to study, now, as if they were sacred writ. The Plath Myth, whatever it meant or means, had been launched like a queen bee on its dangerous flight through everybody's psyche.

The Plath Myth: is there anything legitimate about such a phrase? Is there really, in other words, an identifiable set of forces which nudge the lives and works of women like Plath into certain apparently mythical (or 'archetypal') patterns? In answer, and in justification both of my imagery and of my use of personal material that might otherwise seem irrelevant, I want to suggest that the whole story I have told so far conforms in its outlines to a mythological way of structuring female experience that has been useful to many women writers since the nineteenth century. In Plath's case the shape of the myth is discernible both in her work and in the life that necessitated that work. In addition, the ways in which as woman and as writer she diverges from the common pattern are as interesting as those ways in which she conforms to it [. . .]

Women writers, especially when they're writing *as women*, have tended to rely on plots and patterns that suggest the obsessive patterns of myths and fairy tales. For instance, what Ellen Moers has called 'Female Gothic' is a characteristically mythological genre: it draws heavily upon unconscious imagery, apparently archetypal events, fairy-tale plots, and so forth.[64] And, to use Frank Kermode's distinction between myth and fiction, it implies not an 'as if' way of seeing the world but a deep faith in its own structures, structures which, to refer briefly to Levi-Strauss' theory of myth, offer psychic solutions to serious social, economic, and sexual-emotional problems. [. . .]

An important question then arises: why do so many women writers characteristically work the mythological vein? Some critics account for the phenomenon – following Bachofen, Neumann, and others – with what I regard as a rather sentimental and certainly stereotypical explanation. The dark, intuitive, Molly Bloomish female consciousness, they would say, just naturally generates images of archetypal power and intensity.

But it seems to me that a simpler, more sensible explanation might also be possible. Women as a rule, even sophisticated women writers, haven't until quite recently been brought to think of themselves as conscious subjects in the world. Deprived of education, votes, jobs, and property rights, they have also, even more significantly, been deprived of their own selfhood. [. . .] it is no wonder women haven't been able to admit the complex problem of their own subjectivity – either to themselves or others. Rather, they have disguised the stories of their own psychic growth, even from themselves, in a multitude of extravagant, apparently irrelevant forms and images.[65] □

Gilbert proceeds to explore these disguises and evasions in Plath's writing, suggesting that she escapes enclosure and restriction, both in her life and writing by offering myths of transcendence and liberation similar to the strategies employed by many nineteenth-century women writers. Within a feminist discourse, Gilbert centrally explores metaphors of maternity and creation, suggesting ways in which the creative self is determined through the maternal self.

■ [. . .] the great poems of *Ariel* often catapult their protagonist or speaker out of a stultifying enclosure into the violent freedom of the sky. 'Now she is flying,' Plath writes in 'Stings,' perhaps the best of the bee-keeping poems,

> More terrible than she ever was, red
> Scar in the sky, red comet
> Over the engine house that killed her –
> The mausoleum, the wax house.
>
> *Ariel*, p.63

And in the title poem of the collection, the one that describes the poet's runaway ride on the horse Ariel, she insists that 'I/Am the arrow,/The dew that flies/Suicidal, at one with the drive/Into the red/Eye, the cauldron of morning' (*Ariel*, p.27) [. . .]

Being enclosed – in plaster, in a bell jar, a cellar, or a wax house – and then being liberated from an enclosure by a maddened or suicidal or 'hairy and ugly' avatar of the self is, I would contend, at the heart of the myth that we piece together from Plath's poetry, fiction, and life, just as it is at the heart of much other important writing by nineteenth- and twentieth-century women. The story told is invariably a story of being trapped, by society or by the self as an agent of society, and then somehow escaping or trying to escape. [. . .]

The enclosure – the confinement – began early, we learn. Though her childhood was free and Edenic, with the vast expanse of ocean before her (as she tells us in the essay 'Ocean 1212-W') when she was nine, 'my father died, we moved inland' – moved away from space and playfulness and possibility moved (if she had not already done so) into the black shoe. 'Whereupon,' she concludes, 'those first nine years of my life sealed themselves off like a ship in a bottle – beautiful, inaccessible, obsolete, a fine, white flying myth.' And this is an important but slightly misleading statement, for it was she who was sealed into the bottle, and what she longed for was the lost dream of her own wings. Because, having moved inland, she had moved also into a plaster cast of herself, into a mirror image alien as the image that frightened Jane [Eyre] in the Red Room or the stylish mirrors of the pages of *Mademoiselle* into the bell jar, into the cellar where she curled like a doped fetus, into the mausoleum, the wax house.

In this state, she wrote, 'the wingy myths won't tug at us any-more,' in a poem in *The Colossus* (p.81). And then, in poem after poem, she tried to puzzle out the cause of her confinement. 'O what has come over us, my sister! . . . What keyhole have we slipped through, what door has shut?' she asked in 'The Babysitters,' a piece addressed to a contemporary (*Crossing the Water*, p.15). 'This mizzle fits me like a sad jacket./How did we make it up to your attic? . . . / . . . Lady, what am I doing/With a lung full of dust and a tongue of wood . . .?' she com-plained in 'Leaving Early,' a poem written to another woman (*Crossing the Water*, p.19). 'Soon each white lady will be boarded up/Against the cracking climate. . . .' she wrote in 'Private Ground' (*Crossing the Water*, p.21). [. . .] For her central problem had become, as it became Jane Eyre's (or Charlotte Brontë's), how to get out. How to reactivate the myth of a flight so white, so pure, as to be a rebirth into the imagined liberty of childhood?

Both Jane and Charlotte Brontë got out, as I suggested, through the mediating madness of the woman in the attic, Jane's enraged, crazed double, who burned down the imprisoning house and with it the con-fining structures of the past. Mary Shelley, costumed as Frankenstein, got out by creating a monster who conveniently burned down domes-tic cottages and killed friends, children, the whole complex of family relationships. Emily Dickinson, who saw her life as 'shaven/And fitted to a frame,' got out by persuading herself that 'The soul has moments of Escape –/When bursting all the doors –/She dances like a Bomb, abroad.' Especially in *Ariel*, but also in other works, Plath gets out by 1) killing daddy (who is, after all, indistinguishable from the house or shoe in which she has lived) and 2) flying away disguised as a queen bee (in 'Stings'), a bear (in the story 'The Fifty-Ninth Bear'), superman (in the story 'The Wishing Box'), a train (in 'Getting There' and other poems), an acetylene virgin (in 'Fever 103°'), an arrow (in 'Ariel,' *The Bell Jar*, and 'The Other'), or a baby (in too many poems to mention).

Of these liberating images or doubles for the self, almost all except the metaphor of the baby are as violent and threatening as Dickinson's bomb, Shelley's monster, or Brontë's madwoman. 'I think I am going up./I think I may rise –/The heads of hot metal fly, and I, love, I/Am a pure acetylene/Virgin . . .' Plath declares in 'Fever 103°,' ascending '(My selves dissolving, old whore petticoats) –/To Paradise' (*Ariel*, pp. 54–55). But not a very pleasant paradise, for this ascent is 'The upflight of the murderess into a heaven that loves her,' to quote from 'The Bee Meeting,' and rage strengthens her wings, rips her from the plaster of her old whore life (*Ariel*, p. 57). As the bridegroom, the 'Lord of the mirrors,' approaches, the infuriated speaker of 'Purdah,' trapped at his side – 'The agonized/Side of green Adam . . .' from which she was born – threatens that '. . . at his next step/I shall unloose –/From the small jewelled/Doll he guards like a heart –/The lioness,/The shriek in the bath,/The cloak of holes.' (*WT*, pp. 40–42). 'Herr God, Herr Lucifer/Beware/Beware' cries Lady Lazarus. 'Out of the ash/I rise with my red hair/And I eat men like air.' 'If I've killed one man, I've killed two – ' Plath confesses in 'Daddy.' 'And the villagers never liked you./They are dancing and stamping on you' (*Ariel*, pp. 9, 51). [. . .]

Flying, journeying, 'getting there,' she shrieks her triumph: 'The train is dragging itself, it is screaming –/ . . . The carriages rock, they are cradles./And I, stepping from this skin/Of old bandages, bore-doms, old faces/Step to you from the black car of Lethe,/Pure as a baby' (*Ariel*, pp. 37–38). *Pure as a baby!* [. . .] Esther Greenwood in *The Bell Jar* plummets down 'through year after year of doubleness and smiles and compromise' toward 'the pebble at the bottom of the well, the white sweet baby cradled in its mother's belly' (*The Bell Jar*, p. 79). *Sweet as a baby!*

How do we reconcile this tender new avatar with the hairy bear, the ferocious virgin, the violent and dangerous Lady Lazarus? That Sylvia wanted to be reborn into the liberty of her own distant child-hood – wanted once more to be 'running along the hot white beaches' with her father – is certainly true (*The Bell Jar*, p. 60). Yet, at the same time her father represented the leathery house from which she wished to escape. And the baby images in her poems often seem to have more to do with her own babies than with her own babyhood. In fact, crit-ics often puzzle over the creative release childbirth and maternity apparently triggered for Plath. That she loved her children is indis-putable, but does not seem any more immediately relevant to an understanding of the self-as-escaping baby than her longing for her own childhood. Yes, the baby is a blessing, a new beginning – 'You're [. . .] Right, like a well-done sum,' says Plath to her child in the poem 'You're.' [. . .] But what have these blessings to do with the monster-mother's liberation? Doesn't the baby, on the contrary, anchor her more firmly into the attic, the dark house, the barn?

The answer to this last question is, I think, *no*, though with some qualifications. In fact, for Plath the baby is often a mediating and comparatively healthy image of freedom (which is just another important reason why the Plath Myth has been of such compelling interest to women), and this is because in her view the fertile mother is a queen bee, an analog for the fertile and liberated poet, the opposite of that dead drone in the wax house who was the sterile egotistical mistress of darkness and daddy.

We can best understand this polarity by looking first at some poems that deal specifically with sterility, nullity, *perfection.* 'Perfection is terrible, it cannot have children,' Plath wrote in 'The Munich Mannequins.' '[. . .] It means : no more idols but me,/Me and you' (*Ariel*, p.73). Snow, menstrual blood, egotism, childlessness, the moon, and, later in the poem, the (significantly) *bald* mannequins themselves, like 'Orange lollies on silver sticks,' – all together these constitute a major cluster of images which appears and reappears throughout *Ariel* and the other books. Women like the frightening godmother Jay Gee seemed to be are what they equal for me, and I'm sure what they equaled for Plath. [. . .] Bald, figuratively speaking, as 'the disquieting muses' of Plath's poem and Chirico's painting, these emblems of renunciation were Plath's – and perhaps every academically talented girl's – earliest 'traveling companions.' They counseled 'A's, docility, working for *Mademoiselle,* surrendering sexuality for 'perfection,' using daddy's old red-leather thesaurus to write poems, and living courteously in daddy's shoe, not like a thumbtack, irascible and piercing, but like a poor white foot, barely daring to breathe or Achoo. [. . .]

But 'Two girls there are,' wrote Plath in 'Two Sisters of Persephone' [. . .] The first girl, like the 'childless woman' of another poem, sees her 'landscape' as 'a hand with no lines,' her sexuality as 'a tree with nowhere to go.' The second girl, on the other hand, producing a golden child, produces flight from the folds of her own body, self-transcendence, the dangerous yet triumphant otherness of poetry. For, as Simone de Beauvoir acutely observes in *The Second Sex,* the pregnant woman has the extraordinary experience of being both subject and object at the same time. Even while she is absorbed in her own subjectivity and isolation, she is intensely aware of being an object – a house – for another subject, another being which has its own entirely independent life. Vitality lives in her *and* within her: an ultimate expression of the Shelley-Brontë-Dickinson metaphors of enclosure, doubleness, escape. 'Ordinarily,' de Beauvoir remarks, 'life is but a condition of existence; in gestation it appears as creative . . . [the pregnant woman] is no longer an object subservient to a subject [a man, a mother, daddy, Jay Cee]; she is no longer a subject afflicted with the anxiety that accompanies liberty; she is one with that equivocal reality: life. Her body is at last her own, since it exists for the child who belongs to her.'[66]

That this liberating sense of oneness with life was precisely Plath's attitude toward childbirth and maternity is clear from 'Three Women,' a verse-play on the subject in which the voice of the First Woman, the healthily golden and achieving mother, is obviously the poet's own, or at least the voice for which the poet strives. [. . .] And when the child appears later on, he appears in flight – like the escaping virgin, the arrow, or the lioness – a 'blue furious boy [. . .]' who flies 'into the room, a shriek at his heel.' And again Plath stresses the likeness of babies, poems, and miraculous escapes: 'I see them,' she says of babies, '[. . .] These pure small images . . . Their footsoles are untouched. They are walkers of air.' Living babies, in other words, are escaping shrieks – as poems are; pure small images – as poems are; walkers of air – as poems are: all ways for the self to transcend itself.

Conversely, Plath speaks of dead poems, the poems of jeweled symmetry that would please the disquieting muses, as being like still-born babies, an analogy which goes back to the male tradition that defines the offspring of 'lady poets' as abortions, stillbirths, dead babies. 'These poems do not live,' she writes in 'Stillborn.' '. . . it's a sad diagnosis . . . they are dead and their mother near dead with dis-traction' (*Crossing the Water*, p.20). It becomes clear that certain nineteenth- and twentieth-century women, confronting *confinement* (in both senses of the word) simply translated the traditional baby-poem metaphor quite literally into their own experience of their lives and bodies. 'I, the miserable and abandoned, am an *abortion*, to be spurned. . . .' said Mary Shelley's monster – and he was, for he escaped from confinement to no positive end.[67] I 'step to you from the black car of Lethe/Pure as baby,' cried Plath – meaning, my poems, escaping from the morgue of my body, do that. And 'I was in a boundary of wool and painted boards . . .' wrote Anne Sexton. But 'we swallow magic and we *deliver* Anne.'[68] For the poet, finally, can be delivered from her own confining self through the metaphor of birth.

Can be, but need not necessarily be. And here we get to the quali-fication I mentioned earlier. For while, as de Beauvoir pointed out, the processes of gestation link the pregnant woman with life even as they imply new ways of self-transcendence, they are also frightening, dan-gerous, and uncontrollable. The body works mysteriously, to its own ends, its product veiled like death in unknowable interior darkness. Just as the poet cannot always direct the flow of images but instead finds herself surprised by shocking connections made entirely with-out the help or approval of the ego, so the mother realizes, as de Beauvoir notes, that 'it is beyond her power to influence what in the end will be the true nature of this being who is developing in her womb . . . she is [at times] in dread of giving birth to a defective or a monster.'[69] (In other words, in Plath's case, to the ugly bear or the acetylene virgin that she both fears and desires to be.) Moreover, to the extent that pregnancy depersonalizes the woman, freeing her from her own ego and instead enslaving her to the species, it draws her backward into her own past (the germplasm she shelters belongs to her parents and ancestors as well as to her) and at the same time catapults her forward into her own future (the germplasm she shelters will belong to her children and their survivors as well as to her). 'Caught up in the great cycle of the species, she affirms life in the teeth of time and death,' says de Beauvoir. 'In this she glimpses immortality; but in her flesh she feels the truth of Hegel's words: "the birth of children is the death of parents."'[70] To Plath, this network backwards and forwards was clearly of immense importance. For, if having babies (and writing poems) was a way of escaping from the dark house of daddy's shoe, it was also, paradoxically, a frightening re-encounter with daddy: daddy alive, and daddy dead.[71] □

Gilbert goes on to discuss the bee sequence, describing 'Stings' as exploring the 'interrelated anxieties of poetry and pregnancy', reading Plath's metaphors of bee-keeping as 'a way of coming to terms with her own female position in the cycle of the species'. Gilbert concludes with underlining the positive significance of Plath's poetry, which she sees as going some way towards resolving the paradox of simultaneously desiring and fearing freedom, through the poetry's 'optimistically feminine redefinition of traditions that have so far been primarily masculine' by reaffirming the strength of Plath's lyrical 'I'.[72]

We will conclude this chapter with an extract from Carole Ferrier's 1979 essay 'The Beekeeper's Apprentice', which argues for a critical approach capable of clarifying the 'essentially *political* interrelations of critic, society, and audience, and author', arguing against her understanding of the reductively biographical approaches of Holbrook and Oates. Ferrier's interest in the extent of Plath's knowledge and conscious critique of Freudian analysis in her poetry leads us to debates and arguments we will see developed in the following chapters, but in the extract below Ferrier considers Plath's complicated relationship with patriarchy and the ways in which this is explored through the father figure. In opposition to critical approaches which 'reflect rather than challenge the hegemonic ideology', Ferrier reads Plath's poems as progressively empowering and positive. Here, she interprets the 'bee poems' as narratives of female endurance and strength, interpreting Plath's use of mythic structures in explicitly feminist terms:

■ An activity that figures prominently in a number of Plath's poems, early and late, is beekeeping. Plath's father and, subsequently, the poet herself engaged in it, and in her poems on this subject beekeeping is invested with a various and complex symbolic significance. An early poem, 'The Beekeeper's Daughter,' portrays a relationship between father and daughter in which the father is seen as moving about in a garden, 'hieratical' among the 'many-breasted hives,' like a priest of Diana or Cybele. The 'queenship no mother can contest' involves a relationship with the father that has sexual undertones: the scene of the poem evokes the Garden of Eden with its 'fruit that's death to taste,' and where the knowledge of death follows ritual initiation into certain mysteries:

> Father, bridegroom, in this Easter egg
> Under the coronal of sugar roses
>
> The queen bee marries the winter of your year.

[. . .] In earlier bee poems, the presiding figure of the beekeeper is the father, but then the poet herself becomes beekeeper, thereby gaining symbolic control over her own life and actions.

The bee poems in *Ariel* chart a progress in consciousness that begins with the initiation ritual of 'The Bee Meeting.' The presence of the white goddess is indicated by various references.[73] Present as symbolic figures are the midwife (bringer forth of life) and the sexton (digger of graves), and also a mysterious 'man in black,' who in earlier poems was identified with the figure of Plath's father, the original beekeeper. Prominent in the ritual is a male figure in white, '. . . the surgeon my neighbors are waiting for,/This apparition in a green helmet,/Shining gloves and white suit,' who is also a kind of unidentified executioner. There is a sense that knowledge waits somewhere just beyond the limit of consciousness, but that to gain it could mean death. [. . .] there is an identification of the speaker with the queen bee, who is also being hunted; and, in the connection of the hive with a coffin – the 'long white box in the grove' – there is a clear threat of death.

The dual identification of the central character with both the woman who expects to be sacrificed and the queen bee suggests the two sides of the female personality as conceived of by patriarchal archetype – the victim and what Butscher calls the 'bitch goddess' – that recur in Plath's work. [. . .]

The ritual of the bee meeting leads to the delivery of the bee box in the next poem in the sequence ['The Arrival of the Bee Box']. In this poem the box of bees becomes a metaphor for the fertile, swarming, and potentially destructive chaos that the poet senses within herself. The line 'I have to live with it overnight' indicates that she is dealing with her own unconscious, in which she finds a mass of conflicting and incoherent messages that she is almost powerless to understand, let alone control (play Caesar to):

> It is the noise that appalls me most of all,
> The unintelligible syllables.
> It is like a Roman mob, . . .
>
> I lay my ear to furious Latin.

The evocation of incomprehensible disorder within recalls the earlier account of the 'colossus' who dominated her unconscious – 'Mule-bray, pig-grunt and bawdy cackles/Proceed from your great lips' ['The Colossus'] – but instead of the father, central here are the bees; and though they remain connected with the father, they embody, through the queen bee especially, a sense of the persona's separate female identity. Plath frequently uses metaphors of a box, a windowless room, or a cellar as analogies for the unconscious, and there is also a pervasive sense of the potential danger of breaking into, or out of, this enclosed space. Sometimes the archetype represents the boundaries of the identity, threatened by what is outside; at other times it represents the mysterious and frightening aspects of the inner, unconscious mind, from which things intermittently rise up into consciousness.

[. . .] The persona knows in 'The Arrival of the Bee Box' that she must set the bees free, but is afraid of what they will do once they are loosed: 'I am no source of honey/So why should they turn on me?' The nature of the antinomy here comes through in 'Stings.' The bee-keeping activity threatens the beekeeper; she must organize and discipline her hive and attempt both to understand and master the craft of beekeeping, which involves centrally the liberation of the queen into the bride flight and subsequent fertility. The poet is both beekeeper, the practising craftsperson, and the queen bee that soars into the sky. The conclusion of 'Stings' is an image of triumph and escape from constraint and confinement:

> [. . .] but I
> Have a self to recover, a queen.
> [. . .]
>
> Now she is flying
> More terrible than she ever was, red
> Scar in the sky, red comet
> Over the engine that killed her –
> The mausoleum, the wax house.

The imagery strongly recalls that at the end of 'Lady Lazarus,' where there is a phoenixlike rebirth:

> Out of the ash
> I rise with my red hair
> And I eat men like air.

The ominous conclusions of these two poems are not accidental. A familiarity with details of the life cycle of the bee (which we can be sure Plath possessed) clarifies her intentions and her irony in the poems. The theme of repression and isolation building up a violence that turns on things outside rather than to self-destruction is central to the poem 'Purdah,' which ends:

> I shall unloose –
> From the small jeweled
> Doll he guards like a heart –
>
> The lioness,
> The shriek in the bath,
> The cloak of holes.

Here we have a reference to the murder of Agamemnon by Clytemnestra. The figure of Clytemnestra contrasts strongly with the two famous daughters in Greek drama, Electra and Antigone, whose only course appears to be to resist and to refuse to say 'yes': they are essentially passive female stereotypes who cannot take any positive action to free themselves (though Electra tries to work through Orestes). A patriarchy of family and possessiveness that turns women into 'small jeweled dolls' Plath suggests, can sometimes only be adequately combated by the knife of Clytemnestra, and there is an increasing awareness in her poetry of the need to fight 'the boot in the face,' to abandon the passive and masochistic acceptance of authority. Her references to Greek drama give a wider context to the personally based material of her poetry and are also in some cases an incidental gloss on her use of Freudian categories.[74] □

Ferrier goes on to read 'The Swarm' as an attempt by Plath to relate the personal to a wider historical context, a debate which we will see developed in the next chapter. Ferrier concludes with a reading of 'Wintering' where she suggests there is an empowering 'shift away from the centrality of the father or indeed any male figure – [. . .] and toward an assertion of the persona's own separate identity independent of any "other"'.[75]

The following decade is marked by the publication of Plath's *Collected Poems* in 1981, which confirms Plath as a major poet, and increases the critical interest in her work. Sophisticated psychoanalytic and historical approaches start to develop in Plath criticism. In contrast to the dominant approach of the 1970s, which was one of encompassment and simplification through thematic and mythic readings, critics begin to problematise their readings, interested in the complications and contradictions of Plath's poetry. Mary Lynn Broe's *Protean Poetic: The Poetry of Sylvia Plath*[76] (1980), indicates the shift in critical thinking from the desire for unification to an acceptance of multiplicity and diversity. Broe can be seen to be in opposition to the dominant desire in the seventies for the affirmation of identity in Plath's work, through her exploration of the dissolution of identity and her advancement of protean, shifting identities in Plath's writing, a move that corresponds to much of the recent critical debate.

CHAPTER THREE

'Waist-Deep in History': Cultural and Historical Readings

THE 1980s and the 1990s are a period of astonishing innovation in Plath criticism. The appearance of her *Collected Poems* in 1981, and the American publication of *The Journals of Sylvia Plath* in 1982, confirmed and intensified the continuing critical interest in her writing. Further volumes of collected essays dedicated to her work appeared, most notably *Critical Essays on Sylvia Plath*, edited by Linda W. Wagner, alongside *Ariel Ascending*, edited by Paul Alexander, and *Modern Critical Views: Sylvia Plath*, edited by Harold Bloom. As Plath studies continued to develop in many areas, it becomes increasingly difficult to arrive at a representative selection, and maintain a linear, chronological approach to publications. Rather, we will consider recent Plath studies in three broadly defined, dominant areas of concern: feminism, cultural materialism and psychoanalysis. However, as you will discover, these are not rigid boundaries, and there will be many critical cross-currents, especially in the area of feminist studies that explores, questions and incorporates other disciplines.

This chapter will concentrate on broadly cultural materialist readings that explore the relationship in Plath's poetry between the self and the world. Critics such as Pamela Annas and Alan Sinfield consider the boundaries between the inner self and the culturally figured self, while historically informed critics such as Stan Smith and James E. Young, reinvigorate the debate on Plath's use of Holocaust imagery by suggesting that Plath can be read as a 'profoundly political poet'.[1] Chapter four is more concerned with the advances in feminist debate concerning Plath which, throughout the 1980s, become increasingly theoreticised, partly through an engagement with psychoanalytically informed criticism which redirects critical attention towards poems that explore issues of sexuality and selfhood. Critics such as Alicia Ostriker and Liz Yorke reveal the influence of European feminist thought, and move towards psychoanalytically informed readings, although again it is important to stress the extent and success of a multi-disciplinary approach to Plath's work, perhaps most creatively achieved by Jacqueline Rose, who concludes chapter four, and invites many of the current, ongoing debates of the final chapter.

First, however, we will briefly consider the critical response to the long anticipated *Collected Poems*, a volume that prompts many reviewers to reappraise their earlier evaluations and question many of the myths that developed around Plath's creative power.

Collected poems

After nearly two decades of critics' complaints and publishers' promises, Sylvia Plath's *Collected Poems* was published in 1981 and welcomed as the 'literary event' of the year. An instant critical and commercial success, the *Collected Poems* unexpectedly received the Pulitzer Prize for Poetry in 1982, an award rarely granted posthumously, and was greeted with excitement and admiration by reviewers welcoming it as 'the most important book of poetry this year' and 'a triumph of hard work and artifice'.[2] After years of struggling with vaguely arranged volumes of 'transitional' and 'late' poetry, most commentators were very pleased with the careful dating of the *Collected Poems*, praising the 'care and tact' of Hughes's editing, and welcoming the 'indispensable notes and introduction . . .'.[3] Although much of the *Collected Poems* had been previously published and discussed, critics were often prompted by the complete presentation of the oeuvre to reconsider and re-evaluate Plath: 'Sylvia Plath's poetry is better – more accomplished, assured, original – than its current reputation; it stands with the best American poetry of the fifties and sixties. Misconceived, it has exercised a baleful influence [. . .] Reread chronologically, it should give a new life to contemporary poetry.'[4] William H. Pritchard, in a review ironically entitled, 'An Interesting Minor Poet?', suggests that his reappraisal lies partly in the power of the poems when read in a collected volume:

■ The result is to make her appear an altogether larger and more satisfying poet than this reader had taken her to be. [. . .] For years I have endorsed Irving Howe's limited judgment of Sylvia Plath as an 'interesting minor poet'. But I don't think anyone who submits to this collection is likely to be comfortable with that judgment. She was rather, was indeed – as the expression goes – something else.[5] □

This congratulatory mood is not shared, however, by Marjorie Perloff who severely criticises the editing of the volume as 'curiously inadequate', finding the inclusion of juvenilia inappropriate, Hughes's control of the material problematic, and the edition to be, overall, 'sloppy'. Perloff does, however, concur with other critics in recognising the ultimate value of the volume, stating that: 'Nevertheless, Plath remains an extraordinary poet and the *Collected Poems* reveal a side of her we have not seen before.'[6] Perloff proceeds to offer insightful readings of what she classifies as the 'Terrible Lyrics' of 1962, in particular, a fine interpretation of the previously unpublished 'Burning the Letters' – a poem often dismissed as problematically personal.

Dave Smith accurately describes the experience of many, notably, male critics, who had previously marginalised Plath as a 'special interest' poet, who now found themselves surprised by the force and power of this volume: ' . . . I am astonished to discover this poet is not the Plath I have vaguely remembered, the Plath I have called *interesting* . . . [I am] caught up in this cranky, beautiful, maudlin, neurotic, soaring book . . .'.[7]

The most restrained review comes from Helen Vendler, who feels Plath's poetry suffers from a ' . . . narrowness of tone, [and] her scrupulous refusal to generalize, in her best poems, beyond her own case'; and yet she also acknowledges Plath's 'claim on us – a genius for the transcription in words of those wild states of feeling which in the rest of us remain so inchoate that we quail under them, speechless'.[8]

Michael Hulse articulates the consensus of many critics when he concludes a perceptive review with the comment: '*Collected Poems* is not only the most important collected volume of the last twenty years, it is also a corrective to many of the myths and misunderstandings.'[9] Many critics see the volume as challenging the now mythic admiration for Plath's almost supernatural creative breakthrough; Laurence Lerner maintains that: '[*Collected Poems*] undercuts at least one popular view of Sylvia Plath, that her early work is controlled, formal, even superficial, and the later poems make true contact with her anxieties . . .', reflecting many of the reviews of *Crossing the Water*; while Dave Smith takes to task another common myth indulged in when reading Plath's poetry: 'It is perverse logic which begins with the facts of Plath's suicide and works back to find the poems as scripts of illness.'[10] As many other reviewers do, Smith dismisses Plath's classification as a 'confessional' poet, a term that becomes fairly redundant in Plath studies as critics increasingly view her in less restrictive, what could even be described as old-fashioned, terms. In an incisive comment that stresses the increasing difference between the critical response and analysis of the early 1960s and that of the 1980s, Perloff foreshadows the direction of much contemporary debate; she recognises the significant replacement of criticism informed by the theories of R.D. Laing with criticism developed from the writing of the immensely influential French psychoanalyst and theorist Jacques Lacan when she describes Plath studies as becoming 'more interested in unmasking the verbal strategies of "sane" discourse than in dealing with individual psychosis'.[11]

Cultural discourses

Jerome Mazzaro's 1979 essay 'Sylvia Plath and the Cycles of History' is one of the earliest attempts to consider Plath's poetry from a historical perspective, identifying her move from a 'myth of nature to social and political concerns' as being a symptom of the atomic age. Mazzaro echoes the earlier observations of Lucas Myers in his comment on the changing political atmosphere of the late 1950s and Plath's relationship to it:

■ [. . .] No reader of *The Bell Jar* (1963) will mistake the impact of Lowell's 'Memories of West Street and Lepke' (1958) on the structure of the novel. As that poem had seen his own breakdown, shock treatment, and recovery in terms of the electrocution of Czar Louis Lepke of Murder Incorporated, Plath's heroine sets her own breakdown, shock treatment, and recovery against the electrocution of Ethel and Julius Rosenberg.

Few readers, too, can avoid the coincidences of her interests in fallout, militarism, and concentration camps and the public discussions of militarism and the massive literature that attended the capture and impending trial of Adolf Eichmann.

[. . .] The economy of the country seemed increasingly to owe its stability to what President Eisenhower called a 'military-industrial complex,' [. . .] Fred J. Cook had developed the history and implications of this 'wedding' of arms and industry for an issue of *The Nation* (28 October 1961), and Plath cites the issue as important. She could not have missed the equally 'sensational' capture of Eichmann in Argentina in June of 1960. [. . .] The year also saw the release of the motion picture *Judgment at Nuremberg*, in addition to lengthy controversies about the jurisdiction and legality of the upcoming Eichmann trial. Like others of her generation, Plath felt an era of noninvolvement ending. Her concern with these issues would mark an emergence from 'silence' into an era of political and social activism. This new era would, in turn, require new attitudes toward both her surroundings and her self.[12] □

Later, we will see the way in which Jacqueline Rose and James E. Young fully explore the impact of these historical events on Plath's poetry but, here, Mazzaro is more interested in the conflict between self and society, rather than the ways in which society is explored through the self. Considering such later poems as 'Getting There', 'Cut' and 'Lady Lazarus', Mazzaro concludes by echoing the terminology of Joyce Carol Oates's earlier objections, arguing that: '. . . if one is to grant relevance to Plath's cycles of history, one must grant it on the same terms that Auden grants history to Yeats – as a conflict between Reason and Imagination, objectivity and subjectivity, and the individual and the masses rather then between good and evil will, integrated and diffuse thought, and personality and the impersonal state.'[13] Yet he views the conflict in Plath's work in more sympathetic terms than Oates, suggesting that Plath shares a literary tradition and dilemma with Yeats; they both struggle to shape and order contemporary history, a process, Mazzaro suggests, that is further complicated for Plath by being situated in a post-Freudian society.

Stan Smith progresses this debate into a Marxist area of discussion in his valuable 1982 study *Inviolable Voice: History and Twentieth-Century Poetry*, which includes the significant chapter, 'Waist-Deep in History: Sylvia Plath'. Guided by Georg Lukács's *History and Class Consciousness* (1922), Smith proposes his argument for the reading of poetry in an introduction that engages with and questions T. S. Eliot's 1919 essay 'Tradition and the Individual Talent':

■ Most poetry seems to function at a level remote from history, where a dissociated mind confronts a landscape innocent of social meaning. [. . .] But there is no such thing as an 'innocent' poem. All poetry, at its deepest levels, is structured by the precise historical experience from which it emerged, those conjectures in which its author was formed, came to consciousness, and found a voice. A writer is always the creature of circumstance: a particular set of social relations, of class, family, sex and generation, offer their own cultural, ideological and emotional forms, which he or she acquires even before it has become a matter of personal choice, of acceptance and rejection. [. . .] Lurking behind Eliot's formulae . . . is a central problem for understanding the way a poem relates to history. A poem is produced at the intersection of two histories: the history of the formal possibilities available to the poet – conventions, themes, language – and the history of the individual as a particular expressive 'medium', a product of his own time and place.[14] □

In a study dominated by canonical male writers, such as T. S. Eliot and Ezra Pound, Plath's appearance with such historical heavyweights further establishes her stature as a central figure of the twentieth century. In the introduction, Smith questions the concept of Plath as an intensely personal poet and, instead, identifies her as being absorbed in the historical moment, being concerned with articulating the relationship between the individual and the world: 'For Sylvia Plath . . . identity itself is the primary historical datum: the self is a secretion of history, and therefore not initially "my" self at all, but the voice of its antecedents, its progenitors, a "mouthpiece of the dead".'[15] The chapter begins with an acknowledgment of Plath's status as an 'intensely private poet' before proceeding to argue that Plath's work engages deeply with history, through considerations of such divergent poems as 'Winter Trees' and 'Morning Song'; Smith surmises that:

■ All these poems have a common preoccupation: the relation between the individual self and the process in which it comes to iden- tity, to which it is always irreparably bound, and which, sooner or later, reclaims it. What they embody, as their primary premise, is the *historicity* of the personal life, its status as an historical secretion, the precipitate of an order which precedes and will re-absorb it. In such a perception, Plath poetry goes beyond the polarised, antithetical image of self and world, of transcendent subject and immanent object, which characterises the poetry of most of her contemporaries. It is precisely because her poetry is intensely private that it records so profoundly and distinctly the experience of living history. In Plath's poetry, there is no gap between private and public.[16] □

Smith goes on to consider the early 'Poem for a Birthday' sequence, sug- gesting that these poems explore the 'complications which arise from . . . interweaving relations between self, other and third'.[17] This crisis of identity and gender, then, is central to an understanding of the intersec- tions between self and history in Plath's poetry which lead to the radical internalisation of historical experience in 'The Colossus' and 'Daddy':

■ Though male and female principles struggle, [after 'Maenad'], throughout ['Poem for a Birthday'], this is not just a conflict *out there*, in the realm of 'Time', but something which is also inside, on the very terrain which constitutes the self. History is internalised by the self at the moment that it acquires these antithetical principles as its moral and emotional baggage. In Plath's poetry, the self is radically double in its sexual identity, only arbitrarily declined into male and female inflexions. In a famous comment on one of her poems, 'Daddy', for the BBC Third Programme, Plath spelt this out in explicitly Freudian terms:

The poem is spoken by a girl with an Electra complex. Her father died while she thought he was God. Her case is complicated by the fact that her father was also a Nazi and her mother very possibly part Jewish. In the daughter the two strains marry and paralyse each other – she has to act out the awful little allegory before she is free of it.

Though the daughter identifies with the 'Jewish' mother, by the end of 'Daddy' she has become a phallic aggressor herself, rejoicing as 'the villagers' drive a stake through the 'fat black heart' of the vampire father, cutting the black telephone off 'at the root', in an inescapable image of emasculation, so that 'The voices just can't worm through'. Cutting off the telephone means asserting independence from the voices of the past out of which the self has been shaped.

In that almost unnoticed progression from a single speaker to the collective image of the villagers, Plath gives a further twist to the revolt. She refuses the unitary self imposed by the parental images – a unity always splitting into two opposed principles, of male and female, active and passive, Nazi and Jew, etc. Instead, the self becomes almost what Freud spoke of as the 'brother clan' which overthrows the child-devouring primal father, replacing the single tyrant by a collectivity of equals. [. . .]

['The Colossus'] speaks not just of a particular relationship, with the father who died while Plath was still a child, but of the whole relationship between self and history, mediated through the institutions of a patriarchal society. This is revealed in the fourth stanza, which moves rapidly from the mythic origins of things in the *Oresteia* (where Electra finds herself by sharing in matricide with her brother Orestes) through Rome, to the anarchy of the present:

A blue sky out of the Oresteia
Arches above us. O father, all by yourself
You are pithy and historical as the Roman Forum.
I open my lunch on a hill of black cypress.
Your fluted bones and acanthine hair are littered

In their old anarchy to the horizon-line.
It would take more than a lightning-stroke
To create such a ruin.

The father as colossus is here both an external and an internalised history, symbolised by those horizons which are simultaneously out there and the internal limits of consciousness which extends to the skyline. [. . .] The struggle to dredge the silt from the throat of the colossus is a struggle to hear clearly the voices of history, to discern what it is trying to say to her – a struggle which in 'Daddy' leads to the final destructive refusal of that past, the tearing-out of the telephone wires, that last rebellion of the historical being against its own historicity, a rebellion soon to issue in the only exit that remained open, an abandonment of the human world altogether, in suicide.[18] □

While the 'bee sequence' remains a compelling narrative for feminist critics, it also becomes of central interest to critics exploring issues of history and selfhood. In a slightly later essay, Ellin Sarot concentrates her discussion on 'The Swarm', stating that: 'With the exception of "The Swarm", the bee poems are ahistorical', a view that contrasts with Smith's description of 'The Swarm' as the 'least historical'. Sarot offers a fine reading of the figure of Napoleon, suggesting that the relevance of this individual historical figure can be enlarged to correspond with modern history: 'With the naming of these countries, as if by compulsive anachronistic reference, the victims of Napoleon's war instantly become analogous to victims of the European Holocaust of more than a century later.'[19]

Smith's readings of 'The Swarm' and 'The Arrival of the Bee Box', exploring both the 'political and psychological, . . . social and linguistic ordering of reality', are central to his argument and are worth full consideration, but I have chosen to concentrate on Smith's discussion of the 'Holocaust' poetry, specifically 'Mary's Song'. Marxist approaches to Plath enliven the debate over her use of 'Holocaust' imagery, more often than not arguing for the cultural and political justification of the relationship between self and history, as we will see in Alan Sinfield's 'case for extremism'. Here, Smith, by highlighting the textuality of Plath's poetry, releases his argument from accusations that Plath unjustifiably appropriates these images and, instead, displays the 'deeper correspondences between the personal and the collective tragedies':

■ Plath's poems are, first and foremost, carefully constructed *texts*. If their meaning cannot be reduced to the conscious intentions of their author, it equally cannot be reduced to spirit-messages from the unconscious, over which the literary talent has no control. The full meaning of the text lies in the interplay of *all* its levels, *on the terrain of language*. These levels are not only personal (conscious and unconscious) but cultural and social, deriving from both a literary and linguistic tradition and a public and collective history.

Just as the poem, for Plath, derives from its linguistic and poetic antecedents, so the self too is a secretion of its inherited languages. [. . .]

It would be wrong to see Plath's use of the imagery of the concentration camp simply as unacceptable hyperbole, in which a merely private anguish is inflated to the proportions of global atrocity. Rather, concerned that 'personal experience shouldn't be a kind of shut box and mirror-looking narcissistic experience', but 'should be generally relevant, to such things as Hiroshima and Dachau and so on', Plath has seen the deeper correspondences between the personal and the collective tragedies, their common origins in a civilisation founded on repression at the levels both of the body politic and of the carnal body. 'Mary's Song' uses a gruesome analogy to bring home this correspondence, linking, through the image of the 'Sunday lamb', the familiar and the monstrous. For if 'The Sunday lamb cracks in its fat./[. . .]

Sacrifices its opacity . . .', this heart which renders the opaque trans-
lucent, 'A window, holy gold', is a brutal travesty of that
'incandescent' sacrifice in which the Paschal lamb died for man, and
the homely domestic oven is transformed rapidly into the gas ovens of
Nazi Germany, which in turn becomes a landscape burnt out by fire-
bombing: [. . .] The heart becomes, by the final lines, the 'holocaust I
walk in,/O golden child the world will kill and eat'. The collective
deaths have their origins here, in the burnings of the heart, the gall
and heartburn of each individual being. The 'golden child' who is
held precious will be murdered. The sacrifice, the poem insists, goes
on in each heart, and for each heart. The 'cicatrix' that marks a whole
people has its sources in those wounds out of which the bourgeois ego
has been shaped, those scars which are also emblems of our freedom.

Plath is, in fact, a profoundly political poet, who has seen the
generic nature of these private catastrophes, their origin in a civilisation founded on mass manipulation and collective trickery, which
recruits its agents by those processes of repression and sublimation,
denial and deferment which bring the ego to its belated birth in a family, a class, a gender. [. . .][20] □

Although Smith's study is concerned with literary criticism, Plath's
'Holocaust' poetry is also of interest to other disciplines considering
issues of ideology and historical consciousness. James E. Young includes
a chapter on Plath in his excellent study *Writing and Rewriting the
Holocaust: Narrative and the Consequences of Interpretation*, a study that questions 'precisely how historical memory, understanding, and meaning are
construed in Holocaust narrative'.[21] By considering metaphorical uses of
the Holocaust, both by survivors and non-Jewish writers such as Plath,
John Berryman and Anne Sexton,[22] Young aims to 'examine how both
writers and readers of this literature apprehend events through figurative language, and how we understand our contemporary world in light
of the Holocaust figures we inevitably bring to it'.[23] James shifts the critical focus on Plath by suggesting that rather than 'asking whether a
writer coming after the Holocaust *should* be traumatized by a memory
she may have inherited only literarily, we might ask to what extent the
writer *was* traumatized by her literary historical memory of the
Holocaust'[24] (my italics). In 'The Holocaust Confessions of Sylvia Plath',
Young explores the historical and social developments which meant the
Holocaust became 'not just public knowledge but public memory', arguing that the Holocaust becomes an 'available figural lexicon' for Plath.
Young culturally justifies the reciprocal relationship between personal
suffering and historical suffering in Plath's use of Jewish and Japanese
imagery by suggesting that Plath was responding to a shared, national
consciousness, or historical memory, of the Second World War.

■ Of the many poetic references to the Holocaust by nonvictims, those in Sylvia Plath's last book of poems, *Ariel*, remain among those most bitterly contested. For unlike John Berryman, who became an imaginary Jew in order to explore the idea of antisemitism, or Anne Sexton, who explicitly represented the impact of Auschwitz on herself, or even Yevgeny Yevtushenko, who called himself (and all Russians) Jewish in order to remember Babi Yar, Sylvia Plath represented herself – her inner life – in the figure of the Holocaust Jew. Whether or not these poets and other nonvictims like William Heyen, Charles Reznikoff, Irving Fieldman, and Barbara Helfgott Hyett can be read as Holocaust poets may be debatable. Sylvia Plath's case is more straightforward: she is not a Holocaust poet, simply because she does not write about the Holocaust. She writes about herself figured as a Holocaust Jew, among other contemporary images of suffering. As poets like Abraham Sutzkever, Yitzhak Katzenelson, Nelly Sachs, and Paul Celan inevitably figured the Holocaust in the shapes of unrelated events, Plath has now figured her own – outwardly unrelated – life in the image of the Holocaust itself.

Alvin Rosenfeld is therefore correct to question the assumption that Plath's poems can 'expose the atrocity of the age through exposing self-inflicted wounds,'[25] echoing Edward Butscher, who writes on this point: 'There is no way that the poetry of an American girl writing from the remote perspective of the 1950s could ever capture the actual, brutal reality of the Holocaust.'[26] But then, to some extent, this would also be true of any young American-born poet, boy or girl, Jewish or non-Jewish writing safely in the fifties, including Heyen, Reznikoff, Feldman, or even Randall Jarrell, to name a few of the American poets who have responded most eloquently to the Holocaust. But unlike these poets, who attempted to capture – or at least, respond to – aspects of the Holocaust, Plath has not tried to reimagine these events in any way. The Holocaust exists for her not as an experience to be retold or described but as an event available to her (as it was to all who came after) only as a figure, an idea, in whose image she has expressed another brutal reality: that of her own internal pain.

[I will] explore the ways in which the poet's world and personal experiences are perceived and represented in light of the Holocaust. Specifically, it is to examine how the Holocaust – once it became its own archetype and entered the public imagination as an independent icon – also became a figure for subsequent pain, suffering, and destruction. In this discussion of Plath, I would like to shift our critical emphasis away from the poet's 'right' to Holocaust imagery, in order to explore: (1) how Holocaust imagery functions in non-Holocaust poetry; (2) how its figures organize and create meaning in the poet's world [. . .]

During the months preceding her suicide, it may thus be impossible to discern at what point images of the Holocaust entered her imaginative world and then, taking root there, at what point every domestic scene, every daily bump and bruise evoked in her images of mass suffering. For it was in this period that the events of the Holocaust broke into the public domain and became not just public knowledge but public memory. Between April and December 1961, when the Eichmann trial in Jerusalem riveted public and media attention on the heretofore neglected details of the Holocaust, Plath was pregnant (after having miscarried in February) and moving to Devon from London with her husband, Ted Hughes. Between Eichmann's conviction in December 1961 and his execution in April 1962, Plath lived and wrote in Devon in their new country home, which she left in September after discovering Hughes's infidelity. Between September and December 1962, in her darkest hours, Plath wrote 'Mary's Song,' 'Lady Lazarus,' and 'Daddy,' her so-called Holocaust poems. [. . .]

Of history's innumerable victims, what aspect of the Jews' victimization during the Holocaust lent this catastrophe to Plath's imagination more than others? Why is she not Armenian here, or a black slave, or a Russian from the Gulag? The choice of the Holocaust Jew as a trope here by Plath has less to do with its intrinsic appropriateness than it does with its visibility as a public figure for suffering. As was the case to some extent with the Rosenbergs' execution, the salient aspect of the Holocaust was its wide public knowledge, its place as a figure in the public mind. Where figures of destruction had traditionally taken generations to enter the literary imagination, being passed down an epoch and a book at a time, in America's mass media of the fifties and England's of the sixties, generations of inherited memory were compressed within the space of months. Images selected by the media for their spectacular and often horrifying qualities became the most common figures of all. For the writer and poet immersed in letters and media, as Plath was, these figures seem to have become a kind of currency by which she traded her ideas with the rest of the world, literally absorbing the shape of these figures only to return them to the public sphere with her own imprint on them.

In fact, as Alvarez reminds us, the 'Holocaust Jew' was not Plath's only figure for victimhood. Mixing metaphors slightly in an early version of 'Lady Lazarus,' Plath drew also upon the Japanese victims of the atomic bombs. Again, it was not for any actual correspondence between these kinds of suffering, but as Alvarez suggests in the case of the Japanese, it may only have been for the rhyme. The figure of victimized Japanese was presumed already to be part of an available figural lexicon, which she now searched for the right sound:

Gentlemen, ladies

These are my hands
My knees.
I may be skin and bone,
I may be Japanese . . .

'"Why *Japanese*?" [Alvarez] niggled away at her. "Do you just need the rhyme? Or are you trying to hitch an easy lift by dragging in the atomic victims? If you're going to use this kind of violent material, you've got to play it cool . . ." She argued back sharply, but later, when the poem was finally published after her death, the line had gone.'[27] As Alvarez acknowledges in retrospect, however, she *did* need the rhyme, even if her allusion to the Japanese was not quite relevant. Form and sound may have thus influenced her choice of metaphors at this point, not just the supposed meaning created in such allusions.

In the cases of both Japanese and Jewish figures, mass and anonymous suffering were drawn from the war period, an era contemporary with her own life. Her historical memory was thus constituted both by history books and classical poetry, as well as an infusion of images from the mass media, from newsreels, newspapers, and radio, which create public figures and icons not by using them as figures so much as by saturating the imagination with them. For Plath, it may have been important that events were drawn from the era of her own life, if not from the experiences of her own life. In this way, she shared the era of victimhood, victimized by modern life at large as the Jews and Japanese had been victimized by specific events in modern life.

In Plath's case, her metaphors are built upon the absorption of public experience by language itself, experience that is then internalized and made private by the poet, used to order her private world, and then reexternalized in public verse. If 'The public horrors of Nazi concentration camps and the personal horrors of fragmented identities become interchangeable,' as Arthur Oberg suggests,[28] it is not because they are actually analogous; it is just that the movement between public and personal horrors is at once historical and private. As long as these images of the Holocaust are public, they inevitably enter the private imagination at some level, where they are invariably evoked to order personal experiences. To use the camp experience as a 'ready made modern example' (Alvarez's words) of one's personal pain need not be a conscious or deliberate act, but only a way of knowing one's inner life in the languages and figure of an outer world. In fact, we might ask here if it is ever possible to separate 'private' from 'historical' worlds, insofar as we may neither express our private lives without recourse to public (i.e., historical) language, nor know history except by ordering it privately. In embodying the extremity of this reciprocal exchange between the private and historical realms, Plath's poems seem not to 'exploit atrocity' so much as they merely draw upon a public pool of language that is necessarily informed by atrocity.

Thus, in 'Mary's Song,' a 'Sunday lamb crack[ing] in its fat' suddenly turns sacrificial as the speaker glimpses it through the oven window. The fire that 'makes it precious' becomes

The same fire

Melting the tallow heretics,
Ousting the Jews.
Their thick palls float

Over the cicatrix of Poland, burnt-out
Germany.
They do not die.

Gray birds obsess my heart,
Mouth-ash, ash of eye.
They settle. On the high

Precipice
That emptied one man into space
The ovens glowed like heavens, incandescent.

It is a heart,
This holocaust I walk in,
O golden child the world will kill and eat.[29]

From associations that reveal more her imaginative preoccupations than her sense of self, she moves suddenly from peering inside her oven to entering it – at which point, it seems to enter her. The Jews' pall floats over and through her, and they do not die but obsess her heart. Even the ambiguity of her syntax (is she addressing a golden child or describing one who will be killed and eaten?) seems to reflect the confused exchange between her associations; she moves from seeing, to figuring what she sees, to entering her metaphor as both agent and victim of it.

Like her other poems, 'Mary's Song' is not about the Holocaust, but it still betrays some understanding, a particular figure, of it. She has, after all, recalled only certain images, which in themselves reveal her personal access to them. In 'Mary's Song,' it is not the personal pain of the victims she draws upon, or the mass murder, or the history of Jewish persecution, but rather it is an idea of victimhood and sacrifice of innocents that constitutes the core of her figure. She did not thereby suffer 'as a Jew' so much as she represented her suffering through her own grasp of how (even why) Jews suffered. And as Edward Butscher hints, this vision is necessarily Christian: 'Like the victims of Hiroshima, Sylvia suffers innocently for the crimes of others' (p. 322). That is, she suffers martyrlike, Christlike, and in her mind, Jewlike for others' sins: through this figure and its exchange with her own victimhood, Plath's Holocaust seems to be a kind of calvary.

In this way, she also reveals a surprisingly acute sensitivity to the paschal valences in a 'lamb crack[ing] in its fat [that] sacrifices its opacity,' seemingly conscious of the etymological resonances of sacrifice and burnt offering in her reference to 'this holocaust I walk in.' But by making herself the sacrifice here, she also betrays her own limited understanding of the figure of Jewish suffering itself: again, it is a particularly Christian remembrance of events automatically figured by her idea of a 'holocaust' as a sacrifice of Jews, however innocent. So even as she uses a knowledge of the Holocaust to figure her pain, her own victimhood, this knowledge itself is necessarily prefigured in an essentially Christian frame.

In 'Lady Lazarus' and 'Daddy,' the contours of her own grasp of the Holocaust Jew are less exposed than the manner in which the figure itself organizes, expresses, and perhaps even inflames her private pain. On 'Daddy,' Plath has said, 'The poem is spoken by a girl with an Electra complex. Her father died while she thought he was God. Her case is complicated by the fact that her father was also a Nazi and her mother very possibly part Jewish. In the daughter or in her imagination, the two strains marry and paralyse each other – she has to act out the awful little allegory once over until she is free of it.'[30] The salient point here is that Plath did not believe in the literality of her figures: the poem is spoken by a girl (not written by one), and it is the speaker's (not her own) father who is a Nazi and whose mother is Jewish. The irony here, however, is that by 'acting out the awful little allegory once over [to be] free of it,' neither the speaker nor the poet seems to have freed herself of it but has only incorporated the allegory and its pain all the more deeply. Indeed, . . . insofar as these figures lay in some measure at the base of her unhappiness, she may have simultaneously represented them and used them to represent herself. [. . .]

The Nazis had nothing to do with her feelings of oppression at the hands of her father (he now a figure for her husband), but she was oppressed just the same. In fact, given the reciprocal transfer of imagery between men in these lines, Plath may even be going beyond her personal relationships to husband and father to suggest the larger experiences of women at the hands of men. She might have used slave and master, or even czar and Jews; but insofar as the speaker began in the figure of a Jew, she saw fit to see it through. Whether she became a Jew because her father was already 'Nazi-like' or turned her father into a Nazi because she already identified as a Jew may never be clear, but it is possible that one side of the equation ultimately determined the other, thus completing itself. For once she became a 'bit of a Jew,' both speaker and poet began to know and to represent her world in 'the Jewish way.'[31] □

Young suggests that Plath, as a non-Jew, relates to the Holocaust 'principally [as] a figure, a universal point of reference for all kinds of evil, oppression, and suffering'. Specifically suggesting Irving Howe and Alvin Rosenfeld, Young proposes that for Jewish critics, however, 'these events are inevitably grasped in all their literality . . . Where Auschwitz and Belsen are symbols of suffering for Plath – public ones, which carry no "sacred" charge – they are for the Jewish community at once symbols of specifically Jewish suffering . . .'[32] Young locates the resistance and objections to these poems in Plath's figuring of the Holocaust as a communal memory, yet insists on a historical justification for this: 'rather than disputing the authenticity of her figures, we might look to her poetry for the ways the Holocaust has entered public consciousness as a trope, and how it then informs both the poet's view of the world and her representation of it in verse.'[33]

But not all critics interpret Plath's use of Holocaust imagery so sympathetically: Harold Bloom, in the introduction to *Modern Critical Views: Sylvia Plath* (1989), reads the 'Holocaust' poetry as aesthetically unsuccessful, lacking the notion of literature as 'life-enhancing': '"Lady Lazarus," with its gratuitous and humanly offensive appropriation of the imagery of Jewish martyrs in Nazi death camps (an appropriation incessant in Plath) seems to me a pure instance of coercive rhetoric, transforming absolutely nothing.'[34] Seamus Heaney, himself a poet concerned with intersections between the self and history, protests in an otherwise admiring memorial essay on Plath in 1988, that in a poem such as 'Lady Lazarus' 'the cultural resonance of the original story is harnessed to a vehemently self-justifying purpose . . .'[35]

While the Holocaust poetry remains central to discussions of the social and historical dimensions of Plath's poetry, other critics, many from a sociological background, begin to locate Plath's writing within its social context, namely, the political and social developments of the 1950s and 1960s, and the subsequent cultural changes. Studies such as Benita Eisler's *Private Lives: Men and Women of the Fifties*, and Wini Breines's *Young, White and Miserable: Growing Up Female in the Fifties*,[36] study the dominant ideological forms of the 1950s, looking at the ways in which a commercial mass media shaped an increasingly consumerist society, often reinforcing gender roles which were especially restrictive for women. Historical pressures such as McCarthyism and the Cold War are recognised as underlying tensions in an era frequently remembered as carefree and prosperous. Depicted as an era of sexual and political anxiety, the tensions of this generation often seem to speak directly to the tensions in Plath's work: 'Secrets, lies, evasions, and role-playing: As adolescents we created a precocious public persona, acceptable and accepted, in order to be left alone.'[37] In the chapter 'Sexual Puzzles', Breines recognises *The Bell Jar*'s protagonist Esther Greenwood as a woman restricted by the gender narrative of the era, an era in which women were simultaneously exaggerated and reduced: although the roles of wife and mother were increasingly venerated in American society, they effectively symbolised the limitation of women's expectations. Although Plath herself was a college graduate and women remained in the work place after the Second World War, in the American consciousness they were primarily wives and mothers. Elaine Showalter's brilliant, cultural study, *The Female Malady: Women, Madness and English Culture, 1830–1980*, includes some valuable insights into Plath's work when it is considered within a gendered context of prescription and treatment, stating that '. . . *The Bell Jar* offers the most complex account of schizophrenia as a protest against the feminine mystique of the 1950s'.[38]

Margaret Dickie's essay, 'Sylvia Plath's Narrative Strategy', is a welcome addition to Plath criticism, which illustrates the shift towards considering Plath as a socially informed poet. Dickie suggests that the social context and commentary of the 1950s and 1960s evident in Plath's prose often informs the narrative strategies of the poetry, a view that directly questions the idea of Plath as an isolated, socially withdrawn poet: '. . . the fact that this poet devoted a major portion of her creative energies to writing realistic fiction opens up the possibility that the acknowledged narrative bent in her poetry should be read in that context as social commentary rather than as the rantings of an isolated victim.'[39] While many feminist critics concentrated on the mythic parallels of the 'bee sequence', powerful poems that seem to emphasise flight and rebirth from patriarchal restrictions, Plath's domestically situated narrative poems, often bitter in tone, were frequently sidelined.[40] Considering four often ignored interpretative poems, 'The Tour', 'Eavesdropper', 'Lesbos' and 'Medusa', Dickie explores the narratives embedded in these poems to suggest that their 'metaphorical development works in the context of certain social facts';[41] but, significantly, she locates the speaker's torment and disturbance as her own and private:

■ Although the speaker in all four poems feels estranged from the people around her, she sees herself as part of a community or family and even more she presents herself as a housewife and mother. While she admits to being beleaguered and harried in these roles, she never

wider said andère

abandons them, and they give her at the same time a kind of privilege. [. . .] If it is hard to reconcile someone who calls her neighbor 'Sister bitch' and her mother 'God-ball' with the champion of domestic virtue, it must be remembered nonetheless that such a champion might have expected to find support for her social position in the small-town community and the family, and thus would be doubly hurt by gossip and inquisitiveness. [. . .] Plath . . . harbored hopes for a community of values and meaning where [she] discovered only pettiness, destructive gossip, even viciousness. In Plath's poetry, of course, this slightly old-fashioned point of view of the sanctity of domesticity is wedded to a tormented modern consciousness. [. . .] Plath's woman seems to have suffered some private disaster, some violent emotional upheaval totally unconnected with the sociology of the small town.[42] □

Dickie's view contrasts with that of Linda W. Wagner in her article, 'Plath's *Ladies' Home Journal* Syndrome'. This suggests that the tensions and anxieties found in Plath's own life and her writing are directly controlled and informed by the dominant ideological structures of the era: 'Woman as the willed product of her culture rather than the person she truly is: surely this is Plath's conflict.'[43] Wagner sums up the critical perspectives on Plath over the last twenty years, the 'bitch-goddess', 'martyr' and 'chronically mad poet', and counters them with the idea of Plath as a culturally determined woman, an idea partly substantiated by the publication of the *Journals*: 'Perhaps one of the most supportable views of Plath is none of these, but rather that of the fifties achieving woman, caught in the pervasive cultural rise of conformity.'[44] Concentrating on the short stories Plath wrote specifically for women's magazines, Wagner explores the way they reflect the 'confining 1950s patriarchal structure,' identified in the advertisements and editorial of *The Ladies' Home Journal*, essential reading material for generations of American housewives, and one of the magazines to which Plath submitted her stories. Recognising Plath's stories as reinscribing the dominant ideology of the time, Wagner characterises them as 'predictable, plot-orientated fiction in which women consistently relinquish their dreams and abilities in order to support those of their husbands'.[45] Wagner understands the conflict between these narratives, and the expectations and ambitions of Plath's own life, to be the defining factor:

■ The contradiction between Plath's being submerged in *The Ladies' Home Journal* – and trying repeatedly to write stories for the women's magazines – while she yet dreamed about being a great writer, living independently, traveling across Europe alone, is enough to have driven any mid-century woman to madness.[46] □

Although largely concerned with Plath's fiction, Wagner does briefly consider 'The Applicant', another often neglected poem rescued by critics discussing Plath as a socially specific writer:

■ Judging from illustrations throughout the magazine (this year [1949] and the subsequent five years), women wear either formal gowns or bathing suits; and are interested only in romance or recipes. Or, perhaps, in Mother-Daughter fashions. Patterns for mother-daughter 'look alike' dresses, robes and sportswear abound in many of these issues, and one must conjecture that the message is not only the natural sexual affinity but the similarity in role; whether adult or child, the female is a doll-like object, needing protection, capable of only limited activities. Or as Plath wrote in 'The Applicant':

> Now your head, excuse me, is empty.
> I have the ticket for that.
> Come here, sweetie, out of the closet.
> Well, what do you think of *that*?
> Naked as paper to start
>
> But in twenty-five years she'll be silver,
> In fifty, gold.
> A living doll, everywhere you look.
> It can sew, it can cook,
> It can talk, talk, talk. . . .
>
> *CP*, pp. 221–22

With 'Paper Doll' as background music, the reader flips through page after page of the Journal, and no amount of intelligence can keep the single-minded emphasis from reaching even an antagonistic mind. 'She's married – She's happy – She drives a Mercury' (*Ladies' Home Journal*, July 1950).[47] □

An example of the increasing sophistication of readings of the social and ideological meaning of femininity in the 1950s is Garry M. Leonard's article '"The Woman is Perfected. Her Dead Body Wears the Smile of Accomplishment": Sylvia Plath and *Mademoiselle* Magazine' (1992). Influenced by Luce Irigaray's understanding of 'woman' as a culturally constructed sign, Leonard states:

■ That fashion magazines sell products by persuading women that they need various accessories in order to be 'feminine' is common knowledge; but what Plath explores in her novel, journals, letters, and poetry is the extent to which this commercial product can pervade a

woman's personality until that 'personality' is nothing more than a package designed to catch the eye of the discerning masculine-consumer [. . .][48] □

Leonard intelligently explores both Plath's susceptibility to the dominant ideology of the 1950s, and her attempts to subvert or parody the socially constructed commodity 'woman' in, mainly, *The Bell Jar* and poems such as 'In Plaster' and 'The Applicant'. Although recognising the complexity of Plath's relationship to the dominant culture, Leonard does identify Plath's dismissal of women's magazines in her later poetry, suggesting that poems such as 'Lady Lazarus' reflect her 'defiant liberation' from the ideology of femininity:

■ Advertisements invite women to 'discover the new you' by murdering some personalities and celebrating others through the use of cosmetics. The pursuit of perfection, as outlined by the process that commodifies 'femininity,' is both self-deluding and self-destructive. The perfectly commodified 'woman' (that is, a female consumer) is presumed to have no essential subjectivity, but only an assortment of assumed personalities that the advertised products make possible. Perfection 'cannot have children,' as Plath writes in 'The Munich Mannequins,' and as she observes in one of her last poems, the 'perfect' woman is therefore a corpse (the closest approximation a woman can make to the 'perfect' appearance of a lifeless mannequin): 'The woman is perfected./Her dead/Body wears the smile of accomplishment,' ('Edge' 1–3). By saying *'the* smile of accomplishment' rather than *'a* smile,' Plath implies that the 'look' of a successful 'woman' is as consistent and mass-produced as a registered trademark.[49] □

In the brief article 'Icon of the Fifties', Marjorie Perloff proposes a similar view of Plath as culturally determined: '. . . precisely because Plath's poetry so perfectly embodies, at one level, the dominant ideology of the Fifties and early Sixties, she speaks to the women of her generation as perhaps no other woman poet can.' Yet Perloff ultimately sees the source of this appeal as restrictive: 'Plath's limitations emerge most clearly when she tries to make forays into the "larger world": commenting on the Holocaust or on Christianity, Plath is nothing much more than the average bright and sensitive Smith girl of her time.'[50]

Pamela J. Annas's *A Disturbance in Mirrors: The Poetry of Sylvia Plath* is one of the first full-length studies devoted to exploring the relationship between self and society in Plath's poetry from a feminist perspective, and one that moves the cultural discussion of Plath from a largely biographically based criticism to a more theoretically engaged form of analysis. Annas's title refers to her recognition of the mirror as a potent and recurrent symbol in Plath's work which enables: 'her exploration of the boundary between self and world, her struggle to be reborn into a transformed world, her concern with what is true and what is false, what is real and what is unreal, her interest in the process of perception and creation, her self-consciousness and above all, her ambivalence.'[51] Annas explores the potential of the mirror in the initial chapter 'Reflections', and although it is an image that is employed throughout the study, the title of her book is slightly misleading: the mirror serves more as a motif, or facilitator, for the central argument which concerns the complex relationship between self and society. In the following extract, Annas states the objective of her study, and comments on the society from which Plath emerged, before considering two statements by Plath which are central to a cultural discussion: 'Context', and the BBC interview from 1962:

■ [This] study . . . looks at the way the poems embody the tensions between images of self and images of world, or context within which the self exists, and it looks at the struggles within the poems to achieve transformation of self and of self in relation to the world. A major American poet writing in a period of transition from modernism to postmodernism, Sylvia Plath determinedly and fiercely wrote of and out of female experience and in the context of the time and place that shaped her – the mid 1950s to the early 1960s, in a post-World War II and prefeminist United States. Sylvia Plath is in many ways transitional. She wrote in a period of retreat in American life and art from the explicitly political, in a period of postwar prosperity and political passivity accompanied by a resurgence of American individualism and the success ethic [. . .] Plath's life exemplifies the tension and stresses of the success ethic and the role expectation conflict faced by any woman who had creative talent and a calling ('The blood jet is poetry,/There is no stopping it' ['Kindness', 1963]) and who also wanted to fulfill the conventional roles expected of women. [. . .] Plath does indicate in two separate 1962 comments about her own work, her concern about connecting personal experience with political commitment or at least with putting personal experience into a political context. Employing again the mirror image, she said in a BBC interview:

> I think that personal experience is very important, but certainly it shouldn't be a kind of shut-box and mirror-looking, narcissistic experience. I believe it should be relevant, and relevant to the larger things, the bigger things, such as Hiroshima and Dachau.[52]

'Context,' . . . illustrates Plath's awareness of the dangers of nuclear war and monopoly capitalism; it also demonstrates that, as an artist writing about her own work, Plath has not yet resolved the current separation between personal and political or seen her poetry as a direct and conscious way of connecting the two or mediating between them.[53] □

Annas perceives Plath's late poetry as an attempt to resolve this separation between 'personal and political'. Chronologically arranging her argument, she questions the popular perception of Plath's creative burst of October 1962 by suggesting that Plath's work gradually evolves into a dialogue between self and society, moving away from the initial influence of Hughes and Roethke to a more socially and historically centred poetic: '. . . Sylvia Plath increasingly places herself within a social context, one that is historical and linear rather than natural and cyclical, . . .'[54] Exploration of this process is developed in her excellent discussion of the social implications of *The Colossus*'s mythic imagery and her description of the transitional poetry as representing: '. . . a movement from a world of fluidity and potentiality to a world seen as increasingly rigid and narrow'.[55] With a feminist, post-structuralist understanding of language, Annas argues that in the shift from a natural landscape into a historical one, the self experiences entrapment and containment within a language which is inscribing a culture with which Plath is in conflict:

■ As Plath moves toward the *Ariel* poems, she no longer becomes in her poetry some aspect of animate or inanimate nature. What had before been animistically projected outward onto the natural world is now internalized as Plath faces the social world. Rather than a projection of self outward, she begins to feel trapped inside the self. [. . .]

The change in Plath's poetic voice and the transformation of her central image are both tied to a change in her conception of self-image, image of the world, and relation between self and world. This developing awareness of self is exemplified most clearly in Plath's suspicion of language. [. . .]

If language is a reflection of one's culture, if its structure is based on the assumptions of that culture, a poet uncomfortable with those assumptions is likely to feel uncomfortable with language as well. Language structures our perceptions of self and other; in the act of labeling, it tells us what to see and what not to see; through its syntax, it tells us what the relations are between the things we do see. As a woman poet trying to work out a redefinition of self through her poetry, Plath found herself in a linguistic trap. If she accepted her language without question, she would be accepting a set of assumptions which devalued her, confused her about her priorities, and limited her sense of personal possibility. As a consequence of this dilemma, what begins to develop in these middle poems is a suspicion about the nature and function of language itself and the beginnings of an analysis of the connection between language and society. In both imagery and in attitude toward language in these transitional poems, the sense of entrapment is crucial.[56] □

Annas develops this argument in her final chapter, illustrating the shift from metaphors of nature offering a fluid sense of self, to the socially defined, and thus contained, self. In a statement that reflects Mary Lynn Broe's concept of Plath's late work, Annas states that Plath '[creates] her own system of mythology based on modern historical images and events, a mythology whose central figure is a protean female protagonist, hero, victim, goddess'.[57] The section 'The Social Context' touches on aspects of Plath's work which we will see developed by Alan Sinfield, but here, Annas offers incisive readings of 'The Applicant', 'Cut' and 'The Munich Mannequins', which she recognises as containing 'recurring metaphors of fragmentation and reification – the abstraction of the individual – [which] in Plath's late poetry are socially and historically based'.[58] A valuable contribution to Plath studies, Annas's book considers the difficulty of expressing a female self within a restrictive society and phallocentric language. To illustrate Annas's approach, the following extract is from her chapter on the prose-play 'Three Women', a text of increasing interest to feminist critics as issues of sexuality and selfhood become central. Annas offers a feminist, broadly cultural materialist approach, reading the hospital setting as a metaphor for contemporary society, which expresses feelings of 'impersonality, depersonalization, loss of control of one's own body, sterility, and flatness'.[59] Her unsympathetic reading of 'the Wife' provides an effective contrast to Gilbert's view, which was discussed earlier, of the maternal woman as celebratory. Annas thinks 'the Wife' develops into a 'paean of praise to normality', protesting that 'By the end of the play . . . [she] has become a possessive, self-deceiving stereotype of motherhood'.[60] Annas's cultural approach, and her concern with the perception and definition of 'normality' is best illustrated however, in her discussion of the Second Voice, who she presents as experiencing the tensions between the individual woman and the society she lives in, a conflict Annas identifies as being at the heart of Plath's poetry:

■ The center of Plath's art is a tension between words and wordlessness, stasis and movement, entrapment and potentiality. Her one dramatic piece, *Three Women*, . . . explores this tension through its focus on a crisis situation uniquely female, the act of giving birth. [. . .] Grouped around an apparently straightforward biological act are complicated questions of communication, creativity, and the nature of the relation between an individual woman and her society. Finally, *Three Women* is about what stands in the way of creativity – biological and aesthetic – in a bureaucratized society that confuses the word with the thing, the signifier with what is signified, and in a capitalist society that alienates the producer from what is produced, including babies, and commoditizes most products, including poems. [. . .]

The failure of communication within the formal structure of the play is an important aspect of Sylvia Plath's developing image of the world and herself as woman and as poet in relation to it. In making pregnancy and birth the center of her play, Plath brings us back to the literal question of the possibility of creativity in an alienated world. The 'specific content' of *Three Women* is the isolation of each of these women inside her own experience and more crucially, inside the social definitions of that experience. The form of the play, three inter-cut monologues, is a direct reflection of its content.

Recurring throughout the speeches of the Wife, the Secretary, and the Girl is a concern with the perception and definition of 'normality'. The self-image of each of the three women in Plath's play is in large part founded upon how near (or distant) she feels from the postwar American definition of woman as mother. Betty Friedan writes in 1963 in *The Feminine Mystique* that:

> . . . stories in women's magazines insist that woman can know ful-fillment only at the moment of giving birth to a child. They deny the years when she can no longer look forward to giving birth, even if she repeats that act over and over again. In the feminine mystique, there is no other way for a woman to dream of creation or of the future. There is no other way she can even dream about herself, except as her children's mother, her husband's wife.[61]

It is the very tension or opposition between an individual and his environment that determines the development as well as the expression of his personality suggests George Lukács in 'The Ideology of Modernism.'[62] In such poems as 'The Applicant' in *Ariel* and in the characterization of the Secretary, the Second Voice of *Three Women*, Plath grapples most directly with the numbing effect of a bureau-cratized society upon the creative potential of the individual. She juxtaposes pregnancy and childbirth on the one hand, and the failure to produce children on the other hand, with this attitude toward motherhood as the sole means of fulfillment for a woman. In *Three Women*, she carefully distinguishes between the actual experience of giving birth and the social definition of that experience. [. . .]

. . . The Secretary has an awareness of her self, her world, and the conflict between self and world that the other two voices in the play lack. The Secretary has more lines than either of the other two speak-ers and she has the last word; her seventh speech ends the play. The world she lives in, like the world imaged in much of Sylvia Plath's poetry at this period, is closed, static, and sterile. [. . .]

The ambivalent and uncomfortable relationship between self and world in the Secretary's speeches is characteristic of Plath's late poems. The Secretary's first words connect and oppose the world of bureaucracy (the office where she works) to her own pregnancy, the social to the biological. In contrast, the First Voice and the Third Voice are alone. Plath makes a similar connection between bureaucracy and sterility in 'The Applicant' (*Ariel*), where relations between men and women are equated with the personnel office matching of employer and employee. In both 'The Applicant' and *Three Women*, a world of mechanized and frustrated labor corresponds to a world of mechanized and frustrated love, sexuality, and reproduction. A bureaucratized society will vitiate both the relation of one person to another and of a person to his or her work. The two will be mirror images. What the Secretary has caught from the flat world, from the men in the office, is some quality like cardboard which symbolically and really causes in some way her recurrent miscarriages. This paper imagery occurs often in the *Ariel* poems ('Lady Lazarus,' 'Cut,' 'The Applicant') and suggests that the self so described lacks substance, depth, and color; that is, reality. As in Theodore Roethke's 1948 poem about office work, 'Dolor,' people are two-dimensional in a world of three-dimensional artifacts.

The Secretary in *Three Women* lives in a world of men and machines, and has begun to take on those qualities of flatness, abstractness, rationality, and rigidity which Plath has, in the post-*Colossus* poems, consistently seen as directly inimical to sensuality, transcendence, roundness, and the possibility of change and creativity. In this first speech, the Secretary directly images herself as an extension of a machine.

> The letters proceed from these black keys, and these black keys proceed
> From my alphabetical fingers, ordering parts,
>
> Parts, bits, cogs, the shining multiples.
> I am dying as I sit. I lose a dimension.

The most often repeated word in the Secretary's first speech is 'death.' As the birth of her child is for the Wife also a rebirth of herself, so here the death of the child is a kind of death for the Secretary as well. Her imagery is of bare trees, empty sky, and herself with no relation even to a barren nature. Instead: 'These are my feet, these mechanical echoes./Tap, tap, tap, steel pegs.' If the Wife is described in Christian imagery and the Girl in pagan imagery, then the imagery of the Secretary and her world is first from modern technology and second from the grimmer of Grimm's fairy tales and the folklore from which those tales derive.

[. . .] The Secretary's speeches constantly move back and forth between her own situation and the society outside of yet still mirroring her own inability to create. The world loves death and sees in death its goal. 'It is a love of death that sickens everything./A dead sun stains the newsprint. It is red.' [. . .] Finally, the earth is 'the vampire of us all,' an image that often appears in the *Ariel* poems ('Lady Lazarus,' 'Mary's Song,' 'Daddy'). [. . .] Sylvia Plath's vampire imagery is for the individual what her World War II imagery, with its impersonal massacres and its concentration camps, is for society. Often one shades into the other, as in 'Daddy,' where the central figure is both vampire and gestapo officer.

The connection between the situation of the individual woman and the society she lives in is also clear in the Secretary's fourth speech. Here the moon is a connecting link between her own self-image and her image of her world. Like the moon, the Secretary sees herself as barren, pale, and empty; she is forced to start over again each month and each beginning leads nowhere. She identifies herself as well with what the moon shines on because they all empty: 'that chalk light/Laying its scales on the window, the windows of empty offices,/Empty schoolrooms, empty churches.' All of these – offices, schoolrooms, churches – are of course metaphors for social ordering: business and government, formal education, and organized religion.

The Secretary is the only one of the three women concerned with and self-conscious about her identity, largely because she is unsure about it. (The Third Voice is also self-conscious but seems to know who she is.) The Secretary does not fit the social definition of woman as mother, and so she says, 'I see myself as a shadow, neither man nor woman.' She is the only one of the three who ultimately, and unsatisfactorily, has to find her identity in more abstract social terms: 'The nurses give back my clothes, and an identity.' Even her situation, she finds, is not unique, does not possess a tragic singularity. 'I am not hopeless,' she says. 'I am beautiful as a statistic.' Her clothes, the lipstick she puts on, her job (the fact that she has one and therefore has to be at a certain place at a certain time) are what give her her identity. She is so much a part of the well-oiled nine-to-five machinery that even her personal crises occur on weekends. 'I can go to work today,' she says, and function 'a little sightless,' 'on wheels, instead of legs,' 'speak with fingers, not a tongue.' As in 'The Applicant,' Plath uses metonymy here to describe the woman not only as a collection of parts (literally fragmented) but as parts which are artifacts.

In her last speech, which is also the last speech of the play, the Secretary is at home with her husband, being a wife. She says twice that she feels she is healing and that she feels a tenderness both in nature (the spring air) and in the human world (the lamp light). And certainly the last words of the play are hopeful: 'The city waits and aches. The little grasses/Crack through stone, and they are green with life.' But even within this last speech, an explicit statement of warmth and hope, her own activity is activity leading nowhere.

> . . . My hands
> Can stitch lace neatly on to this material. My husband
> Can turn and turn the pages of a book.
> And so we are at home together, after hours.
> It is only time that weighs upon our hands.

What distinguishes the Second Voice of *Three Women* from the other two speakers is not only her inability to create biologically but also through most of the play her tragic self-awareness, her consciousness of the conflict between her creative needs and the world she lives in. The other two women are in some measure blind in their narcissism. The Girl is blind in her selfishness and in her refusal to connect acts to consequences. The Wife, in her need to protect and possess her child, wants to believe in a nursery-plate vision of normality, where motivations are benign and proportions harmonious. But the Secretary, in her desire to have children and in her inability to have any, is forced toward sight. Further, she is the only one of the three women who is a worker and who therefore participates in the reality of alienated work. She is the only one of the three women whose world is imaged consistently in the harsh and blindingly stark colors which characterize Sylvia Plath's late poems. She is the only one who is aware of the hostility in purpose between her biological and personal goals and the goals of the larger society she lives in. And yet she also sees herself as part of this world which is finally inimical to her creativity. She is fatally involved in it. Her 'flaw,' which makes her the tragic center of this play and which distinguishes her from the Wife and the Girl, is her at least partial rejection of illusion based on her knowledge that she is inextricably a part of the world she lives in. [. . .]

The ambivalence with which *Three Women* ends is a prelude to many of the poems collected in *Ariel*, which move beyond ambivalence to a bitter satire that uses the socially based and worldwide horrors of World War II as a structure of imagery to define her own personal situation. Here in *Three Women* Plath seems to be still working out what the nature of the society she lives in is and what the possibilities are for coming to terms with this necessary involvement

of the individual woman in her society. Her conclusions are not opti-
mistic. The experience of birth should be the Dionysian transcendence
of self and merging with self which the Wife alone among the three
women experiences, but even she loses this when she returns to her
socially defined self. Mid-twentieth-century corporate bureaucracy
undercuts the creative possibilities of the self. The Secretary's world is
this social world, bureaucratic, machine-dominated, populated by
cardboard people who seem finally not quite as real as the artifacts
that surround them. In such a world, real and sustained creativity is
difficult. All three women survive by choosing blindness in varying
degrees, from the Wife's almost total retreat into a nursery world of
illusion through the Girl's abdication of responsibility to the
Secretary's conscious decision to be numb. What *Three Women* finally
says is that one can no longer be a heroine of the central and the real,
merely a heroine of the peripheral.[63] □

The final extract in this chapter is from Alan Sinfield's seminal study
Literature, Politics and Culture in Postwar Britain (1989) in which he explores
the ideological intersections between society and art. Sinfield includes an
absorbing chapter on women's writing and chooses to concentrate on the
figure of Sylvia Plath since: 'All the main positions have been taken through
her, and therefore she is a key point at which to attempt an intervention
. . .'[64] Significantly, Sinfield places Plath within a British context, in contrast to previous cultural critics who consider her firmly within
American culture and society. The debate on national identity becomes
more focused in the following decade's interest in 'transatlantic' writing,
as we will see in Tracy Brain's 1998 article, but here, Alan Sinfield resolves
Plath's 'dual nationality' by stating: '. . . I have found it appropriate to
use evidence from Britain and the United States with only occasional
discriminations. [. . .] Plath lived and worked in the United States and in
England, and appropriations of her by Modernism, academic English and
the Women's Movement have also been international.'[65]

Expertly considering much of the initial Plath criticism from a cultural and historical perspective, Sinfield exposes the way in which male
critics in particular disempowered Plath, suggesting that the tendency to
'[put] everything down to emotional instability is of a piece with the customary stereotyping of women'.[66] Sinfield accuses critics of ignoring the
specificity of history, politics and society in Plath's writing while privileging 'psychic disorders and generalized horror', critical positions which
served the political conjuncture.[67] Holbrook's psychoanalytic analysis is
charged with prescribing 'normative gender roles', while the acceptance
of Plath as a 'mad genius [driven] onward to desperate expression and
death' is viewed as part of the 'concurrent recycling of Modernism'
espoused by Alvarez and Spender.

Sinfield begins with a Marxist analysis of women's experience of the postwar society: 'Placing the topic in a larger perspective, we are looking at an inflection in the historic exploitation of female labour – comparable with exploitation of the working class and the subjects of imperialism.'[68] Sinfield argues that the dominant ideology of domesticity which was conservative and conformist, and the consumer society which 'was targeted on the housewife and mother', was a direct response to the instability of gender roles following the war. Recognising that 'male and female roles became uncertain and disputable, problematizing marriage and the heterosexual relation in all aspects',[69] Sinfield suggests that these tensions can be found in the representative nature of Plath's writing. In contrast to most other critics who tend to read Plath's short stories as facile and conformist, Sinfield locates resistance and tension in her magazine fiction:

■ In so far as she chose to tell her story through the *Ladies' Home Journal* and the *New Yorker* – to herself and to her readers – Plath collaborated with patriarchy in the scripting of herself and other women. This is how cultural production works: we read our experience in the stories that we know. But the stories are contradictory and the point of intersection at which Plath was situated was particularly fraught. In so far as she allows us to see the strain she contributes to political understanding.[70] □

Sinfield proceeds to read Ted Hughes as an almost archetypal figure. He creates distance between the actual person Ted Hughes, and the man who is figured as TH, explaining that this is not: '. . . out of coyness, but because it was the *idea of a certain kind of man* that seemed to answer Plath's demand, and the relation between that idea and the historical Ted Hughes can only be speculative'.[71] Concerned with the presence of TH in the poetry, Sinfield suggests that TH 'accommodate[s] Plath's contradictory and challenging negotiation of current ideology'; this powerful masculine figure allows Plath to enter into a complex discourse of gender relations, sexuality and identity. These gender relations and negotiations, which Sinfield understands as representative of the postwar era, are explored in Plath's writing, particularly in the section 'Rabbit Catcher'. After briefly considering the bee sequence, which Sinfield recognises as embodying a new confidence but lacking a 'distinct model of gender relations', he considers the representation of male violence in Plath's later poetry, suggesting that this indicates her growing realisation of the links between the personal and the political:

■ The critical force of Plath's late poems is in what they do with violence – bees signify danger as well as honey. 'Letter in November'

(*CP*, p.204), where a woman walks around her territory alone, is one of the most positive late poems. Even so, male violence appears at the last moment, extending the final line as if an unanticipated thought breaks in:

> O love, O celibate.
> Nobody but me
> Walks through the waist-high wet.
> The irreplaceable
> Golds bleed and deepen, the mouths of Thermopylae.
>
> *CP*, p.254

Atlas in 'By Candlelight' is represented with 'five brass cannonballs' (*CP*, p.237). In 'The Swarm' (*CP*, p.179) TH is the beekeeper; he is Napoleon, and the swarming bees are the peoples of Europe who think to rise against him. He plays with them as if they were 'chess people', 'The mud squirms with throats' (*CP*, p.216), and he is only apparently defeated:

> The man with gray hands smiles –
> The smile of a man of business, intensely practical.
> They are not hands at all
> But asbestos receptacles.
> Pom ! Pom ! 'They would have killed *me*.'
>
> *CP*, p.217

Plath invokes Napoleon because she had been reading a biography of the Empress Josephine, and related Josephine's marriage to her own. Napoleon is transmuted into 'a man of business' because she had been profoundly disturbed by articles in *The Nation*, 'all about the terrifying marriage of big business and the military in America' (*LH*, p.437). She spoke to Elizabeth Sigmund 'with bitter anger of the involvement of American big business with weaponry'.[72] Plath was reaching towards the idea that her experience with TH was of a piece with the violence and oppression that are produced generally in patriarchy.[73] □

This powerful argument is extended through the section 'The Case for Extremism', in which Sinfield brings a gendered cultural perspective to the continuing debate over the 'holocaust' poetry, considering in particular the use of the Holocaust, or similarly extreme situations, by women writers. As we have already seen in the work of Jerome Mazzaro and James E. Young, there is an argument for recognising Plath's legitimate political concern: the trial of Adolf Eichmann and the increasing awareness of the horrors of the 'Holocaust' in the 1960s, the pressure of Cold

War America and the execution of the Rosenbergs, alongside the increasing anxiety over atomic weaponry, are all issues of concern to Plath evident in her journals and letters. Sinfield states that 'Plath's anxieties about war, militarism and state violence were by no means sudden. Despite what most critics say, she had long expressed political commitment',[74] which he outlines in her fears over the Korean War, McCarthyism, Suez, and her strong response to the Campaign for Nuclear Disarmament; she took part in the 1960 annual CND march in London. Having established Plath's political commitment, and her increasing sense of a connection between personal relationships and patriarchy, Sinfield suggests that her poetry begins to establish further, powerful links:

■ So Plath had the basis for seeing connections between the personal defection of TH, her long-standing resentment of male attitudes, and state violence. In her radio poem 'Three Women' (*CP*, p.157, March 1962) one woman says:

> And then there were other faces. The faces of nations,
> Governments, parliaments, societies,
> The faceless faces of important men.

> It is these men I mind :
> They are so jealous of anything that is not flat! They are jealous gods
> That would have the whole world flat because they are.
> I see the Father conversing with the Son.
> Such flatness cannot but be holy.

CP, p.179

Recognition of a pattern of male violence in patriarchy informs 'Daddy' (*CP*, p.183, October 1962). The poet scornfully identifies her father with the devil, God, Nazis, torturers of early modern times, and TH – in the marriage ceremony she said 'I do':

> I made a model of you,
> A man in black with a Meinkampf look
> And a love of the rack and the screw.
> And I said I do, I do.

CP, p.224

They are all instances of male power. And in 'Lady Lazarus' (*CP*, p.198) she identifies her body with the abused remains of gassed Jews – 'my skin/Bright as a Nazi lampshade' (*CP*, p.244).

It is a bold move – 'monstrous, utterly disproportionate', declared

Irving Howe, the voice of ex-radicalism in the United States. In the last poems, Howe found, Plath illustrates 'an extreme state of existence'. She couldn't illustrate 'the general human condition' because she was 'so deeply rooted in the extremity of her plight'. This is not a new accusation for the woman writer: Matthew Arnold found Charlotte Brontë's *Villette* 'disagreeable' because 'the writer's mind contains nothing but hunger, rebellion and rage'.[75] The reasonable man finds Plath's last poems extreme; my project is to look at the social construction of that writing and that judgement.

Plath is saying – and I don't claim it is fully articulated, which is not surprising since it was a thought struggling into consciousness, scarcely anticipated in its period; she is saying that Jews and women, both, have been among the victims of institutionalized violence in Western civilization. Certainly those oppressions differ. Nazi persecution of Jews, as with other scapegoatings, was focused, systematic and directly lethal. Other oppressions have been more long-term and uneven, and that is generally the case with the subjection of women. Nonetheless, the treatment of women through the centuries of Western man constitutes one of the great offences. 'Society as we know it fears and tries to destroy "the Other"', writes Mary Daly – with the Jews, women, and the Vietnamese in mind; Daly links rape, genocide and war as the most unholy trinity.[76] If, as Plath suggests, 'Every woman adores a Fascist' ('Daddy', p.223), it is because there is indeed a continuity between the patriarchal structures that legitimate state violence and violence against women. TH is male power in western society; and this is an extreme view.

Furthermore, Plath writes of violence against men. 'I've killed one man, I've killed two' ('Daddy', p.224); 'I eat men like air' ('Lady Lazarus', p.247). 'Purdah' (*CP*, p.197), spoken from within a harem, conjures Clytemnestra, slayer of the hero Agamemnon:

I shall unloose –
From the small jeweled
Doll he guards like a heart –

The lioness,
The shriek in the bath,
The cloak of holes.

CP, p.244

Men in our culture are generally anxious about female power, which Adrienne Rich identifies as 'first of all, to give or withhold nourishment and warmth, to give or withhold survival itself.' And this produces male fear: 'the hatred of overt strength in women, the definition of strong independent women as freaks of nature, as unsexed, as frigid, castrating, perverted, dangerous; the fear of the maternal woman as "controlling", the preference for dependent, malleable, "feminine" women.'[77] Hence, Rich says, the domestication of women: domesticity is supposed to contain female power. But in Plath's poems domesticity and hostility to men tangle together, threatening that containment. This is specially true of the last poem in the published *Ariel*, 'Edge' (*CP*, p.224), which invokes Medea, who revenged herself on the man who deserted her, the heroic Jason, by killing their children. By such an action, the poem says, 'The woman is perfected'. Now her children are hers alone, 'She has folded/Them back into her body as petals' (*CP*, pp.272–73); at last she is entire in her motherhood, free of TH. Adrienne Rich, telling of a woman who killed her children, asks what woman, caring single-handed for her children or struggling to retain her personhood against the idea that she must be only a mother, 'has not dreamed of "going over the edge", of simply letting go, relinquishing what is termed her sanity, so that she can be taken care of for once'.[78] It is not for a man to reply.

Of course, Plath failed to transcend the violence that she identified. She was unable to live in her own instance the vision that made her support CND and want her brother to be a conscientious objector. The conditions for that were scarcely available, so mystified was the whole topic. In part the customary idea of woman as victim rather than assailant triumphed, and she turned her violence upon herself. Yet she also turned it upon TH: I believe that the poems, and the suicide that showed she really meant it, were partly vengeance on TH. As such, they were not unsuccessful, though they could be recuperated through male myths about the monstrous independent female (Robert Lowell wrote in the introduction to the US *Ariel* of Plath's voice as that of 'the vampire – a Dido, Phaedra, or Medea'). But the violence is not just Plath's: it is the violence of patriarchy, unleashed out of manipulation and entrapment in a woman who had taken on the contradictory demands of patriarchy at their widest and deepest. Plath had tried to tell the acceptable stories and realized their stresses in herself. Now she turned upon their prime scriptors.

The L-Shaped Room, The Pumpkin Eater and *Franny and Zooey*[79] are not extreme because they fit the woman back, albeit uncertainly, into the social order. For moderation, maturity and good sense are defined normatively, by patriarchy. I drew attention in chapter three to Nancy K. Miller's argument that plausibility is normative: that which is not conventionally thought to be the case will seem incredible and perhaps extreme.[80] Miller quotes Freud's belief that men's daydreams are ambitious, egoistic and erotic, whereas women's are mainly erotic (since, of course, that is where their ambitions are supposed to reside).

But, Miller asks, if women have ambitious daydreams, how do they appear? As 'a fantasy of power that would revise the social grammar in which women are never defined as subjects'.[81] That is what we see in 'Daddy' and 'Lady Lazarus': a fantasy of power reversal, which appears extreme not only to many readers, but to Plath herself. The violence and extremity indicate the scale of social change that would have to occur for Plath to become acceptably powerful. For, Miller argues, verisimilitude and the 'truths' of 'human' experience to which it appeals are male in our culture and that is why words such as 'extravagant' suggest the feminine.[82] Speaking as a woman, of women's oppression, is extreme because the language – the credible stories – are written by patriarchy. Plath's extremity is a necessary and necessarily limited strategy of the oppressed.[83]

The same argument applies to 'hysteria'. Juliet Mitchell locates hysteria as 'the woman's simultaneous acceptance and refusal of the organization of sexuality under patriarchal capitalism. It is simultaneously what a woman can do both to be feminine and to refuse femininity.'[84] If Plath's poetry appears hysterical, that is because the power of naming is Adam's, and women (and other subordinated groups) who want to tell a different story must either adapt to prevailing discourses or force a way through. The latter produces hysteria – as a discursive feature and, indeed, in the writer herself, scripted by her stories.[85] □

CHAPTER FOUR

Feminist and Psychoanalytic Strategies

A T THE same time as important historical and materialist approaches to Plath's poetry were developing, so too were significant psychoanalytic and deconstructive readings of her work. These readings further shifted the emphasis from the early attempts at identifying unifying strategies in the poetry, evident in the Plath critics of the 1970s, towards modes of interpretation that produce more ambiguous and multiple meanings, confronting the contradictions, pluralities and conflicts involved in reading. This was part of a more general change in literary criticism in which language was increasingly viewed as a condition, rather than as a realistic reflection, of experience. The implications for reading Plath are neatly summarised by Susan Bassnett:

■ Only by accepting that Sylvia Plath's writings are filled with contradictions existing in a dialectical relationship with each other can we move beyond the dead-end 'reading to find out the truth' kind of process. [. . .] It is worth bearing in mind two simple points when approaching a writer like Sylvia Plath. The first is to recognise the impossibility of consistency. [. . .] It is impossible to try to discover the 'real' Sylvia Plath, to work out the 'real' reason for her suicide, because there is no 'real' person and no 'real' explanation. [. . .] The second point arises out of the first. Just as it is impossible to discover the 'truth' about anyone else's heart, so it is impossible to have a single true reading of a work. Post-structuralism has shown us that there are as many versions of a text as there are readers reading it and though there have been some attempts to restrict the anarchy of that suggestion . . . we are today offered the prospect of a text as an open entity.[1] □

This chapter will explore the impact of these theoretical developments on Plath studies as critics begin to engage with an increasingly psychoanalytically informed criticism, an approach that particularly advances feminist readings of Plath's poetry. We will initially consider the continuation of comparative and canonical discussions of Plath within the context of women's writing, then explore the growing interest in psychoanalysis that leads many feminist critics, such as Liz Yorke and Alicia Ostriker, to adapt the ideas of European feminist thought in order to complement their predominantly Anglo-American feminist criticism, and finally concentrate on increasingly deconstructive and psychoanalytical readings from Stephen Gould Axelrod and Jacqueline Rose.

Influenced by the insightful arguments of earlier feminist studies, many critics continue to consider Plath within a feminist canon and women's tradition, often sharply comparing and contrasting Plath with other poets. Paula Bennett's *My Life a Loaded Gun: Dickinson, Plath, Rich and Female Creativity* claims that the gender of these poets is 'central to their poetic development', and identifies the explosion of a repressed poetic self as the major feature of their texts. Largely informed by *Letters Home* and Plath's *Journals*, Bennett offers an intelligent biographical reading of the poetry which examines Plath's struggle to be confidently creative while seeking acceptance within a patriarchal society, a dialectic Bennett accurately describes as 'the conflict between the needs of her gender and the requirements of her genre . . .'[2] In the following extract, Bennett's author-centred approach locates Plath's fascination with the divided self as extending beyond the often discussed 'In Plaster' to the poems from 1961.

■ 'In Plaster,' written on March 18, 1961, indicates that Plath knew her façade was cracking. [. . .] 'In Plaster' presents a clear, unequivocal picture of the struggle going on inside the poet between her two selves. The 'close, explicit, and murderous' relationship between these two selves forms [. . .] the substance and theme of this extraordinary and, for Plath, artistically novel poem.

    [. . .] Although not as specifically, virtually all the poems Plath wrote in 1961 suggest the same sense of isolation, frustration, and internal division as 'In Plaster.' The titles alone seem to evoke Plath's sense of self-alienation and inner loneliness: 'Zoo Keeper's Wife,' 'Face Lift,' 'Barren Woman,' 'I Am Vertical,' 'Insomniac,' 'Widow,' 'Wuthering Heights,' 'The Surgeon at 2 a.m.,' 'Last Words,' and 'The Moon and the Yew Tree.' In these poems, as in poems with more innocuous titles including 'Parliament Hill Fields,' 'Morning Song,' 'Stars Over the Dordogne,' and 'Blackberrying,' the poet presents herself as alone in a landscape. She is cut off not just from that 'country far away as health' (*CP*, p.162), but apparently from all human contact and consolation. [. . .] In 'Morning Song,' she is a statue in a 'drafty museum,' blank as a wall and no longer part of the child she mothers (*CP*, p. 157). [. . .] And in 'Blackberrying,' based on an actual family outing, there is 'Nobody in the lane, and nothing, nothing but black-berries.' Whatever the real circumstances of the event, in the poem the speaker confronts the 'intractable' sea by herself (*CP*, pp. 168, 169).[3] □

By privileging 'biographical and gender elements' as a response to the marginalisation of women writers within a Western canon, Bennett continues the feminist groundwork of the 1970s; yet even in a reading that parallels Plath's biography and poetry, giving particular emphasis to the dynamics of the relationship between mother and daughter, Bennett does effectively employ the rhetoric of psychoanalysis: 'But all [three poets] finally learned how to discard the mask and speak directly from the unacceptable core of their beings, to claim their loaded guns.'[4]

Feminist critics increasingly become preoccupied with exploring Plath's portrayal of family relationships within domestic settings, but, significantly, they begin to focus less on the representation of self as traumatised, even victimised daughter, and more on the transformation of self through motherhood. Gilbert and Gubar go so far as to say that: '[B]y choosing to *celebrate* maternity . . . Plath virtually initiated what has become a significant genre for the mid- and late-century women whom we call "mother poets."'[5] This increasing emphasis on the experiences of the female body, centering on menstruation, pregnancy, birth and mother-hood, enables critics to explore fully the complexities of a gendered self in Plath's writing. Developing her earlier argument for the enlargement of metaphor in Plath's poetry, Barbara Hardy further recognises that many poems, such as 'Metaphors' and 'The Babysitters', are circum-scribed by the female experiences of pregnancy and motherhood.[6] Janice Markey's critique of Plath's poetry, *A Journey into the Red Eye* (1993) is a helpful introduction arranged in thematic sections, and includes an exploration of the presence of a lesbian erotic in poems such as 'Leaving Early' and 'Ariel'.[7] Susan Bassnett's accessible study *Sylvia Plath* (1987) is a useful introduction to Plath's life and work which offers balanced and intelligent readings of the poetry. In the chapter 'Writing the Family', Bassnett discusses the societal taboo of menstruation in Plath's work, an area that becomes increasingly theoreticised by feminist critics: '[In a journal entry from 20 March 1959] Sylvia Plath linked the imagery of the blood flow to her own creativity/productivity and . . . shows also that this is an image that is fundamentally ambiguous.'[8] Natalie Harris's essay 'New Life in American Poetry: The Child as Mother of the Poet' (1987), intelligently reads Plath's representation of children in her poetry as 'both fact and symbol of the mother's experience in the world.'[9] Through close readings of three poems, which offer very different representations of the experience of motherhood, 'Nick and the Candlestick', 'Tulips', and 'Edge', Harris claims that while the child consistently represents change, wholeness and participation in life, the mother's response changes, moving through loving embrace, to painful ambivalence and destructive rejection.

Lynda Bundtzen's incisive study *Plath's Incarnations: Woman and the Creative Process* (1983) explores issues of subjectivity and selfhood in Plath's writing, signalling the shift towards considering Plath's more obscure, even mystical poems in terms of sexual identity, a proposal we will later see explored by Anna Tripp's reading of 'I Am Vertical'. Bundtzen locates in Plath's poetry the desire for an androgynous self, signalling an escape from the limitations of sexual identity, and also a wish for the celebration or fulfilment of the physical self. For example, Bundtzen recognises the powerful sensuality of 'Ariel', suggesting that the masturbatory movement of the poem contains a protean sexual identity: 'She is defiantly female like Godiva, but she assumes the masculine power of her horse. She is both female "furrow" of earth, ready to be sown with male seed, that "splits and passes" and also "The brown arc /Of the neck I cannot catch".'[10] This interest in 'the body', exploring the ways in which the physical, sexual self is inscribed in Plath's poetry, is tentatively theoreticised by critics such as Alicia Suskin Ostriker and Liz Yorke who are influenced by the innovations of European feminist theorists, Julia Kristeva, Luce Irigaray and Hélène Cixous – theorists broadly associated with the idea of *écriture féminine*.[11]

Alicia Suskin Ostriker's excellent study of women's poetry, *Stealing the Language: The Emergence of Women's Poetry in America* (1986), offers a generous account of Plath's poetry. Her insightful, wide-ranging and inclusive approach places Plath in an expansive canon of women writers by examining both their influences upon her and her influences upon later poets. Ostriker progresses through an exploration of the condition of marginality, the centrality of the divided self as a motif of women's poetry, and the representation of the body and the question of female desire, considering the expression of anger and violence, before concluding with a study of revisionary myth-making in women's poetry, which includes a brief discussion of Plath and Sexton's 'female monsters'.[12] Perceiving women writers as engaged in a struggle for articulation, Ostriker aims to show that: '[T]his sequence of motifs constitutes an extended investigation of culturally repressed elements in female identity.'[13] 'In Plaster', described as 'the most brilliant single split-self poem of our time', is central to her discussion of the divided self in women's poetry, which Ostriker sees as grounded in the authorised dualities of the culture:

■ 'In Plaster' is a tour de force of extreme solipsism. Nothing and nobody exists inside the poem but 'I' and 'she,' and the poem illustrates the tight connection between passivity, dependence, solipsism, and self-loathing. [. . .] There is a public self designed to please others, which is so perfect that it drives all antisocial 'ugly' impulses back into secrecy, where they seethe and increase. Or there is an 'ugly' self so distressing that an unbreakable self of 'whiteness and beauty' must be invented to mask it. Either way, division is self-perpetuating. [. . .]

Wild self and tame self in [Denise] Levertov, strong rational poet and weak emotional woman in [Diane] Wakoski, perfect external and ugly internal selves in Plath – never far from the surface in all this work is the sense that self-division is culturally prescribed, wholeness culturally forbidden, to the woman and the woman poet. The cleavage in the brain is inherited from Dickinson and other ancestresses. It appears conspicuously in Atwood, Sexton, Rich, and many lesser-known poets. Invisibility and muteness, dissolving and distorted selves are images of it.[14] □

Plath's work also features prominently in Ostriker's discussion of rage in women's poetry: 'Herr God, Herr Lucifer: Anger, Violence, and Polarization'. Identifying 'Daddy' as the 'earliest and most famous of female vengeance poems',[15] Ostriker offers an incisive reading of Plath's 'suicide fantasies', which explore the tensions of passivity and aggression, victimisation and vengeance, but I have chosen to concentrate on Ostriker's illuminating comments on Plath's inscription of the body. She subtly adapts the stimulating ideas of French feminist thinkers to strengthen her argument for a gendered cultural determination. Opening with a short discussion of influential theorists, beginning with Simone de Beauvoir's seminal *The Second Sex*, Ostriker starts to read Plath's poetry in the light of contemporary feminist debates:

■ Historically, de Beauvoir explains female subordination as a necessary outcome of advancing technology and civilization, [. . .] Identified with the Nature which men have sought to conquer, woman has remained trapped, forced by her body to serve as the eternal Other, an emblem perhaps of sacred mysteries, but a physical, social, and political inferior. Biologically a victim of the species, she becomes by extension a victim of culture.

[. . .] De Beauvoir's rejection of female subordination is forceful and combative. But below the ring of her battle cry sounds a heavy drone, difficult to distinguish from the voice of patriarchy itself, with its metaphors of attacking, wrestling and profit. [. . .] [*The Second Sex*] indicates that in order for a woman to achieve full humanity, she must reject or minimize whatever is imposed on her by the physical body. The inferior life of 'immanence' dictated by feminine anatomy must become the superior life of 'transcendence' willed and dictated by the striving individual ego.

[. . .] From her privileging of 'transcendence' over 'immanence,' it follows that de Beauvoir cannot take women artists seriously. She allows that they aptly describe 'their own inner life, their experience, still warm, through savory adjectives and carnal figures of speech',[16] and they are good at recording facts. But for her these strengths are weaknesses, dooming a woman to intellectual mediocrity. [. . .]

While contemporary feminist critics have found these positions highly debatable, de Beauvoir's ideas nevertheless powerfully articulate the dominant assumptions of a phallocentric culture and literature. Consequently, radical French feminists of the school of *l'écriture féminine* have contended that to 'inscribe the body' for a woman writer does not simply promote female self-expression but constitutes a subversion of patriarchy and patriarchal discourse, substituting female libido for male, sexual pleasure or *jouissance* for logic and convention.

For the Marxist linguist Julia Kristeva, founder of the avant-garde journal *Tel quel*, women's linguistic essence is 'negative, at odds with what already exists . . . something that cannot be represented, something that is not said,' and preoedipal, representing the blissful fusion with the mother that all social organization attempts to overcome and deny; woman's role as writer is then to 'reject everything finite, definite, structured, loaded with meaning, in the existing state of society.'[17] Hélène Cixous' manifesto 'The Laugh of the Medusa' identifies women's writing with an illimitable, explosive physicality and sexuality: 'Almost everything is yet to be written by women about femininity; about their sexuality, that is, its infinite and mobile complexity . . . More body, hence more writing . . . Her libido is cosmic, just as her unconscious is worldwide.'[18] The post-Lacanian psychoanalyst Luce Irigaray similarly claims that the unique disruptiveness of women's writing derives from the diffuseness of her sexuality:

> . . . woman has sex organs just about everywhere. She experiences pleasure almost everywhere . . . That is undoubtedly the reason she is called temperamental, incomprehensible, perturbed, capricious – not to mention her language in which 'she' goes off in all directions and in which 'he' is unable to discern the coherence of any meaning.[19]

[. . .]

Among American writers, Mary Daly, Susan Griffin, and Adrienne Rich have championed the transformative power of a writing grounded in the body: 'In order to live a fully human life,' argues Rich in *Of Woman Born: Motherhood as Experience and Institution*, 'we require not only control of our bodies . . . we must touch the unity and resonance of our physicality, the corporeal ground of our intelligence.'[20]

Such writers have been challenged by other feminists as re-iterating an unacceptable biologism and as reinforcing a dualism in language and society which has always been used to justify the marginalization of women. The demand that the woman writer must embrace a disintellectualized, preoedipal carnality may be as prescriptive as the demand that she remain disembodied.[21] It is with this debate in mind, however, that we must examine what happens when contemporary American women poets 'inscribe the body.'

[. . .]

To understand the connection between physical vulnerability and ironic self-rejection in women poets, it is useful to consider Sylvia Plath, who appears most thoroughly to have internalized the larger culture's principles of flesh-rejection and aspiration towards transcendence. Plath's work is filled with body images both internal and external: skin, blood, skulls, feet, mouths and tongues, wounds, bone, lungs, heart and veins, legs and arms. She writes of both male and female bodies. She also projects human anatomy into the natural world. . . . Tulips, when the poet is hospitalized, have 'sudden tongues' and 'eat my oxygen.' They breathe

> Lightly, through their white swaddlings, like an awful baby.
> Their redness talks to my wound, it corresponds . . .
> They are opening like the mouth of some great African cat.
>
> *CP*, pp. 161–62

In 'Totem,' the projection of biology outward is global and primitive: 'the world is blood-hot and personal' (*CP*, p. 264). [. . .]

A number of Plath's persistent motifs can be decoded with de Beauvoir's help as referring to the feminine body specifically. Plath's imagery of strangulation implies in extreme form the woman fatally imprisoned and stifled by her own body. An infant is 'stealer of cells, stealer of beauty' in 'The Fearful.' Children are hooks sticking in one's skin, and placenta and umbilical cord threaten the poet in 'Medusa.' Most painfully, her imagery of laceration suggests woman's essential anatomical condition, shameful to endure, difficult to confess – as in 'Cut,' where the poet runs through a set of brilliant metaphors for the thumb she has just sliced with a kitchen knife 'instead of an onion.' All the metaphors are masculine and military: 'Little pilgrim . . . Redcoats . . . Homunculus . . . Kamikaze man,' until the finale:

How you jump –
Trepanned veteran,
Dirty girl,
Thumb stump.

CP, pp. 235–36

What, after all, is more humiliating in our culture than being a bleeding, dirty girl? As in [May] Swenson's 'Bleeding,' the coded allusion to menstruation points to a primary locus of woman hatred in our culture and hence of woman hatred within the female self.

At the same time, the landscape of war and mutilation in a poem like 'Getting There,' the references to Jews and Nazis in 'Daddy' and 'Lady Lazarus,' the 'Hiroshima ash' of 'Fever 103°,' and even the sour commercial comedy of 'The Applicant,' in which a wife is sold like a household appliance and only the mutilated man can be normal enough to marry, reinforce Plath's vision of worldly existence as at worst holocaust, at best tawdry sideshow. The drama of social and political life plays out, on a nightmarishly large scale, the victimization of the body. [. . .]

As Plath's artistic control increased, so did her vision of possible release, into a state of purification and perfection equivalent to the perfection of art. The implicit equation is clear as early as 'Two Views of a Cadaver Room,' which places a real-life scene with corpses next to the 'panorama of smoke and slaughter' in a Brueghel painting. In 'The Disquieting Muses,' Plath rejects her mother's cheery songs and stories for the three bald and faceless figures she accepts as artistic guides. And in *Ariel*, the poet 'unpeels' herself from her body in poem after poem, lets her body 'flake' away, annihilates the 'trash' of flesh which disgusts her because it would make her kin to the ogling peanut-crunching crowd. She transforms herself from gross matter to 'a pure acetylene virgin' rising toward heaven or to dew evaporating in the sunrise – but transcendence always means death. When self-inflicted, it spells triumph. And if she fears and scorns death's perfection as well as life's imperfection ('Perfection is terrible, it cannot have children' [*CP*, p. 262]; 'This is what it is to be complete. It is horrible' [*CP*, p. 198]), self-annihilation is nevertheless the ultimately artistic, ultimately ironic response to humiliation.

Had Plath lived, she might have discovered another exit from the locked compartment; possibly through motherhood, about which she wrote her only poems of unambiguous sensual pleasure. As it is, she imagined one further form of transcendence. The veiled and jadelike woman in 'Purdah,' who says of her bridegroom 'I am his,' proceeds to envision herself the tigress who will kill him. The daughter in 'Daddy' who lives passively and fearfully 'like a foot,' adores 'the boot in the face,' and lets her 'pretty red heart' be bitten in two, finally accomplishes her ritual murder of the father she loves and hates. 'Lady Lazarus' reduces Lucifer, God, the killer of Jews, and the poet's doctor to a single brutal exploitative figure. [. . .]

In the Plath scheme, then, if transcendence is a solution to the problem of the body, it merely means joining the killers instead of the killed. It is not this vision which de Beauvoir anticipates when she asks women to 'attack the world.' But when the physical self is made an object, trash, subject to harm and worthy of destruction, its most ardent impossible dream may be to destroy its maker.

Plath is, as Alvarez earlier recognized, a poet whose 'particular gift is to clarify and intensify the received world.'[22] We may view her work aesthetically as a radical extension of the mode of disenchanted alienation in the Eliot–Auden–Lowell line. We may view it morally as a capitulation to weakness, a self-indulgence. Perhaps it is both. In any case, the identification of woman and body, body and vulnerability, vulnerability and irony – which in effect responds to the implacable indifference or cruelty of the world by internalizing it – is a common phenomenon in women's poetry of the last twenty years.[23] □

While Ostriker seems to suggest that Plath's figuration of the body is closest to de Beauvoir's concept of transcendence, Liz Yorke's *Impertinent Voices: Subversive Strategies in Contemporary Women's Poetry* (1991) engages with the ideas of *écriture féminine* to suggest that Plath's work develops into an empowering sense of the body. Reading poetry by women as wilfully disruptive, challenging a patriarchal discourse which has traditionally excluded them, Yorke offers readings of Plath, H.D., Rich and Audre Lorde. She begins by outlining the flexibility of her theoretical approach, which illustrates a combination of *écriture féminine* with a broadly Anglo-American cultural reading:

■ It will be clear that, in my reading of the French feminist writers, I have not privileged one theoretical approach over another. This is because I have found that each vision presents an aspect of the truth which can be considered a valid trajectory of thought in its own terms. Yet each in itself is not enough. . . . Thus, I give attention to the specificity of women's biological difference from men, to the complexities of the mother–daughter bond, to the erotics of a decensored writing of the body. In studying the innovative strategies employed by poets, I move between women's material and historical (socio-economic) oppression and their construction as subjects. In so doing, I construct a both/and model for criticism in which both psychoanalytical/ mystic/intuitive and rational/historical/materialist approaches are held in tension.[24] □

In arguing for Plath to be read as a precursor, a literary innovator for contemporary women poets attempting to construct the female subject, Yorke begins by suggesting that Plath's poetry should be seen as transgressive and subversive, challenging the prevailing culture, both in cultural and sexual terms:

■ [Plath's] illicit poetry repeatedly brings to consciousness what fifties' and sixties' respectability would have wished silenced, excluded and suppressed. We find in this poetry the compulsive intensities, the fragmentations and splits, the insistent aggressions, the hatred and complaint of the woman who radically refuses to hold back on her grievances. She refuses to be the silenced hysteric – to be the woman having nothing to say, the woman whose suffering never reaches language. In Irigaray's words, the hysteric is the woman who does not know herself because:

What she 'suffers,' what she 'lusts for,' even what she 'takes pleasure in,' all take place upon another stage, in relation to already codified representations.[25] □

Yorke's consideration of Plath's poetic strategies when confronting the idea of the mother reflects an area of increasing interest to critics informed by psychoanalysis, and it is worth comparing Stephen Gould Axelrod's and Toni Saldivar's intricate discussions of language and silence, exploring the creation of Plath's 'poetic voice' with Yorke's more culturally determined discussion; but, for reasons of space, I have decided to focus on Yorke's much stronger analysis of femininity in Plath's poetry.[26] Yorke argues that Plath's work becomes increasingly concerned with the study of women, exploring the construction of femininity in poems from the early 1960s, such as 'In Plaster' and 'Three Women'. She contests Pamela Annas's negative analysis of the Third Voice, or 'Girl', by choosing to read the girl's actions as reflective of Plath's 'poetic project [of] going beyond the bounds of censorship to find the repressed of patriarchal culture, seeking the "inner voice" that resists both the damaging cultural edict and the acts of domination'.[27] Yorke illustrates this by her close readings of 'Tulips' which she describes as 'a very self-conscious and aware critique of myths of femininity'.[28]

Yorke concludes by proposing that Plath's struggle, evident in these 'transitional' poems, with a language and society that exclude female sexuality and subjectivity leads to a strategy of revision, arguing that Plath's construction of mythic selves is ultimately a subversive act of defiance. Referring to Catherine Clement's and Hélène Cixous' writing on the revision of patriarchal history, Yorke suggests that Plath's position on the margins, her exclusion from the symbolic order, results in the self-conscious and self-reflexive irony of her later poetry. Her discussion of 'Lady Lazarus' is the centrepiece of this analysis:

■ A rather different mythic 'set' [than the previously discussed 'Daddy'] is broken in the slightly later poem: 'Lady Lazarus'. The persona of Plath's 'Lady Lazarus' can be seen as a feminine hysteric/exhibitionist/sorceress who, in choosing to suffer spectacularly before her voyeuristic audience, stages for the reader a dramatic transformatory passage – from colonised female victim to phoenix-like avenger (CP, p.244). Following Freud and Michelet, Cixous suggests that 'the repressed past survives in woman; woman, more than anyone else is dedicated to reminiscence' – that the hysteric is one 'whose body is transformed into a theatre for forgotten scenes, relives the past, bearing witness to a lost childhood that survives in suffering.'[29] Undoubtedly, in writing this poem, Plath drew obsessively on her own long-standing inner suffering, her own attempts to commit suicide and her own murderous anger against her 'oppressors'. But the poem becomes more than an individual statement, for it, in Cixous' and Clement's words, 'resumes and assumes the memories of the others' who have suffered. In targeting the fascistic and authoritarian aspects of patriarchy for critique, Plath also holds up to ridicule the mythic patterns of fascism, with its many forms of fetishistic ritual.

As the fascinating, feminine woman, [Lady Lazarus] entices [her audience] into a series of pathological, repugnant, and pornographically captivating scenarios only to turn on them vengefully. This subversive feminine position is not that of passivity but rather that of actively entering into her role as dispossessed other. She deliberately and purposefully abases herself, enters into these compulsive perverse rituals in order *to cash in*. The woman, dispossessed, possessed, enters fully into the position created for her – as macho-male-defined woman/fascist defined Jewess.

Symbolically this demonic seductress, this sardonically 'smiling woman', becomes the horrific, destroyed and self-destructive other, the ultimate victim – who provocatively confronts her 'enemy'. Here, she reveals the appalling outcome of fascism, of its obscene, sadistic acts:

A sort of walking miracle, my skin
Bright as a Nazi lampshade,
My right foot

A paperweight,
My face a featureless, fine
Jew linen.

> Peel off the napkin
> O my enemy.
> Do I terrify? –

This revelation, this 'theatrical' demonstration – her dying, her miraculous 'Comeback in broad day' – are ostensibly for benefit of 'The peanut crunching crowd', but the real targets of her hatred who must 'Beware', are symbolic figures, male representatives of medical, militaristic, heavenly or diabolical patriarchal power: Herr Doctor, Herr Enemy, Herr God, Herr Lucifer.

A prostitute ready to flaunt herself, this persona would make them pay – a lot – to indulge their fetishistic attachments to women as part-objects. To gaze upon the woman or to hear her, to touch her fragmented body, smear her blood or feel her hair or her clothes –

> There is a charge
>
> For the eyeing of my scars, there is a charge
> For the hearing of my heart –
> It really goes.
>
> And there is a charge, a very large charge
> For a word or a touch
> Or a bit of blood
>
> Or a piece of my hair or my clothes.

[. . .] In this passage Lady Lazarus spectacularly immolates her old self: the used and abused woman/the despised, violated and massacred Jewess (whom Sartre recognised as having 'a very special sexual signification' in the literature of pornography).[30] She transfigures herself to ashes: [. . .] This menacing, sardonic ritual of self-immolation, as an exhibition carried out before her enemies' eyes, allows the woman, even as she poses before them, to escape their look of possession, to slip away from the gaze which had seized her, had regulated her, held her. She is no longer willing to fulfil their desires of her: she has left the ritual exchanges of macho-fascist patriarchy. She has absented herself:

> Ash, ash –
> You poke and stir.
> Flesh, bone, there is nothing there –
>
> A cake of soap,
> A wedding ring,
> A gold filling.

From that stage to another stage: from the looked-at, exploited and degraded woman, circumscribed by male economic or fascist military power, Plath imagines a liberating transfiguration to an engulfing furious female. Out of this transfiguring fire, a new woman is created out of the old, a woman capable of repudiating the dysfunctional patterns of hysterical femininity. Lady Lazarus, as vindictive sorceress, seizes the stage, transgresses the codes that have enslaved her. Phoenix-like, Plath's emerging, avenging woman tells her readers: 'Out of the ash/I rise with my red hair/And I eat men like air.'

It is a symbolically effective metamorphosis – a magical transcendence is achieved. It is fictive rather than real, but it brings to articulation a fiendish force-field of dissident, if not paranoid, female hatred and anger. Ultimately, it is not a convincing restitution: Hélène Cixous and Catherine Clement suggest that:

> This feminine role, the role of sorceress, of hysteric, is ambiguous, antiestablishment, and conservative at the same time. Antiestablishment because the symptoms – the attacks – revolt and shake up the public, the group, the men, the others to whom they are exhibited . . . . The hysteric unties familiar bonds, introduces disorder into the well-regulated unfolding of everyday life, gives rise to magic in ostensible reason. These roles are *conservative* because every sorceress ends up being destroyed, and nothing is registered of her but mythical traces.[31]

As I read this poem, these roles – of hysteric and sorceress – Plath both enjoyed and pressed to their limits. As Cixous and Clement go on: 'both sorceress and hysteric, in their way, mark the end of a type – how far a split can go'. Perhaps Plath knew that too. But, in opening up the field of subjectivity to furious female anger with its potential for transforming social relations between oppressor and victim, Plath was a poet before her time.[32] □

It is useful to compare this reading to Susan Van Dyne's analysis of 'Lady Lazarus' in her valuable *Revising Life: Sylvia Plath's Ariel Poems* (1993). A Professor at Smith College, Van Dyne's access to Plath's manuscripts of the *Ariel* poems produces a unique and detailed discussion of Plath's poetry, which recognises 'a richly significant aspect of all of Plath's *Ariel* poems: how biographical events and earlier texts deeply interpenetrate each other in the composition process'.[33] Developed from her earlier excellent essay on Plath's bee poems,[34] Van Dyne studies the revisions of twenty-five manuscripts chosen from Plath's original ordering of *Ariel*, developing significant links between poetry drafts that were written on the reverse of Hughes's poetry, and *The Bell Jar* manuscripts. For example, Van Dyne explores the relevance of Plath's often disparaged 'Burning the Letters', which was drafted on the reverse of Hughes's 'The Thought Fox' manuscripts, convincingly arguing that rather than being merely the bitter poem of a rejected wife, 'Burning the Letters' is a revisionary reply to 'Hughes's visionary equation of his own poetic genius with the mysterious powers of nature . . .'[35] While biographically driven by her reading of Plath's journals, Van Dyne's approach remains grounded in a broadly cultural analysis of Plath's poetry, confirming the female subject as 'a product of historicized experience'; but like many feminist critics of this decade, her analysis is considerably influenced by psychoanalytic feminist strategies. In the section, 'The Body, O Bright Beast I,' Van Dyne begins with a helpful discussion of feminist attempts to theorise the body and the debate on essentialism, primarily concerned with identifying ways in which 'the carnal female subject may express an I which is not merely Other.'[36] Although Plath often depicts the body as monstrous, whether in terms of revulsion as in 'Medusa' or empowerment as in 'Lady Lazarus', Van Dyne's discussion of the manuscripts for 'Ariel' suggests the successful fusion of the creative and sexual self into an articulate, female 'I' through Plath's revision of the Godiva legend:

■ In 'Ariel,' Plath is the most reckless in enacting her poetics through the fiery transubstantiation of the female subject. Yet even here creative liberty is expressed through figures that are emphatically corporeal and transgressively sexual. In her drafts Plath progressively obliterates the distance and difference between the speaker and the animal energy of her horse, Ariel, and interpolates a revised legend of Godiva in which the heroic wife performs a rebellious striptease. She also transposes the imagery of burning first associated with Godiva, to the 'red/Eye, the cauldron of morning' in yet another mutation of the poet's volatile form. Each of these changes, I would argue, produces a fusion of poetic identity and the carnal subject, not a rejection of it. The poem originally began by marking more explicitly an initial dichotomy between the raw, unguided material force of the horse and the speaker as controlling, yet desiring subject: 'God's lioness also, how one we grow/Crude mover whom I move & burn to love.' Compared to the hurtling velocity and unitary drive of the finished poem, the earliest draft reveals a pervasive, unresolved tension between alternative figures for the speaker's transformation in the grip of her muse. In the first of these, her presence is dispersed into the landscape:

Something else
Hauls me through air, // (I foam), O (I) flakes from my heels, (I)
Foam (In) to white wheat, a glitter of seas.

[. . .] The first of three handwritten drafts is incomplete; it breaks off, significantly, at a point at which the speaker's rising, melting motion is confused and contradicted by her embodiment in 'plunging hooves':

> (I rise, I rise, now)
> (I am) the arrow (I am) the (rain) dew that flies
> (Into the sun's)
> In the cauldron of morning
> One white melt, upflung
> to the lover, the plunging
> Hooves I am, that over & over.

Plath tries and rejects in each of the three drafts phrasing about the female subject's dawn 'rise' in favor of more urgent and purposeful motion. It seems even more significant that here the attraction that compels the union of dew and sun is not suicidal but sexual. All of Plath's figures in this draft are alike in stressing energy and mutability, but they lack the bodily integrity of the 'acetylene virgin' of 'Fever.'

As she revises, Plath refocuses the poem along a single trajectory, Godiva's daredevil ride at breakneck speed in which horse and rider are merged. The most significant changes occur in the third hand-written draft. The kinship that is claimed at the beginning of the poem ('Sister to the brown arc/Of the neck I cannot catch') is reconfirmed at the close of this draft. The final movement opens with an image in which horse and rider appear to coalesce: 'O bright//beast, I/Am the arrow.' The line breaks encourage the reader to interpret this vocative as an appositive, a fluid exchange of identities between radiant carnality and female subjectivity. Plath also reconnects the speaker to flesh in this draft by introducing the figure of Godiva. When, in the sixth stanza, Plath sexualizes the rider by adding 'thighs' and 'hair,' she also considers a much longer treatment of the legend in a digression that covers a full page, or space equal to the draft for the entire poem so far. These stanzas, which are all later discarded, show the intrusion of material addressed in earlier poems. The 'old dead men' that had been repeatedly killed in the drafts and finally eliminated from the last version of 'Stings' reenter here: 'Hands, hearts, dead men/Dead men/Hands, hearts, peel off –.' In another stanza, Godiva appears an amalgam of the suffering martyrs of the rage poems and the avenging temptress of 'Lady Lazarus':

> In a season of burning, I
> Am White Godiva
> On fire, my hair
>
> My one resort.

In the legend of Godiva, the importance of her naked ride to relieve the town of her husband's unjust tax is that it is an unseen spectacle. Her body is modestly veiled by her hair, and her chastity is protected by the town's willing refusal, except for peeping Tom, to look. The potency of the icon in the popular imagination, however, is not in its inscription of female purity and its function to validate communal norms of propriety, but precisely in the repressed content of the legend, that is, our fascination with the forbidden image of the unclothed female body as a gesture of female daring and an object of male desire. In her transformation of Godiva, Plath exploits the erotic charge of her self-display and yet refocuses our attention on Godiva as subject rather than spectacle. Plath omits any reference to the male gaze, so prominent in the legend and so essential to 'Fever,' because she would free her speaker even more unequivocally from this dependence. In the single stanza Plath retains in the final poem, Godiva is defiantly anti-social, her desire an unconstrained liberty of self-definition: 'White/Godiva, I unpeel – /Dead hands, dead stringencies.' She is un-ashamed of her guilty pleasure in the exhilarating ride that eludes even maternal obligations and ignores the child's cry that 'melts in the wall.'

In the close of the poem Plath confronts what I take to be two opposing images for the next incarnation of her speaker and, in them, contrary implications for her poetics. Although the ending forges another blazing signature for the singular poet 'at one with the drive' toward morning, the images she would merge have an ambiguous instability. Even more dramatically than in the willed triumph of the close of 'Wintering,' this poem incompletely suppresses a residual ambivalence between an identification with the flying arrow and the suicidal dew. Both images serve to retell the decade between her twentieth birthday and her thirtieth in a poetic shorthand. The phallic arrow recalls a maternal maxim about gender roles that Plath records in her journals and later revises in *The Bell Jar*. ['What a man is is an arrow into the future and what a woman is is the place the arrow shoots off from.' (*BJ*, p.74)] On the same morning in December 1958 that Plath reports the germ of her novel, she also complains of Hughes's lack of masculine drive: 'Dick Norton's mother was not so wrong about a man supplying direction and a woman the warm, emotional power of faith and love. I feel we are as yet directionless' (*J*, p.285). Three years later when Plath reworked these journal entries in draft-ing *The Bell Jar*, she was the mother of a daughter herself, struggling to prove she was also a writer. [. . .] In 'Ariel,' the dichotomy between male ambition and envious female desire is erased in her assertion: 'I/Am the arrow.' [. . .]

Finally, the compelling evidence of Plath's revisions demonstrates that 'Ariel' represents not an urge to disintegration but to articulation.

[. . .] In the original handwritten draft almost the whole poem is composed in complete sentences. By disrupting and fragmenting these in her revision, Plath creates the illusion of pure energy in motion. The shift to intelligible, complete sentences, which comes only with the entrance of 'White/Godiva' in the seventh stanza, is especially pronounced. At the same time, in the final third of the poem, Plath relocates the pronoun 'I' to the ends of several lines. The poem ends with an intensification of identity rather than with its negation as the speaker's self-assertive 'I' is magnified in the 'red/Eye' (initially 'heart') of the rising sun.[37] □

While Van Dyne understands the sexual energy of 'Ariel' as affirmative, Sandra M. Gilbert, in her valuable essay 'In Yeats' House: The Death and Resurrection of Sylvia Plath', claims that the sexual dynamics of Plath's poetry suggests an allusive sexual self, arguing that 'Ariel' embodies an androgynous being. Initially published in Wagner's *Critical Essays on Sylvia Plath* (1984), Gilbert includes a revised version of this essay in the final volume, *Letters From the Front* (1994), of Gilbert and Gubar's stimulating three-volume series *No Man's Land: The Place of the Woman Writer in the Twentieth Century*. A major contribution to feminist studies, *No Man's Land* is an author-centred discussion of the social, literary and linguistic conflicts between male and female writers, considering the strategies used by women writers who find themselves 'situated on an embattled and often confusing cultural front', with Plath emerging as a major figure through which to consider contemporary female selfhood.[38] 'In Yeats' House' responds to many of the debates and issues circulating in Plath studies, looking at questions of influence, selfhood, sexuality, culture and the potentially liberating use of mythology.

The essay begins powerfully by suggesting that the cultural memory of World War II becomes a 'trope of sexual battle' informing Plath's work:

■ The conflation in these two stories ['Superman and Paula Brown's New Snowsuit,' and 'The Shadow'] of human guilt and divine innocence, of the fall from innocence to experience and the rise of warfare, of struggles between children and battles between and within nations foreshadows a complex set of references to warfare that was increasingly to mark Plath's writing as, in the spring of 1962, she began to break through into the vivid style of the *Ariel* poems. [. . .] But as Plath evolved what was to become her mature style, metaphors drawn from World War II frequently replaced delineations of combat between individuals, not only to enact conflict within the poet herself, torn between guilt over her German ancestry and grief for her German father, but also to explore sexual battles, literary campaigns, the horrifying ruptures of all human history, and the ghastly torpor of a god who, as Plath writes in 'Lyonesse,' has 'had so many wars' that 'the white gape of his mind [is] the real Tabula Rasa.' (*CP*, p. 234).[39] □

Concerned with the way in which historical conflict intersects with sexual conflict, the earlier version of this essay offered a cultural reading of Plath's poetry, focusing on her dialogue with her modernist mentors, Woolf and Lawrence, and exploring her engagement with the rhetoric of World War II. While continuing to suggest that World War II is a central trope of Plath's literary imagination, this revised essay extends the discussion to raise questions of sexual identity and gender transformation: '. . . World War II offered Sylvia Plath a trope of sexual battle which modulated into a search for new ways of (feminine) being . . .'[40] In contrast to Van Dyne's argument that Plath is confirming her gender in 'Ariel', Gilbert understands this imaginary female self as an attempt to escape the constrictions of gender, raising questions of androgyny and gender transformation:

■ [I]n many of her most compelling texts Plath fantasized escapes from sexual difference which parallel some of the strategies for imagining the 'sexchanges' of the *new* that were deployed by such artists as Woolf and H.D. Most obviously, perhaps, in *The Bell Jar* as well as in 'Getting There,' she imagined her own rebirth. [. . .] The speaker of 'Getting There' rides a train that 'is dragging itself, it is screaming . . . Insane for the destination' and ultimately decides:

> The carriages rock, they are cradles.
> And I, stepping from this skin
> Of old bandages, boredoms, old faces
>
> Step to you from the black car of Lethe,
> Pure as a baby.
>
> CP, p. 249

And, by implication at least, the 'baby' self to be reborn here is a pre-oedipal creature whose innocence signals an ontological freedom from the contaminations of gender [. . .]

That the rebirth of such a purified fantasy self is achieved only at great risk – the screaming train is full of dangers, the ski ride breaks Esther's leg – proves just how radical as well as how crucial the poet's struggle toward the new has become and suggests that from Plath's conflicted perspective the new can only come into being through an annihilation of the old. The poem 'A *Birth*day Present' makes this point explicitly by defining the 'knife' of change that will 'not carve, but enter' to slice the universe from the speaker's 'side' as 'Pure and clean as the cry of a baby' (*CP*, p.208; emphasis ours). But some of the assertive self-definitions . . . formulate the violence associated with gender transformation even more directly.

'Ariel''s self-as-'arrow' flying toward rebirth in the 'red . . . cauldron of morning' (*CP*, p.240), for instance, incorporates the definition of masculinity proposed by Buddy Willard's mother in *The Bell Jar* . . . into a prophetic figure of ferocious androgyny. Similarly, the 'pure acetylene/Virgin' of 'Fever 103°,' shedding her sexuality like 'old whore petticoats' as she rises into a future whose mysterious objects ('whatever these pink things mean') she can hardly define, regresses to a virginity that, like the innocence of the baby, predates difference but is also as searingly dangerous to the ordinary reality of the past as an acetylene torch. And that, as several commentators have noted, this speaker's obliquely confessed eroticism is feverishly masturbatory ('All by myself I am a huge camellia/Glowing and *coming* and going') reemphasizes her metaphorically androgynous self-sufficiency (*CP*, p.232; emphasis ours).

But if both Plath's fantasized arrow-self and her virgin-self are dangerous in their quasi-androgynous transcendence of traditional gender categories, some of her most vengeful yet stereotypically *'female'* selves are equally deadly in their construction of a kind of *super* femininity that also, paradoxically enough, strives toward the new in its elision or evasion of traditional sex roles. In her sardonic revision of biblical parable, the heroine of 'Lady Lazarus' achieves, in the seductively (albeit parodically) eroticized body of a woman, the resurrection that Jesus had bestowed on a man whose power sisters, Mary and Martha, had watched in wonderment. [. . .] More radically, though, Plath's flaming, red-haired revenant threatens a resurrection of the feminine that will explode the old order by destroying the power of the patriarchal enemies ('Herr God, Herr Lucifer') who had mistakenly identified her as their 'opus' in the first place. Thus, as she brags 'Out of the ash/I rise with my red hair/And I eat men like air,' she preenacts the impassioned warning on which Hélène Cixous was to elaborate later in *The Newly Born Woman*: 'When "*The*" repressed of their culture [*sic*] . . . come back, it is an explosive return, which is *absolutely* shattering.'[41]

Similarly, in 'Stings' the self reincarnated as a queen bee, a 'red/Scar in the sky, red comet,' is neither (like the baby and the virgin) presexual nor (like the male/female arrow) androgynous, but rather *super* sexual in her generative and regenerative femaleness. Yet she too rises out of a tired gender order that forced her into 'a column//Of winged, unmiraculous women,/Honey-drudgers,' and thence out of the 'mausoleum' of sexual domestication that had previously 'killed her' (*CP*, pp.215, 214). And she, too, is murderous, both in her rage against the bee-keeping father figure – that 'great scapegoat' whom her sister bees died to kill when they molded onto his lips, 'complicating his features' – and in her achievement of a sexuality that must destroy every male who mates with her.[42]

Whether they withdraw from the feminine into a preoedipal 'purity,' appropriate a form of androgyny, or fantasize a powerful super femaleness, Plath's dreams of escape from gender and its discontents are usually as 'blood-hot and personal' as are most of the poems in *Ariel*.[43] □

While Gilbert almost celebrates Plath's representation of the body as a potent means of escape from the limitations of gender, Kathleen Margaret Lant insists that representation of the female body in Plath's work reinforces feelings of vulnerability and failure. Her article, 'The Big Strip Tease: Female Bodies and Male Power in the Poetry of Sylvia Plath' (1993), takes issue with the power or assertion which some critics locate in Plath's depiction of the female body, and argues instead that Plath experiences a 'troubled relationship to her body as an emblem of identity . . .'[44] By contrasting Plath's work with that of male confessional poets, Lant contends that Plath's work ultimately reveals a rejection of the female body, which even in its moments of transcendence is defeated by 'the language which shaped her and which constructed her femaleness as vulnerability'.[45] Lant centrally argues that the combination of the culture in which Plath was writing, and a 'figurative system' that devalued women, made it impossible for her to represent the body in affirming terms. The following extract outlines the differences she identifies between Plath and her male contemporaries, and goes on to offer a reading of 'Stings' that dramatically contrasts with Gilbert's.

■ Plath's veneration of personal statement and intimate revelation notwithstanding, it is the differences – especially with regard to figurative nakedness – between Plath and the male confessional poets that are ultimately illuminating. More than peculiarities of individual temperament, these differences hint at provocative discontinuities between the creative experiences of a woman writing at mid-century in America (and, in Plath's case, Britain as well) and of men writing from a similar context. And in many ways such differences reflect the startling dissimilarities in representation we find in the lines of poetry quoted at the beginning of this essay.[46] These lines – drawn, with the exception of those from Whitman's *Song of Myself*, from the works of American poets since the fifties – convey strikingly divergent attitudes toward the body and specifically toward nakedness. For the male writers, the unclothed body of the male speaker betokens joyous transcendence, freedom, power. For the female subject in Louise Gluck's verse, however, nakedness does not bring that female subject closer to the self or to truth or to power. Rather, nakedness for the female subject is experienced, at least within the context of this work, as yet another barrier between the self and the world or even between the authorial self and the persona it inscribes. The disclosure of the female body is, here, merely another false and falsifying gesture.

It does not come as a surprise that we find in Plath's poetry a concern with the body and with the physical, for she seemed – if we may take her poetry, her letters, her fiction, and her journals as reliable sources – a passionate and even sensuous woman.[47] Axelrod asserts that 'Plath enthusiastically traced connections between body and text',[48] and Joanne Feit Diehl, in her consideration of Plath's poetry and the American sublime, argues that Plath's primary trope [is] the engendered body'.[49] But when her use of the body, the metaphorical rendering of the female body specifically, is given close attention, we find that Plath inhabits a universe far removed from that of Ginsberg or Whitman or Lowell. For her, the body stands not as a shimmering emblem of the soul's glory but seems, rather, an embarrassing reminder of the self's failures, an icon of the poet's vulnerability. The speaker of Plath's poem 'The Jailer,' obviously kept violently against her will ('I have been drugged and raped'), clearly naked in her imprisonment ('My ribs show'), remarks pathetically, 'I am myself. That is not enough' (*CP*, p.226). The line is strikingly distant from Whitman's ebullient 'I will go to the bank by the wood and become undisguised and naked' and Robert Lowell's contented 'so much joy has come,/I hardly want to hide my nakedness.' In fact, Plath's lines echo Anne Sexton's searing and hopeless assertion that the bare, unhidden female self is pathetically insignificant: 'Once I was beautiful. Now I am myself'.[50] Somehow, at least in the works of Sylvia Plath, the unadorned, physical self of the female subject cannot function as a metaphor in the same way that it does for the male subject; the female body reminds us only that the female self is unworthy, inadequate, and – ultimately – vulnerable rather than ascendant. [. . .]

In positioning herself as a subject, then, Plath appropriates inappropriate figures with which to shape her subjectivity and her creativity. [. . .]

[Throughout the 'bee sequence'] the bees continue to present a threat to the body of the speaker, and she incessantly – almost in an incantation or ritual – insists upon her unimportance, on her hiddenness as her protection: 'They might ignore me immediately/In my moon suit and funeral veil' ('The Arrival of the Bee Box', *CP*, p.213). The queen is released finally from her isolation; she is permitted to unclothe herself from the honeycomb which has hidden and protected her, to fly naked and triumphant:

> Now she is flying
> More terrible than she ever was, red
> Scar in the sky, red comet
> Over the engine that killed her –
> The mausoleum, the wax house.
>   'Stings' *CP*, p.215

But the queen's triumph is qualified (as the triumph at the end of 'Lady Lazarus,' which this passage foreshadows, is qualified). The queen may now be her free self, but she is a red scar, the result of a wound or some unidentified pain, and she flies *only because* she must die; she flies over the world that decrees that she must die. Her nakedness promises to undo her. It is too easy to say that Plath – as an artist – has found transcendence or triumph in death. The queen, who has lost her 'plush,' is, despite her flight, despite her majestic death, 'Poor and bare and unqueenly and even shameful' (*CP*, p.214). Even if we wish to read the poem as very positive, it is clear that the unclothed body of the female subject here – the queen/speaker – does not experience the exuberance or triumph that Whitman or Ginsberg could express. In fact, she cannot even speak that triumph from the uncovered female body.[51] □

While we have been exploring the ways in which many feminist critics begin to engage with the theories of *écriture féminine* as a complement to broadly cultural readings of Plath's poetry, with the emergence of psychoanalytic criticism as a major trend in literary studies, several critics begin to discuss Plath's work in the light of these new and challenging debates. Steven Gould Axelrod's *Sylvia Plath: The Wound and the Cure of Words* (1990) and Toni Saldivar's *Sylvia Plath: Confessing the Fictive Self* (1992) are valuable contributions to Plath studies which advance sophisticated psychoanalytic readings of Plath, illustrating the progression from Holbrook's initial attempt at psychoanalytic criticism. Axelrod begins by suggesting that his study is 'a biography of imagination', exploring Plath's project of textual self-creation. In the introductory chapter, he interprets Plath's creative drive as a need to '[inscribe] an enduring immanence [. . .] In studying the interactions between her positions as person, author, text, and represented "I," we witness her quest to achieve satisfaction and authority in the symbolic order of language'.[52] Informed by Roland Barthes's conflation of text with the mother's body in *The Pleasure of the Text*, Axelrod concentrates on Plath's essay, 'Ocean 1212-W', to explore these issues, suggesting that, for Plath, the ocean 'seems to have incorporated all elements of this complex into her oceanic drama of the daughter's death and her rebirth as poet, of the mother's death and her rebirth as text'. Succeeding chapters identify the 'systems of her family relations' as central to Plath's poetry, exploring the difficulty of establishing a creative, independent self while under the influence of powerful precursors, both literary and biological, suggesting that Plath 'ultimately converted her experience of the conflict between self and other into a textual issue – the tension between subject and language, . . .'[53]

To give a flavour of Axelrod's analysis, I have chosen an extract from chapter three that focuses on 'Three Women'. As we have previously seen, this is a poem of increasing interest to critics, and Axelrod offers a psychoanalytic reading which, in contrast to Lant's argument for female vulnerability, argues that Plath's work is a powerful challenge to the symbolic order.

■ Plath . . . assumes an unprecedented degree of autonomy in 'Three Women.' First, she denies the prestige of the phallus, refusing either to subordinate female experience to the desires of males or to trivialize motherhood by idealizing it. 'Three Women' refashions the unfortunate 'creature without a penis' of the Freudian text[54] into a being who appears satisfactory and whole. Whereas Freud wrote of male penis and female 'jealousy',[55] Plath's second voice asserts that it is men who are 'jealous' of female anatomy (*CP*, p. 179). Whereas Freud depicted childbirth as a poor substitute for a penis,[56] Plath's poem celebrates childbirth as a 'great event' that allows women to achieve feelings of creativity and power. Whereas Lacan regarded the phallus as a signifier and Ophelia as Hamlet's cry of 'O phallus',[57] Plath's speakers seem to regard their wombs as signifiers. Refusing to entertain Freud's premise that what a girl 'wants' is a penis,[58] these speakers imply that it is men who are wanting. 'Three Women' places women at the center of the symbolic order, substituting a trinity of female originators for the male myth of origins. By positing female norms of experience, anatomy, and language, the poem subverts the patriarchal assumptions that frequently regulate Plath's texts, even her poems of revolt.

Plath pulls free from the mother's hypersymbiosis as well. Surely the woman who advised her daughter to write about 'decent courageous people' would not wish to 'appropriate' these frightened, angry, conflicted, and self-assertive monologues (*LH*, p. 477; *J*, p. 281). If Plath achieved only an illusory independence in 'Medusa,' she attained a more authentic separation in 'Three Women' by inventing female voices that speak beside, rather than against, the mother. In a complementary sense, however, Plath's voices also speak *for* the mother. Nancy Chodorow, revising Freud, argues that women value childbearing not as a substitute for a penis but as an occasion to recover their pre-Oedipal feelings of oneness with their mothers.[59] In a parallel way, Plath restores her mother's voice – the 'one mouth' she 'would be tongue to' (*CP*, p. 132) – through giving birth to voices of her own. She recovers a oneness by creating characters (in both senses of the term) with whom she feels united. Thus, in 'Three Women' Plath achieves a dual misprision. She severs a Western linguistic tradition that, as Margaret Homans has shown, associates entrance into the symbol order of language with the loss or murder of the mother;[60] but at the same time she asserts her difference from her mother by rejecting the progenitor's narrowness and control. This complex act of differentiation within assimilation permits the female subject to transcend both the literality of pre-Oedipal language and the particular configurations of the mother's discourse.[61] □

Axelrod goes on to suggest that the depiction of the maternal self is an inscription of the textual self. First Voice is seen to confirm the link between maternity and creativity, 'giving birth has reaffirmed her femaleness, which she gynocentrically equates with creative "power"', while Third Voice is identified as textually inscribing the apprentice poet: '. . . the very sorrow of her utterance suggests that the necessary precondition for creative success may at last be present. Like the poet-to-be of "Ocean 1212-W," she may stand ready to transform her loss into artistic gain.'[62] However, it is Second Voice which Axelrod locates as a textual challenge to patriarchal language:

■ To pursue our more radical line of interpretation, let us consider the second voice as a figure of the writer whose words have miscarried. From this perspective, the voice resembles that of . . . Plath herself, hiding a rejected poem – 'under a pile of papers like a stillborn illegitimate baby' (*Journals*, p. 106). The second voice is, after all, a secretary, a position that closely associates her with words. Those words, however, are normally dictated by a male executive. That fact helps to account for her anger at men, and it additionally connects her to women's historical role as transmitters of men's texts (a role played professionally by Aurelia Plath and periodically by Sylvia Plath herself). The second voice explains that when she sits at her desk, the letters proceed metonymically 'from three black keys, and these black keys proceed/From my alphabetical fingers' (*CP*, p. 177). She feels simply a 'bit' or 'cog' in the masculine signifying machine, producing a series of 'mechanical' rather than personal 'echoes.' This situation convinces her that she has lost a 'dimension,' which I interpret not simply as her baby but as the creative 'fulfillment' Plath spoke of so often in letters and interviews (e.g., *LH*, p. 298; Interview, 176). [. . .]

If the second voice begins as a silenced artist, a woman forbidden entry into the symbolic order of language except in the role of amanuensis, she ends in revolt:

> I shall not be accused by isolate buttons,
> Holes in the heels of socks, the white mute faces
> Of unanswered letters, coffined in a letter case.
>
> *CP*, p. 182

Prodded by her history of defeats, she intends to uncoffin her letters, to unmute her language, to breathe life into her creative corpses, to answer her call. When she states that losing a child resembles losing 'an eye, a leg, a tongue' (*CP*, p. 183), her implicit equation reads: child = eye, leg, tongue = vision, standing, voice = poem. Just as the starfish grows back its 'arms' (*CP*, p. 184), so she proposes to regenerate the poems that have thus far died aborning. Speaking with 'fingers, not a tongue' (*CP*, p. 184), which I interpret as a substitution of textual for phonic voice, she intends to replace her miscarried texts with viable ones: '. . . nothing has happened/ . . . that cannot be erased, ripped up and scrapped, begun again' (*CP*, p. 184). 'Like a spirit' or a revitalized imagination (*CP*, p. 184), she concludes her discourse at home in an Eliotesque 'lamplight' (*CP*, p. 186), stitching lace onto fabric, an image of nonpatriarchal composition. ('Text,' like 'textile,' derives from *texere*, to weave.) Her last lines allude to three interconnected images that are canonical in our literature: Whitman's 'grass,' which signifies (among other things) the woven green flag of his disposition, a child, an interpretable hieroglyphic, and uttering tongues (*Leaves*, pp. 33–34); Dickinson's 'Grass' that is both a sphere of simple green and a sod hiding a volcano (poems 333, 1677); and Stevens's fiction of the 'green leaves' covering and curing the barren stone of reality ('The Rock'). Transuming all those complex images of vital poetic art, and Plath's own 'flickering grass tongues' as well (*CP*, p. 79), the second voice affirms that for her too, '. . . The little grasses/Crack through stone, and they are green with life' (*CP*, p. 187).

The second voice of 'Three Women' inaugurated Plath's period of textual self-realization after years of artistic miscarriage.[63] □

The following extract is from Toni Saldivar's psychoanalytic study *Sylvia Plath: Confessing the Fictive Self*. Often neglected at the expense of Axelrod's earlier similar study, Saldivar does carve a space for herself within Plath criticism, positioning her work in opposition to what she suggests is the misguided Bloomian approach of previous critics:

■ Feminist critics who have appropriated Bloom's ideal of the strong poet have extended his theory to exalt the woman poet who can overcome 'anxiety of authorship', that is, her doubts about her right to author herself. These readers find Plath a triumphant heroine of self-determination in her later poetry.[64] In contrast, the same Bloomian theory can be used to read Plath as a woman poet who, in trying to subvert the patriarchal symbolic order, subverted her will to create and her will to live.[65] Certainly Plath's allegories can turn monstrous. In my reading, however, they attack, not the symbolic order, but the gnostic will to power that refuses any authority but itself.[66] □

Recalling earlier charges of solipsism, Saldivar reads Plath as possessing and nurturing a gnostic form of the imagination, a poet of self-scrutiny and solitary subjectivity. In the following brief extract, Saldivar asserts the textual nature of her study with a comparison with Sandra Gilbert.

■ [Plath] was afraid of her negating imagination, for it worked against her deepest need. That need was, I believe, not to defy death but to redeem her erotic sense. [. . .] These relations [husband, children] affirmed the rightness and richness of her given world which included her relation to others. This belief underlies the tradition of the symbolic imagination and casts the negating, gnostic imagination, at least for Plath, in a sinister role. I see a conflict of modes of imagination in Plath's poetry, not a 'battle of the sexes' as Sandra Gilbert called Plath's internalized war.[67] Plath's struggle reveals the two different ways of using language imaginatively.

One way Plath affirmed the symbolic imagination was to keep within her poems elements that resisted her will, or seemed to, such as the inscrutable alien crabs in 'Mussel Hunter at Rock Harbor,' [. . .] the nursing infant in 'Morning Song', and the gift of red flowers in 'Tulips'. Such palpable, stubborn things will not allow the speaker to 'have no face,' a line from 'Tulips' taken out of Rhoda's monologue in [Virginia Woolf's] *The Waves*. Their opacity baffles gnostic desires to have everything on one's own terms as an expression of individual will. They will not dissolve, and thus they keep Plath facing them, not a transparent image for a sublime 'self'.

Many of Plath's poems of 1962 strive for opacity as a way of staying within the given. Only when human relations break down does she write her strongest and most furious poetry of the negating imagination. Those poems want to dissolve all limitations on their drive for poetic victory. Plath's gnostic mode is skewed, however, by a vengeance that results from her marginal stance as the 'heroine of the peripheral'. At the edge, not at the center, her unleashed desire sees its discontents too clearly to be able to repress them strongly enough for transumption. [. . .] She etches on 'intractable metal' the horrors of the solitary and arbitrary will, for, like other satirists, she wants to wound. Refusing to dissolve the pain of human existence, she insists on keeping present, that is metaphorically powerful, what is wrong with human will, thus making a satiric triumph out of her refusal of gnostic 'identity'.[68] □

Although Saldivar and Axelrod differ strongly in their discussions of Plath's poetry, they are both concerned with identifying Plath's textual self-realisation, with exploring the formation of Plath's 'poetic voice'. In contrast, the final critic to be considered in this chapter, Jacqueline Rose, decisively deconstructs the idea of 'the poet', and interrogates the accepted subjective, internalised nature of Plath's imagination. Her influential study *The Haunting of Sylvia Plath* (1991) is a major contribution to Plath criticism which opens up the literary debate surrounding the poetry, and allows for a theoretical expansion in the study of Plath's work. Informed by diverse psychoanalytic and cultural approaches, Rose's brilliant, provocative book eloquently explores the circulation of fantasy in Plath's texts, examining the inner psychic processes which unsettle certainties of language, identity and sexuality, and question the boundaries of our sexual and cultural world. Rose's is an in-depth, thought-provoking and original study of considerable subtlety. The following discussion aims to outline some of the major arguments and provide extracts from her more textually based discussions.

In the introductory chapter, 'She', and the later chapter 'The Archive', Rose forces the reader to question prevalent critical responses to Plath, analysing both a masculinist approach to Plath's poetry, and the struggle over the ownership and meaning of Plath's texts. Rose asserts that it is 'impossible to read Plath independently of the frame, the surrounding discourses, through which her writing is presented'.[69] By exposing Plath as 'clearly hystericised by the worst of a male literary tradition', Rose aims to show, citing Holbrook and Alvarez as examples, that much of the sexualised criticism of Plath is a form of projection, 'the casting out by Plath's critics of what is most troubling about her writing, only for it to return all the more luridly as image within their own critical texts'.[70] It is an expertly argued critique that reads Plath as a cultural icon, and considers the problematic cultural investment which society locates in its female poets. Rose develops this position in 'The Archive', an absorbing chapter that questions the idea of Plath which emerges from the editing and ownership of her work, and provides a valuable antidote to much of the biographical writing. Through a critique of Hughes's comments on Plath's writing, Rose locates a debate over high and low art, which she suggests Plath's work explores, an argument fully developed in the later chapter 'Sadie Peregrine'.

Named after one of Plath's magazine pseudonyms, 'Sadie Peregrine' explores Plath's relationship to popular culture, contending that she is at the centre of many debates about the meanings and forms of culture. Although previous critics have discussed the impact of women's magazines on Plath's writing, these discussions are often restricted to identifying similarities in style and imagery, particularly the echoes of advertising slogans in such poems as 'The Applicant'. Rose, however, extends into a discussion of the denigration of popular culture and thus of primarily female forms of expression. Considering chiefly Plath's prose writing, Rose argues that 'it is clear that [Plath] sees a central component of her identity and her ambitions as a writer in terms which are incompatible with – at the opposite pole to – that image of the unique and solitary author which she has come so dramatically to personify'.[71] Rose considers the influence on Plath's own writing of popular texts, such as Philip Wylie's *Generation of Vipers*, mentioned in Plath's poem 'The Babysitters', and *Stella Dallas*, the hugely popular novel by Olive Higgins Prouty, the model for *The Bell Jar*'s Philomena Guinea. Arguing for the recognition of Plath as a culturally involved writer, Rose discusses her intelligent critiques of women's magazines and cinema, closing with readings of 'Superman and Paula Brown's New Snowsuit', and 'The Shadow', stories that raise questions of race, cultural origins, and politics. Although doing much to assert that Plath is a politically engaged writer, as cultural critics such as Alan Sinfield and James Young have previously suggested, Rose explores the contradictions and ambiguities of Plath's position:

■ Plath sits ambiguously in these cultural and political debates. The important point, however, is the extent of her participation in them. Her books on culture and politics, with their underlinings and commentaries, are at least as relevant as those books of literature (Auden, Woolf and Yeats) which have received so much more attention – anxiety of influence as much a cultural-political as a literary effect . . . [72] □

In the chapters we will be considering in more depth, 'No Fantasy Without Protest' and 'Daddy', Rose is primarily concerned with Plath's poetry. As a feminist critic, Rose explores issues of gender, sexuality and power in these chapters, developing her earlier analysis of Kristeva's concept of abjection, explored through a reading of 'Poem for a Birthday'. Rose is concerned with the link between sexual fantasy and writing, and in her introductory chapter she negotiates her approach as a feminist in relation to the dominant feminist discourses:

■ [. . .] For some time now, feminist criticism has seemed to be divided between a reading of women writers which bemoans the lack of – or attempts to retrieve for them – a consistent and articulate 'I', and one which celebrates linguistic fragmentation, the disintegration of body and sexual identity, in the name of a form of writing which has come to be known as *écriture féminine*. The first is expressed most clearly by Sandra Gilbert and Susan Gubar[73] [. . .] The second can be related to a number of French feminist writers, amongst them Hélène Cixous[74] [. . .]

We can recognise the awkward proximity of these conceptions to Alvarez's consistency of representation on the one hand, and, on the other, to Spender's disintegration of writing as a femininity spilling out of itself.[75] In fact, these early responses to Plath provide an early version of a still unresolved drama about femininity and writing. As we read them, we can watch unfold the stark alternative between, on the one hand, a masculinist aesthetic and on the other, a form of writing connoted feminine only to the extent that it is projected on to the underside of language and speech.

But there is also, I would argue, a strange proximity between these two accounts of women's writing, in the way that they each situate the woman inside an exclusively personal struggle to express either the self or the non-self. Both seem to remove the woman writer from historical process, the first through the image of a sustained lineage of women writers across all historical differences (cultural perpetuity for women), the second by dissolving the very possibility for women of any purchase on historical time. And both seem attached to the same valorisation of high culture, whether in its coherent 'realist' or its fragmented 'modernist' mode (it has been pointed out that the argument between them inherits the terms of the realist/modernist dispute).[76] We should also ask – since this will be such a central issue in relation to Plath – what image of sexual relations these different accounts of women's writing seem to imply – a battle of the sexes, meaning a battle between unequivocally gendered and sexually differentiated egos,[77] or a disintegration into a body without identity, shape or purpose, where no difference, and no battle, can take place.[78] □

Rose's negotiation of a feminist approach leads to her exploration of the prominence of fantasy in the chapter 'No Fantasy Without Protest'. In this controversial chapter, Rose consistently stresses that she is writing in the field of textuality, with no recourse to Plath's life. The centrepiece is her contested reading of 'The Rabbit Catcher', but the following extract provides a reading of 'Getting There', which reflects on the meaning of transcendence in Plath's poetry in light of the dominant feminist interpretation, which emphasises an empowering selfhood.

■ This factor [of the dialogism of the later poetry] seems to me to be of particular importance in relation to the concept of an emergent female selfhood which has been so crucial in the reading of these late poems. It is a reading which . . . is strangely shared by one form of feminist criticism and by Ted Hughes. What the two have in common is an image of transcendence – poetic, psychological, political – in which Plath finally takes off from, burns herself out of, whatever it was (false self for Hughes, Hughes himself for feminism) that had her in its thrall. This self enters into no dialogue (with others, with other poems) – it simultaneously sheds all others, as well as any otherness in its relation to itself; it sheds the trappings of language and the world. It is the Queen Bee [. . .]; it is Lady Lazarus [. . .]; it is 'pure acetylene Virgin' of 'Fever 103°,'. . . (*CP*, pp. 214–15, 244–47, 231–32).

This reading . . . tends to be teleological – the rest of Plath's poetry is then read back for the gradual emergence of this selfhood. It also depends on a specific, unitary conception of language as tending, like the subjectivity it embodies, towards the ultimate fulfilment of itself. Any uncertainty in the language, any ambiguity or obscurity, indicates Plath's as yet incomplete knowledge both of her authentic selfhood and of the language she gradually honed to the final perfection of its craft.[79] Thus the taking off of Plath becomes an allegory, not just for female self-emergence but for the flight of poetry and, by implication, for the transcendence of high art.

The arguments against this way of thinking about poetry are now fairly well known, but the issue takes on a very specific significance in relationship to Plath[80] – not because that figure is not there in the poetry, but precisely in so far as it is. By representing it, Plath allows us to examine it, allows us to ask what such a concept of an 'authentic female selfhood' might turn out to be carrying – what, exactly, it might mean. I would suggest that Plath reveals the internal impossibility of this conception of selfhood; that she represents it, while at the same time subjecting it to the most devastating critique. At the most immediate level, how can such a concept work as a model for female (for any) identity, since it involves not the assertion but the sublation of self? Too little or too much of identity, this figure in Plath's late poetry provides no basis for identification either because it propels itself beyond the (gendered) framework of the world: 'My selves dissolving, old whore petticoats'; or because it can rediscover itself – pure, self-generating ego – only in the place of God: 'I am too pure for you or anyone./Your body/Hurts me as the world hurts God' ('Fever 103°'). [. . .]

[. . .] On the same day [as she wrote 'The Night Dances'] Plath writes 'Getting There', one of her clearest indictments of God, man and the logos (the blind thirst for destination of all three) (*CP*, pp. 247–49). In this poem, the history of the world is a train 'insane for the destination': 'All the Gods know is destinations.' A woman drags her body across the terrain of war, attempting at once to repair the ills of history: 'I shall bury the wounded like pupas,/I shall count and bury the dead'; and to get free of patriarchal myth: '. . . It is Adam's side,/This earth I rise from, and I in agony. / I cannot undo myself, and the train is steaming.' The last lines of the poem can be read only as a rewriting of the end of 'Fever 103°':

And I, stepping from this skin
Of old bandages, boredom, old faces

Step to you from the black car of Lethe,
Pure as a baby.

What this poem seems to be saying is that the drive to undo herself ('I cannot undo myself'), which is more than legitimated by the horrors of the world, is self-defeating, for it can work only by means of the very forgetfulness which allows – which ensures – that those same horrors will be repeated. As Uroff puts it: 'The pure baby who steps from [the black car of Lethe] will perpetrate murder because she has forgotten the world's past history of murderousness.'[81] It seems impossible not to read these lines of Plath as her own diagnosis of the very solution that she herself seems to offer in other poems to the violence of the world. Transcendence appears here not as solution, but as repetition. Read together, these late poems offer one of the most stunning indictments of the very image of transcendence for which Plath has become most renowned. What she seems to be offering is a type of reading in advance of the link between phallocentrism, or phallogocentrism (the phallus as logos), and the feminist assertion of selfhood at that point where they both turn on the isolate ego where the second finds itself repeating the great 'I am I' of the first – the slide from 'I am I' to 'I did it, I' and its violence, as we have watched it unfolding here. It is a problem that has been central to much recent feminist aesthetic, as well as political, debate – the risk that feminism might find itself reproducing the form of phallocentrism at the very moment when it claims to have detached itself most fully from patriarchal power.[82]

There is no question, therefore, of denying the force of female transcendence, the presence and importance of such a figure in Plath's later work, nor of denying the narratives of vengeance and/or betrayal which this figure expresses or to which she comes as the response. It is also evident, surely, that the monstrous image of a vengeful feminism constantly conjured up by the executors in relation to Plath criticism is nothing other than this figure of Plath's late poetry. Rather the point is to suggest that, by representing this figure, Plath pushes it to its own vanishing point – self-immolation or an ego that knows nothing other than the void of itself (what would be the crudest rendering of self-transcendence if not 'topping yourself'?). Whether intentionally or not, she exposes the conditions of possibility of this figure *even* as she affirms it in her work. We do not in fact have a term for an identity free of the worst forms of social oppression which does not propel us beyond the bounds of identity in any recognisable form.

This problem seems to me to be far more important than any discussion of the positive or negative, creative or destructive attributes of this figure of female transcendence in Plath's poetry (these discussions seem to rely on taking the concept of identity in the poems as presupposed). Nor, I think can it be dealt with by an appeal to the contrary idea of shifting protean identities which makes lack of identity, rather than its affirmation, the virtue of femininity itself.[83] Neither singular nor protean, this is a tension which resides at the heart of identity – the ego and its other ('identity and its other' or 'the other of identity', to use Julia Kristeva's expression)[84] – in the most specific sense of the term.

The issue here, therefore, is the very form in which (female) transcendence can be thought. Teleology, identity, the ego – Plath's writing, and commentaries on her writing, shows us how this figure of transcendence subordinates all other figures (all other poems) to itself. We read Plath through this figure only by repeating its own ferocious gesture of hierarchisation; only by effacing, therefore, all traces of the sexual and linguistic hesitancy and self-questioning that we have seen running through the body of her work. Awful exigency, which crushes as much as it affirms.[85] □

We will close this discussion with a generous extract from Rose's final chapter, 'Daddy'. While it has been necessary to edit Rose's insightful comparisons between the approaches of Plath and other writers to the Holocaust, and her reading of 'Little Fugue' as a forerunner of 'Daddy', these are essentially preliminary to the central argument we are about to consider. Rose asserts that Plath's use of the Holocaust as metaphor neither trivialises the Holocaust nor aggrandises Plath's personal experience but actually accentuates the realization that the Holocaust has put a question mark over representation itself. Rose begins by entering into the continuing debate on Plath's appropriation of Holocaust imagery, before taking a detour through psychoanalysis, and finally leading us to consider the relevance of fantasy in 'Daddy':

■ For a writer who has so consistently produced outrage in her critics, nothing has produced the outrage generated by Sylvia Plath's allusions to the Holocaust in her poetry, and nothing the outrage occasioned by 'Daddy', which is just one of the poems in which those allusions appear. Here is one such critic, important only for the clarity with which he lays out the terms of such a critique. Leon Wieseltier is reviewing Dorothy Rabinowicz's *New Lives: Survivors of the Holocaust* in an article entitled 'In a Universe of Ghosts', published in *The New York Review of Books*:

Auschwitz bequeathed to all subsequent art perhaps the most arresting of all possible metaphors for extremity, but its availability has been abused. For many it was Sylvia Plath who broke the ice . . . In perhaps her most famous poem, 'Daddy,' she was explicit . . . There can be no disputing the genuineness of the pain here. But the Jews with whom she identifies were victims of something worse than 'weird luck'. Whatever her father did to her, it could not have been what the Germans did to the Jews. The metaphor is inappropriate . . . I do not mean to lift the Holocaust out of the reach of art. Adorno was wrong – poetry *can* be made after Auschwitz and out of it . . . But it cannot be done without hard and rare resources of the spirit. Familiarity with the hellish subject must be earned, not presupposed. My own feeling is that Sylvia Plath did not earn it, that she did not respect the real incommensurability to her own experience of what took place.[86]

It is worth looking at the central terms on which this passage turns – the objection to Plath's identification with the Jew: 'the Jews with whom she identifies'; to the terms of that identification for introducing chance into Jewish history (into history): 'victims of something worse than "weird luck"'; above all, to Plath's failure to recognise the 'incommensurability to her experience of what took place'. Wieseltier is not alone in this criticism. Similarly, Joyce Carol Oates objects to Plath 'snatching [her word] metaphors for her predicament from newspaper headlines'; Seamus Heaney argues that in poems like 'Lady Lazarus', Plath harnesses the wider cultural reference to a 'vehemently self-justifying purpose'; Irving Howe describes the link as 'monstrous, utterly disproportionate'; and Marjorie Perloff describes Plath's references to the Nazis as 'empty' and 'histrionic', 'cheap shots', 'topical trappings', 'devices' which 'camouflage' the true personal meanings of the poems in which they appear.[87] On a separate occasion, Perloff compares Plath unfavourably to Lowell for the absence of any sense of personal or social history in her work.[88] The two objections seem to cancel and mirror each other – history is either dearth or surplus, either something missing from Plath's writing or something which shouldn't be there.

In all these criticisms, the key concept appears to be metaphor – either Plath trivialises the Holocaust through that essentially personal (it is argued) reference, or she aggrandises her experience by stealing the historical event. The Wieseltier passage makes it clear, however, that if the issue is that of metaphor, . . . what is at stake finally is a repudiation of metaphor itself – that is, of the necessary difference or distance between its two terms: 'Whatever her father did to her it cannot be what the Germans did to the Jews.' Plath's abuse (his word) of the Holocaust as metaphor (allowing for a moment that this is what it is) rests on the demand for commensurability, not to say identity, between image and experience, between language and event. In aesthetic terms, what Plath is being criticised for is a lack of 'objective correlative' [. . .] But behind Wieseltier's objection, there is another demand – that only those who directly experienced the Holocaust have the right to speak of it – speak of it in what must be, by implication, non-metaphorical speech. [. . .]

Turn [Wieseltier's] opening proposition [around] and we can read in it, not that 'Auschwitz bequeathed the most arresting of all possible metaphors for extremity', but that in relation to literary representation – or at least this conception of it – Auschwitz is the place where metaphor is arrested, where metaphor is brought to a halt. In this context, the critique of Plath merely underlines the fact that the Holocaust is the historical event which puts under greatest pressure – or is most readily available to put under such pressure – the concept of linguistic figuration. For it can be argued . . . that, faced with the reality of the Holocaust, the idea that there is an irreducibly figurative dimension to all language is an evasion, or denial, of the reality of history itself. But we should immediately add here that in the case of Plath, the question of metaphor brings with it – is inextricable from – that of fantasy and identification in so far as the image most fiercely objected to is the one which projects the speaker of the poem into the place of Jew. The problem would seem to be, therefore, not the *slippage* of meaning, but its *fixing* – not just the idea of an inherent instability, or metaphoricity, of language, but the very specific fantasy positions which language can be used to move into place. Criticism of 'Daddy' shows the question of fantasy, which has appeared repeatedly as a difficulty in the responses to Plath's writing, in its fullest historical and political dimension.

[. . .] I want to address these objections by asking what the representation of the Holocaust might tell us about this relationship between metaphor, fantasy and identification, and then ask whether Sylvia Plath's 'Daddy' might not mobilise something about that relationship itself. The issue then becomes not whether Plath has the right to represent the Holocaust, but what the presence of the Holocaust in her poetry unleashes, or obliges us to focus, about representation as such.

To pursue this question, I want first to take a detour through psychoanalysis, as the discourse which makes language and fantasy the direct object of its concern – specifically through the 1985 Hamburg Congress of the International Association of Psycho-Analysis, as the psychoanalytic event which illustrated most acutely the shared

difficulty of language and fantasy in relation to the Holocaust itself.[89]
[. . .]

[. . .] At the opening session, Janine Chasseguet-Smirgel quoted these famous words from Freud: 'what has been abolished internally returns from the outside in the form of a delusion'.[90] In the memories of the patients, the Holocaust endlessly recurred in the form of such a delusion, demonstrating with painful clarity the detours which lie, of necessity, between memory and this (any) historical event.

No simple memory, therefore, especially for a second generation shown by analysis as in need of remembering to the precise extent that they did not participate concretely in the event. And no simple identification – not for this second generation but, equally and more crucially perhaps, not for the first generation. For if the experience of this generation was, historically, so unequivocal, their identifications at the level of fantasy constantly dislocated that certainty of historical place. I am referring here not only to what one writer described as the 'sacrilege' or 'disjunct parallelism' involved in juxtaposing the cases of the children of survivors to the children of Nazis (and the reverse)[91] but also, and even more, to the internal vicissitudes of identification revealed in the individual case-histories [. . .][92] Over and over again these patients found themselves in fantasy occupying either side of the victim/aggressor divide. Like the daughter of a German military family caught in a double role as victor and vanquished, and who thus mirrored, her analyst commented, the children of Jewish survivors who identify with the aggressor and victim alike;[93] or the two sons of the Third Reich fathers oscillating between the 'polar extremes of submission and exertion of power' as the 'defense of experiencing oneself as a victim' gradually met up with the 'repressed experience of harbouring the intentions of the perpetrator';[94] or the daughter of a member of the SS whose analyst comments – and not only in relation to her – on the conflict between the 'partial identities of the shame of the victim and the guilt of the culprit'.[95]

Suspended between these partial identities, these patients lived in a world of fantasy where actuality and memory both did and did not correspond [. . .] But what did emerge from these case-histories was that the question of historical participation in no sense exhausted that of identification and of fantasy – it did not settle the question of from where, and in what form, memory takes place. For being a victim does not stop you from identifying with the aggressor; being an aggressor does not stop you from identifying with the victim. To which we can add a formula only deceptively tautological – that being a victim (or aggressor) does not stop you from identifying with the victim (or aggressor). Identification is something that always has to be constructed. Wherever it is that subjects find themselves historically, this will not produce any one, unequivocal, identification as its logical effect.[96] [. . .]

. . . what happens if we extend . . . beyond the world of neurosis and repression to that of psychosis and projection, where it is not a socially outlawed object of desire but a psychically and ethically unmanageable identification which is at stake? Could it be that the very different encounter between psychoanalysis and politics precipitated here (partially and tardily of necessity) by the Holocaust cannot help but produce this demand as its effect? Note just how far this takes us from those who criticise Plath for putting herself in the wrong place in 'Daddy', for putting herself – the two are, we will see, inseparable in her poem – in the place of the Nazi as in the place of the Jew.

Go back once again to that criticism of Plath, specifically on the issue of metaphor, and it then appears that such a demand, such an identification, relies on the possibility of metaphor: the problem is not the presence of metaphor, but the risk that metaphor, along with the possibility of language itself, may be lost. Loss of metaphor is in itself a form of defense which threatens memory and identification alike. [. . .] Take metaphor out of language and there is no memory, no history, left.

In the analytic setting, this requires a return to the event, [. . .] in order to *restore* the function of metaphor; to release the essentially metaphorical work of analysis itself [. . .] Only in this way will these patients be freed from the literalness of a language which makes memory impossible – which, paradoxically, is the sign that they have no real knowledge that the Holocaust even took place. Only in this way, too, will they be able to acknowledge the aggressive side of fantasy which the loss of metaphor allows them simultaneously to erase. For metaphor is the recognition and suspension of aggression (the second as the condition of the first), allowing the subject to take up any one of these propositions in turn:

I want X but I do not intend to do it
I want X but I am not doing it
I do want X (in fantasy) but I do not (actually) do it
I want X but I do not want to want it

– all mutations of an unspeakable desire, or rather one that can be spoken only to the extent that, as in poetry (the poetry of Plath, for example), it remains within the bounds of speech.

There is a sense here, therefore, in which we can truly say that metaphor was arrested in Auschwitz, in so far as the figural possibilities of language, without which 'the origins of language are unthinkable', are one of the things that the Holocaust put at risk. We can turn that criticism of Plath around again and ask: not whether the Holocaust is 'abused' by metaphor, but rather under what conditions of representation can the fantasies underpinning metaphor itself be spoken? [. . .]

[In comparison to 'Little Fugue'] 'Daddy' is a much more difficult poem to write about (*CP*, pp. 222–24). It is of course the poem of the murder of the father which at the very least raises the psychic stakes. It is, quite simply, the more aggressive poem. [. . .] Writing on the Holocaust, Jean-François Lyotard suggests that two motifs tend to operate in tension, or to the mutual exclusion of each other – the preservation of memory against forgetfulness and the accomplishment of vengeance.[97] Do 'Little Fugue' and 'Daddy' take up the two motifs one after the other, or do they present something of their mutual relation, the psychic economy that ties them even as it forces them apart? There is a much clearer narrative in 'Daddy' – from victimisation to revenge. In this case it is the form of that sequence which has allowed the poem to be read purely personally as Plath's vindictive assault on Otto Plath and Ted Hughes . [. . .] Once again, however, it is only that preliminary privileging of the personal which allows the reproach for her evocation of history – more strongly this time, because this is the poem in which Plath identifies with the Jew.

The first thing to notice is the trouble in the time sequence of this poem in relation to the father, the technically impossible temporality which lies at the centre of the story it tells, which echoes that earlier impossibility of language in 'Little Fugue' [. . .] What is the time sequence of [the opening three verses]? On the one hand, a time of unequivocal resolution, the end of the line, a story that once and for all will be brought to a close: 'You do not do, you do not do/Any more'. This story is legendary. It is the great emancipatory narrative of liberation which brings, some would argue, all history to an end. In this case, it assimilates, combines into one entity, more than one form of oppression – daughter and father, poor and rich – licensing a reading which makes of the first the meta-narrative of all forms of equality (patriarchy; the cause of all other types of oppression which then subordinates to itself). The poem thus presents itself as protest and emancipation from a condition which reduces the one oppressed to the barest minimum of human, but inarticulate, life: 'Barely daring to breathe or Achoo' [. . .]

If the poem stopped here then it could fairly be read, as it has often been read, in triumphalist terms – instead of which it suggests that such an ending is only a beginning, or repetition, which immediately finds itself up against a wholly other order of time: 'Daddy, I have had to kill you./You died before I had time.' In Freudian terms, this is the time of '*Nachtraglichkeit*' or after-effect: a murder which has taken place, but after the fact, because the father who is killed is already dead; a father who was once mourned ('I used to pray to recover you') but whose recovery has already been signalled, by what precedes it in the poem, as the precondition for his death to be repeated. Narrative as repetition – it is a familiar drama in which the father must be killed in so far as he is already dead. This at the very least suggests that, if this is the personal father, it is also what psychoanalysis terms the father of individual prehistory, the father who establishes the very possibility (or impossibility) of history as such.[98] It is through this father that the subject discovers – or fails to discover – her own history, as at once personal and part of a wider symbolic place. The time of historical emancipation immediately finds itself up against the problem of a no less historical, but less certain, psychic time.

This is the father as godhead, as origin of the nation and the word – graphically figured in the image of the paternal body in bits and pieces spreading across the American nation state: bag full of God, head in the Atlantic, big as a Frisco seal. Julia Kristeva terms this father 'Père imaginaire', which she then abbreviates 'PI'.[99] Say those initials out loud in French and what you get is 'pays' (country or nation) – the concept of the exile. Much has been made of Plath as an exile, as she goes back and forth between England and the United States. But there is another history of migration, another prehistory, which this one overlays – of her father, born in Grabow, the Polish Corridor, and her mother's Austrian descent: 'you are talking to me as a general American. In particular, my background is, may I say, German and Austrian.'[100]

If this poem is in some sense about the death of the father, a death both willed and premature, it is no less about the death of language. Returning to the roots of language, it discovers a personal and political history (the one as indistinguishable from the other) which once again fails to enter into words: [verses 4–6]. Twice over, the origins of the father, physically and in language, are lost – through the wars which scrape flat German tongue and Polish town, and then through the name of the town itself, which is so common that it fails in its function to identify, fails in fact to name. [. . .] Wars wipe out names, the father cannot be spoken to, and the child cannot talk, except to repeat endlessly, in a destroyed obscene language, the most basic or minimal unit of self-identity in speech: 'ich, ich, ich, ich' (the first draft has 'incestuous' for 'obscene'). The notorious difficulty of the first-person pronoun in relation to identity – its status as shifter, the division or splitting of the subject which it both carries and denies – is merely compounded by its repetition here. In a passage taken out of her journals, Plath comments on this 'I':

I wouldn't be I. But I am I now; and so many other millions so irretrievably their own special variety of 'I' that I can hardly bear to think of it. I: how firm a letter; how reassuring the three strokes: one vertical, proud and assertive, and then the two short horizontal lines in quick, smug, succession. The pen scratches on the paper I . . . I . . . I . . . I . . . I . . . I. (*J*, p. 20)

The effect, of course, if you read it aloud, is not one of assertion but, as with 'ich, ich, ich, ich', of the word sticking in the throat. Pass from that trauma of the 'I' back to the father as a 'bag full of God', and 'Daddy' becomes strikingly resonant of the case of a woman patient described at Hamburg, suspended between two utterances: 'I am God's daughter' and 'I do not know what I am' (she was the daughter of a member of Himmler's SS).[101]

In the poem, the 'I' moves backwards and forwards between German and English, as does the 'you' ('Ach, du'). The dispersal of identity in language follows the lines of a division or confusion between nations and tongues. In fact language in this part of the poem moves in two directions at once. It appears in the form of translation, and as a series of repetitions and overlappings – 'ich', 'Ach', 'Achoo' – which dissolve the pronoun back into infantile patterns of sound. Note too how the rhyming pattern of the poem sends us back to the first line, 'You do not do, you do not do', and allows us to read it as both English and German: 'You du not du', 'You you not you' – 'you' as 'not you' because 'you' do not exist inside a space where linguistic address would be possible.

I am not suggesting, however, that we apply to Plath's poem the idea of poetry as *écriture* (women's writing as essentially multiple, the other side of normal discourse, fragmented by the passage of the unconscious and the body into words). Instead the poem seems to be outlining the conditions under which that celebrated loss of the symbolic function takes place. Identity and language lose themselves in the place of the father whose absence gives him unlimited powers. Far from presenting this as a form of liberation – language into pure body and play – Plath's poem lays out the high price, at the level of fantasy, that such a psychic process entails. Irruption of the semiotic (Kristeva's term for that other side of normal language), which immediately transposes itself into an alien, paternal tongue.

[. . .] I think it becomes clear that it is this crisis of representation in the place of the father which is presented by Plath as engendering – forcing, even – her identification with the Jew. Looking for the father, failing to find him anywhere, the speaker finds him everywhere instead. Above all, she finds him everywhere in the language which she can neither address to him nor barely speak. It is this hallucinatory transference which turns every German into the image of the father, makes for the obscenity of the German tongue, and leads directly to the first reference to the Holocaust:

> And the language obscene
>
> An engine, an engine
> Chuffing me off like a Jew.
> A Jew to Dachau, Auschwitz, Belsen.
> I began to talk like a Jew,
> I think I may well be a Jew . . .

The only metaphor here is that first one that cuts across the stanza break – 'the language obscene//An engine, an engine' – one of whose halves is language. The metaphor therefore turns on itself, becomes a comment on the (obscene) language, which generates the metaphor as such. More important still, metaphor is by no means the dominant trope when the speaker starts to allude to herself as a Jew:

> Chuffing me off *like* a Jew.
> I began to talk *like* a Jew.
> I *think* I may well be a Jew
> I may be a *bit* of a Jew.

Plath's use of simile and metonymy keeps her at a distance, opening up the space of what is clearly presented as a partial, hesitant, and speculative identification between herself and the Jew. The trope of identification is not substitution but displacement, with all that it implies by way of instability in any identity thereby produced. Only in metaphor proper does the second, substituting term wholly oust the first; in simile, the two terms are co-present, with something more like a slide from one to the next; while metonymy is, in its very definition, only ever partial (the part stands in for the whole).

If the speaker claims to be a Jew, then, this is clearly not a simple claim ('claim' is probably wrong here). For this speaker, Jewishness is the position of the one without history or roots: 'So I never could tell where you/Put your foot, your root'. Above all, it is for her a question, each time suspended or tentatively put, of her participation and implication in the event. What the poem presents us with, therefore, is precisely the problem of trying to claim a relationship to an event in which – the poem makes it quite clear – the speaker did not participate. Given the way Plath stages this as a problem in the poem, presenting it as part of a crisis of language and identity, the argument that she simply uses the Holocaust to aggrandise her personal difficulties seems completely beside the point. Who can say that these were not difficulties which she experienced in her very person?[102]

If this claim is not metaphorical, then, we should perhaps also add that neither is it literal. The point is surely not to try and establish whether Plath was part Jewish or not. The fact of her being Jewish could not *legitimate* the identification – it is, after all, precisely offered as an identification – any more than the image of her father as a Nazi which now follows can be *invalidated* by reference to Otto Plath. [. . .]

In Plath's poem, it is clear that these identities are fantasies, not for the banal and obvious reason that they occur inside a text, but because the poem addresses the production of fantasy as such. In this sense, I read 'Daddy' as a poem about its own conditions of linguistic and phantasmic production. Rather than casually produce an identification, it asks a question about identification, laying out one set of intolerable psychic conditions under which such an identification with the Jew might take place.

Furthermore – and this is crucial to the next stage of the poem – these intolerable psychic conditions are also somewhere the condition, or grounding, of paternal law. For there is a trauma or paradox internal to identification in relation to the father, one which is particularly focused by the Holocaust itself. [. . .]

One could . . . argue that it is this paradox of paternal identification that Nazism most visibly inflates and exploits. For doesn't Nazism itself also turn on the image of the father, a father enshrined in the place of the symbolic, all-powerful to the extent that he is so utterly out of reach? (and not only Nazism – Ceausescu preferred orphans to make up his secret police). By rooting the speaker's identification with the Jew in the issue of paternity, Plath's poem enters into one of the key phantasmic scenarios of Nazism itself. As the poem progresses, the father becomes more and more of a Nazi (note precisely that this identity is not given, but is something which emerges). Instead of being found in every German, what is most frighteningly German is discovered retrospectively in him:

I have always been scared of *you*,
With your Luftwaffe, your gobbledygoo.
And your neat moustache
And your Aryan eye, bright blue.
Panzer-man, panzer-man, O You –

Not God but a swastika
So black no sky could squeak through.

The father turns into the image of the Nazi, a string of clichés and childish nonsense ('your gobbledygoo'), of attributes and symbols (again the dominant trope is metonymy) which accumulate and cover the sky. This is of course a parody – the Nazi as a set of empty signs. The image could be compared to Virginia Woolf's account of the trappings of fascism in *Three Guineas*.[103]

Not that this makes him any the less effective, any the less frightening, any the less desired. In its most notorious statement, the poem suggests that victimisation by this feared and desired father is one of the fantasies at the heart of fascism, one of the universal attractions for women of fascism itself. As much as predicament, victimisation is also *pull*:

> Every woman adores a Fascist,
> The boot in the face, the brute
> Brute heart of a brute like you.

For feminism, these are the most problematic lines of the poem – the mark of a desire that should not speak its name, or the shameful insignia of a new licence for women in the field of sexuality which has precisely gone too far: 'In acknowledging that the politically correct positions of the Seventies were oversimplified, we are in danger of simply saying once more that sex is a dark mystery, over which we have no control. "Take me – I'm yours", or "Every woman adores a fascist".'[104] The problem is only compounded by the ambiguity of the lines which follow that general declaration. Who is putting the boot in the face? The fascist certainly (woman as the recipient of a sexual violence she desires). But, since the agency of these lines is not specified, don't they also allow that it might be the woman herself (identification *with* the fascist being what every woman desires)?

There is no question, therefore, of denying the problem of these lines. Indeed, if you allow that second reading, they pose the question of women's implication in the ideology of Nazism more fundamentally than has normally been supposed.[105] But notice how easy it is to start dividing up and sharing out the psychic space of the text. Either Plath's identification with the Jew is the problem, or her desire for/identification with the fascist. Either her total innocence or her total guilt. But if we put these two objections or difficulties together? Then what we can read in the poem is a set of reversals which have meaning only in relation to each other: reversals not unlike those discovered in the fantasies of the patients described at Hamburg, survivors, children of survivors, children of Nazis – disjunct and sacrilegious parallelism which Plath's poem anticipates and repeats.

If the rest of the poem then appears to give a narrative of resolution to this drama, it does so in terms which are no less ambiguous than what has gone before. The more obviously personal narrative of the next stanzas – death of the father, attempted suicide at twenty, recovery of the father in the image of the husband – is represented as return or repetition: 'At twenty I tried to die/And get back, back, back to you' . . . 'I made a model of you', followed by emancipation: 'So Daddy I'm finally through', and finally 'Daddy, daddy, you bastard, I'm through'. They thus seem to turn into a final, triumphant sequence the two forms of temporality which were offered at the beginning of the poem. Plath only added the last stanza – 'There's a stake in your fat black heart', etc. – in the second draft to drive the point home, as it were (although even 'stake' can be read as signalling a continuing investment).

But for all that triumphalism, the end of the poem is ambiguous. For that 'through' on which the poem ends is given only two stanzas previously as meaning both ending: 'So daddy, I'm finally through' and the condition, even if failed in this instance, for communication to be possible: 'The voices just can't worm through'. How then should we read that last line – 'Daddy, daddy, you bastard, I'm through'? Communication *as* ending, or dialogue *without end*? Note too how the final vengeance in itself turns on an identification – 'you bastard' – that is, 'you father without father', 'you, whose father, like my own, is in the wrong place'.[106]

[. . .] if ['Daddy'] is a suicide poem, it is so only to the extent that it locates a historically actualised vacancy, and excess, at the heart of symbolic, paternal law. [. . .]

Finally, I would suggest that 'Daddy' does allow us to ask whether the woman might not have a special relationship to fantasy – the only generalisation in the poem regarding women is, after all, the most awkward of lines: 'Every woman adores a fascist.' It is invariably taken out of context, taken out of the ghastly drama which shows where such a proposition might come from – what, for the woman who makes it, and in the worse sense, it might *mean*. Turning the criticism of Plath around once more, could we not read in that line a suggestion, or even a demonstration, that it is woman who is most likely to articulate the power – perverse, recalcitrant, persistent – of fantasy as such? Nor would such an insight be in any way incompatible with women's legitimate protest against a patriarchal world. This is for me, finally, the wager of Plath's work.[107] □

CHAPTER FIVE

New Directions

THIS FINAL chapter will consider recent publications on Plath, suggesting possible new directions and developments in the criticism. While very much connected to the debates of the previous two chapters, as is shown by their continuing interest in psychoanalytic and deconstructive criticism, and their growing awareness of the political and cultural implications of Plath's poetry, these critics seem to offer a fresh and encouraging future for Plath studies, increasingly raising questions of nationality and sexuality. The impact of *The Haunting of Sylvia Plath* is evident; many recent critics feel it necessary to question and respond to elements of Rose's argument.

Al Strangeways' article '"The Boot in the Face": The Problem of the Holocaust in the Poetry of Sylvia Plath' (1996) continues the debate over metaphor and appropriation. Strangeways aims to show that in her use of the Holocaust, Plath's 'motives were responsible, and that the often unsettling appearance of the Holocaust in her later poems stems from a complex of reasons concerning her divided view about the uses of poetry and the related conflict she explores between history and myth [. . .]' Interpreting Rose's argument as an attempt to define Plath as a politically engaged poet, Strangeways suggests that the debate has to be extended, stating that 'little attention has been given to the link between such political concerns and the Holocaust'.[1] His opening argument adopts a vaguely cultural materialist approach, which, in establishing Plath's motives for the use of this material, often concurs with James E. Young's assertion that Plath 'shared the era of victimhood'.[2] However, within the now familiar discussion of the political pressures of the period, Strangeways does briefly, yet effectively, propose that Plath offers a metaphorical link between the Holocaust and the Cold War:

■ Plath, in 'Mary's Song' [. . .] connects the past atrocity of the Holocaust and the future threat of nuclear destruction, exploring the double-edged nature of technological 'progress' that allows both space flight and efficient genocide – historically of the Jewish people, potentially of the whole world [. . .] For Plath, the main link between the Holocaust and a potential nuclear war was the mind-numbing rhetoric that both 'final solution' and cold war discourses employed.[3]

[. . .] Plath's personalized treatment of the Holocaust stems, then, from a combination of two motives: her very 'real' sense of connection (for whatever reasons) with the events, and her desire to combine the public and the personal in order to shock and cut through the distancing 'doubletalk' she saw in contemporary conformist, cold war America.[4] □

Strangeway's central argument, however, is not so concerned with culturally justifying Plath's use of Holocaust imagery as with evaluating how 'effectively or appropriately Plath treats the Holocaust, and whether, indeed, she actually confronts the problem of metaphorization'.[5] Resurrecting a subject that has been fairly dormant since Kroll, Strangeways considers Plath's interest in mythic texts, primarily Graves's *The White Goddess*, alongside her evident political concerns. By arguing that Plath employs the Holocaust on almost mythic terms, Strangeways finally suggests that Plath's work betrays a mid-century conflict over the meaning of poetry:

■ While it is relatively straightforward to chart the complex of reasons behind the abrupt chronological appearance of the Holocaust in Plath's poems, the briefness of the appearance of such material within individual poems poses more complicated problems. Certainly, as Young notes, Plath's poems are not strictly about the Holocaust [. . .] although, as I argued earlier with reference to the influence of Erich Fromm, neither are they as resolutely private as they often appear. Accepting this, however, and notwithstanding her genuine sense of connection to the cultural impact of its horrors, the Holocaust appears in Plath's poems in references that are often emblematic, seemingly untransformed by poetic craft. In 'Daddy,' for instance, it is not so much the style of 'light verse' and the connection of the very personal to the very extreme horrors of, in Seamus Heaney's terms, 'the history of other people's sorrows'[6] that causes unease. Rather, Plath combines myth and history (Electra, vampirism and voodoo rub shoulders with the Holocaust) in such a way that the history of Nazi persecution of the Jews appears almost one-dimensional in comparison to the flexibility of her treatment of the poem's mythic and psychoanalytic aspects. [. . .]

The contrast between the resonance and diversity of Plath's use of myth and the single dimensions of her use of history in the form of the Holocaust and Hiroshima is not simply due to Plath's greater experience and confidence in handling the former, learned from using mythic material throughout her poetic career. Robert Graves in *The White Goddess* (an influential book for Plath and for many mythmaking poets of the 1950s), separates history and myth in their relation to poetry. He writes of 'the tendency of history to taint the purity of myth' and is disdainful of 'originality' in the poet who 'take[s] his themes from anywhere he please[s]',[7] by which Graves appears to mean 'occasional' rather than 'mythic' themes. Yet while Plath agrees with Graves about the importance of a deep personal knowledge of and feeling for myth, she not only dissents from Graves's view of the poetic dominance of myth, but extends his exhortation about the importance of a personal feeling for and connection to myth to reverse the dichotomy he sets between myth as pure, history as impure. In her poetry, it is myth that Plath appropriates (more and less successfully) for more idiosyncratic and personal ends (for instance, in her connection of myth with psychoanalytic themes in poems such as 'Electra on Azalea Path' [1959]). Notwithstanding her sense of involvement with political and historical themes, it is history that stands as somehow unchanging and 'pure,' emblematic and suprapersonal in her poetry. It is this impersonal 'purity' of emblem applied to such horrors of history as the twentieth-century Holocaust that makes poems such as 'Fever 103°' and 'Daddy' so discomfiting.

If, then, this is the root of the dilemma about Plath's treatment of the Holocaust, what were the reasons behind Plath's reversal of Graves's dichotomy? By declaring [in the 1962 interview with Peter Orr] that personal experience should be relevant to such historical events, [Plath] apparently contradicts a statement she made in the same period, where she describes the 'bigger things,' more traditionally, as the timeless universals of loving and creating.[8] This highlights a central conflict for Plath about the uses of poetry, rooted in the watershed period in which she wrote, where the movement was from seeing poetry as mythic and timelessly universal (as Graves did) to its being more a personal and didactic communication that comments on the issues of the day.[9] Indeed, Plath even expresses her ambivalence within the same piece, when she writes, on the one hand, that the importance of poetry does not lie in its ability to communicate with or influence people – 'Surely the great use of poetry is its pleasure – not its influence as religious or political propaganda. . . . I am not worried that poems reach relatively few people' – yet several lines later declares that she sees poetry as communicating something good, teaching or healing by comparing poems' 'distance' as reaching 'farther than the words of a classroom teacher or the prescriptions of a doctor' ('Context' p. 92). It is Plath's own ambivalence about these two uses of poetry that is reflected in the divergent critical reception her use of the Holocaust has generated: whether her poetry is mythic, and thus open to the charge that (notwithstanding the impossibility of legislating history and subjectivity) her figurings are either inappropriate or irresponsible, or whether her poetry is inescapably concerned with contemporary issues, directly confronting the problems surrounding the use of topical material as tropes. [. . .]

[. . .] instead of trying directly to present the cruelty of the Holocaust itself, the feeling Plath's poems generate is one of complicity in the easy assimilation of past cruelties. Her poems try to avoid the anonymity and the amnesia contingent on the 'them and us' and 'then and now' distinctions that characterize the perception of history by highlighting her use of the Holocaust as metaphor. In such poems, readers are *meant* to feel uncomfortable with the suprapersonal, mythical depiction of Jewish suffering, feeling somehow implicated (because of their traditional identification with the lyric persona) in the voyeurism such an assimilation of the Holocaust implies. This feeling of implication that Plath's poems generate may be viewed in broad terms as their success. Such poems are culturally valuable *because* the appearance of the Holocaust in them is like a 'boot in the face' – certainly few readers leave them feeling 'complacent instead of concerned or disturbed.'

While the ultimately inconceivable nature of the horror of the Holocaust means that Plath cannot mobilize the kinds of overt reflexivity apparent in her treatment of traditional myth in, for example, 'Electra on Azalea Path,' her poems that deal with the Holocaust also work to comment on metapoetic concerns. In 'Lady Lazarus,' for example, Plath collapses the 'them and us' distinction by confronting readers with their voyeurism in looking at the subject of the poem. To apply Teresa De Lauretis's theorizing of the cinematic positioning of women to Plath's poem, in 'Lady Lazarus,' the speaker's consciousness of her performance for the readers (who are implicitly part of the 'peanut-crunching crowd') works to reverse the gaze of the readers so that they become 'overlooked in the act of overlooking'.[10] By extension, in parodic overstatement (Lady Lazarus as archetypal victim, archetypal object of the gaze) Plath highlights the performative (that is, constructed rather than essential) nature of the speaker's positioning as object of the gaze, and so (to extend Judith Butler's terms), Lady Lazarus enacts a performance that attempts to 'compel a reconsideration of the place and stability' of her positioning, and to 'enact and reveal the performativity' of her representation.[11] This sense of performativity and the reversal of gaze likewise tends, in 'Lady Lazarus,' to compel reconsideration not only of the conventional positioning of the woman as object, and of the voyeurism implicit in all lyric poetry, but also of the historical metaphors as objects of the gaze. Readers feel implicated in the poem's straightforward assignment and metaphorizing of the speaker in her role as object and performer, and contingently are made to feel uncomfortable about their similar easy assimilation of the imagery (of the suffering of the Jews) that the speaker uses. In 'Daddy,' a similar relationship between reader, speaker, and metaphor is at work. Like 'Lady Lazarus,' 'Daddy' does not attempt to depict the suffering directly for our view (an impossible task, for the reasons given above) but works by confronting readers with, and compounding the problematic distinctions and connections between, the private and the historical (our lives and their suffering). In other words, readers' reactions of unease, discomfort, and outrage are necessarily a response to the surface, the poem itself, rather than to the events the poem uses as metaphors for its subject (be it about individualism, freedom, or memory), because the events themselves are not graspable. The poem is effective because it leaves readers in no clear or easy position in relation to the voyeuristic gazes operating within it (of reader at speaker, reader at poet, poet at speaker, and all at the events which are metaphorized) and able to take no unproblematic stance regarding the uses of metaphor involved.

Ultimately, then, George Steiner's divided attitude[12] towards Plath's treatment of such material most adequately and accurately represents the effect and effectiveness of Plath's project – a project meant to confront readers with their implication in the viewing and metaphorizing of others' lives and suffering, and aimed at foregrounding the complex instability of the boundaries between myth and reality that forms the root of the problematic placement of the Holocaust in our society. The reason such reflexivity, and its resulting complexity, is so often missed is because Plath's conflict between the idea of poetry as timeless mythic object or as political and/or personal communication remains unresolved, or, indeed, unresolvable, due to the modern relation between history and myth. Her critics often fail to see Plath's balanced ambivalence and appear trapped in one of two extremes of judgment about the meanings of, and motives behind, her poetry. Two interpretations of 'Getting There' (1962) sum up this divide. Judith Kroll reads the poem 'as the enactment of a willingly undertaken purgatorial ritual, in which the true self, purified by Lethe of all false encumbrances [of the past] finally emerges . . . [d]iscarding the "old bandages" [in] a symbol[ic] resurrection'.[13] In this interpretation, indeed, the Holocaust has been abused for its immediate value as a metaphor for the past. Margaret Dickie Uroff, however, perceives the poem as expressing a view opposed to that read by Kroll. She writes:

'[T]he train that drags itself through the battlefields of history ultimately becomes the "black car of Lethe," a symbol of the forgetfulness of the past. It becomes a cradle, nurturing a new generation of killers: the pure baby who steps from it will perpetuate murder because she has forgotten the world's past history of murderousness.'[14] These two readings reflect Plath's own foregrounding of her culturally situated conflict about the uses of poetry, between the mythic desire that poetry transcend history and the 'committed' purpose that it name history and thus remember it. An understanding of the 'boot in the face' effect of Plath's treatment of the Holocaust, then, enables the recognition that the dissonances between history and myth in her poetry are not an aesthetic problem but work to prohibit complaisance about the definitions of – and the relationship between – myth, history, and poetry in the post-Holocaust world.[15] □

While Strangeways reveals a sympathy towards Rose's discussion of appropriation in 'Daddy', by contrast, Anthony Easthope offers a forceful reply to Rose's interpretation, in which he questions her complex argument for the recognition of the instability of identity. Easthope insists on the essentially 'lyrical-confessional mode' of Plath's poetry, which, he suggests, like much of modern British poetry, essentially descends from an English Romantic tradition which aims to '[hold] meaning onto word, signified onto signifier'. Modernism seems only to have influenced modern British poets, such as Larkin, Hughes, and Heaney, in their adoption of modernist techniques in vocabulary and metaphor. Easthope explores Eliot's concept of the 'objective correlative', 'the relationship between the I of enunciation and the I of the enounced or statement',[16] suggesting that the radical uncertainty of the subject in Eliot's *The Waste Land* effectively invites both 'personal' and 'historical' readings. Focusing on the operation of the signifier in 'Daddy', Easthope offers a critique of Rose's understanding of 'objective correlative' in 'Daddy', questioning the historical contextualisation of the poem:

■ Jacqueline Rose's extended commentary on Plath's 'Daddy' gives most space to possible meanings of the text, arguing that it is a poem 'of the murder of the father' (p. 222) whose narrative moves 'from victimisation to revenge' (p. 223), a murder in which, according to the logic of the unconscious mechanism of deferred action (*Nachtraglichkeit*), 'the father who is killed is already dead' (p. 224).

The poem has been attacked by critics for its deployment of the Holocaust, a criticism epitomised in one view that 'Whatever her father did to her it cannot be what the Germans did to the Jews' (cited by Rose, p. 206). Rose summarises these criticisms as the views that (1) 'in aesthetic terms, what Plath is being criticised for is a lack of "objective correlative"', and (2) 'only those who directly experienced the Holocaust have the right to speak of it' (p. 206).

In defending Plath, Rose first sustains a long, serious and important argument against (2), affirming the necessity, even at the price of some forms of sado-masochistic identifications, that those who have not directly experienced the Holocaust should encounter it in fantasy as, among things, a means to begin to work it through in the psychoanalytic sense (the argument has recently come alive again over *Schindler's List*). Since the perspective of this argument concentrates on thematic meaning rather than matters of signification I'll not pursue the question of fantasy in 'Daddy' [. . .]

Difficulties in Rose's argument occur, for me, with (1) – not so much (to anticipate) the poem's *lack* of an objective correlative but rather that it uses the Holocaust mainly *as* an objective correlative. The question, as Rose concludes, depends on the 'conditions of representation' (p. 214) operating in the text, that is, I take it, an issue which largely resolves into a formal question.

In her analysis of the poem and its conditions of representation Rose makes three related assertions:

(1) The poem presents 'a crisis of language and identity' (p. 228) caused by a process in which 'identity and language lose themselves in the place of the father whose absence gives him unlimited powers' (p. 227).

(2) This crisis of language and identity is registered in the text especially in two instances. On the lines

Ich, ich, ich, ich
I could hardly speak. . . .

Rose comments that 'The notorious difficulty of the first-person pronoun in relation to identity – its status as shifter, the division or splitting of the subject which it both carries and denies – is merely compounded by its repetition here' (p. 226). Noting that 'In the poem the "I" moves backwards and forwards between German and English', she refers this to 'the dispersal of identity in language' (p. 226).

(3) Rose argues that it is the 'crisis of representation in the place of the father which is presented by Plath as engendering – forcing, even – her identification with the Jew' (p. 227); that identification equates the father with a Nazi, so leading into images of the Holocaust such that, Rose claims, 'Plath's poem enters into one of the key phantasmic scenarios of Nazism itself' (p. 232).

A first response to this would be to ask who is meant in the argument by 'Plath' as when it is said that the crisis of representation in the poem is 'presented by Plath' (p. 227), that the poem exhibits 'Plath's use of simile' (p. 228), that 'Plath stages this (event) . . . as part of a crisis of language and identity' (p. 228). Is this merely a convenient and conventional way of identifying a text or is something deeper at stake? In the third example 'Plath' is distinguished from 'the poem' and its 'speaker' but in the other two, for example, 'Plath' is not separated clearly from the poem's represented speaker.

What to me is so striking about Plath's 'Daddy' is the sustained coherence and stability of its represented speaker, the I which runs across and is confirmed at every instance in:

> . . . I have lived . . .
> . . . I have had to kill you . . .
> I used to pray . . .
> . . . I never could tell . . .
> I never could talk . . .
> I could hardly speak . . .
> I thought every German . . .
> I began to talk like . . .
> I think I may . . .
> I may be . . .
> I have always . . .
> I was ten . . .

and so to the end, '. . . I'm through'. One could argue that such insistent affirmation on self-identity by the represented speaker might deny its own confidence. Identity is always an effect, always in play, but the poem represents a speaker whose identity is substantiated and confirmed throughout by a consistent individual state of mind, a psychological unity which is very much that Rose defines – in imagining the father's death, the represented speaker moves from victimisation to revenge. If you can still say 'I think I'm having a crisis', your subjectivity is very much in place; for an example of a *radical* crisis in identity and language you have to turn to the closing eleven lines of *The Waste Land*.

Identity is never wholly unified but, given this degree of pre-existing integrity in the represented speaker, it is hard to see how it is deeply split by the repetition of the German 'Ich', especially since any momentary disturbance is immediately made good when the speaker comments retrospectively on this disturbance, 'I could hardly speak . . .'. If the speaker is represented as experiencing such a split (an effect with precedents as far back as *Tintern Abbey*), far from producing a crisis that reminds us we are reading a poem, it in fact stages the speaker's state of mind more convincingly. Nor can I see a movement between German and English as entailing a 'dispersal of identity in language' since again that movement is explained by the state of mind of the represented speaker who reflects upon it, 'I thought every German was you'.

In the dominant poetic tradition from Wordsworth on represented speakers frequently refer to themselves and their own thoughts so that a split between subject of enunciation and subject of enounced is represented by the poem as something the speaker feels. And, according to the same strategy, represented speakers often imagine identities for themselves. In Wordsworth's *The Prelude* the represented speaker identifies with a version of his earlier self, just as, in a rather different way, the represented speaker of 'The Wild Swans at Coole' rather imagines himself as a swan. Far from undermining the stability of identity represented by the text such manoeuvres actually tend to strengthen it, by admitting and holding in place what might threaten to dissolve such stability. So it is very much in accord with tradition that the speaker represented in 'Daddy' begins to imagine an identity for herself. For me it is crucial that this kind of slide in identity does not occur, as it does so often in *The Waste Land* or *The Cantos*, as an unanticipated change of discourse, of textuality. Far from it: the represented speaker in 'Daddy' makes the situation clear, 'I think I may well be a Jew'. The first 'I' is firmly in place holding up the second as a provisional and temporary identity.

A temporary identity for what purpose? Here perhaps we should retrieve the points made earlier about 'objective correlative'. How far is the very powerful material in the poem circulating around the fantasies Rose acutely describes made available for contextualisation in historical and social discourses and how far as personal expression? Though of course the two can never be fully separated, the nodal factor is the mode of representation. I would propose that a necessary condition for historical contextualisation ('as historical reference', p. 216) is the kind of relatively unanchored textuality specified earlier in the lines about 'hooded hordes' in *The Waste Land*. But 'Daddy' does not work like this since it seeks throughout to efface and control textuality in the service of representing a speaker and her state of mind. To that extent the images from the Holocaust function as objective correlatives for a personal emotion, are appropriated to express a version of the self. There is, then, justice in the claim that 'Whatever her father did to her it cannot be what the Germans did to the Jews' if it is read to mean something like, 'To adapt some of the most intense and overwhelming historical discourses of the twentieth-century as means to express mental suffering caused to an individual by a personal relationship is to diminish and reduce those discourses'.

Rose accepts that in 'Daddy' there is a 'preliminary privileging of the personal' (p. 223). I find this privileging to be not preliminary but comprehensive, ensuing as it does from the poem's failure to challenge the inherited lyric-confessional mode in which it is written. On my showing 'Daddy' is a humanist poem, and a pretty old-fashioned one, inviting comparison with the work in the confessional voice of Plath's mentor, Robert Lowell, 'The Quaker Graveyard in Nantucket' and so on. The problem with such poetry, aiming as it does to put at the centre of writing a dramatisation of the unified self, is that, as Toril Moi argues, it conforms to a 'humanist ideology' in which 'the self is the *sole author* of history and of the literary text'.[17] □

As Easthope incisively employs post-structuralist practice to explore the subject position in Plath's 'Daddy,' concluding that Plath essentially writes in a humanist, confessional tradition, Anna Tripp's essay 'Saying "I": Sylvia Plath as Tragic Author or Feminist Text?' (1994) also adopts post-structuralist strategies, but to a very different effect, arguing for the primacy of textuality in Plath's poetry. Acknowledging the influence of Rose, Tripp, in her reading of 'I Am Vertical', rejects the conventional 'death-wish' interpretation that underlies many myths of the woman poet. She suggests that feminist critics can circumvent biographically driven interpretations by employing post-structuralist reading practices which free the text from a limited, intentional relationship with the author, and thus enable feminist critics to locate resistance at the level of language. Tripp provides illuminating comparisons with Hughes, Woolf and Martin Amis, to illustrate the way in which 'subjectivity becomes textualized':

■ I would argue that reading practices which seek to extrapolate the figure of the author from Plath's writing may ultimately edit out many fascinating and radical aspects of these texts. Because they construe Plath's work as the transparent self-expression of a tragic or self-destructive victim, and attempt to look 'through' her writing to her life, these readings neglect the surfaces of her texts. And perhaps it is precisely *on* these surfaces – on the level of textuality, word-play, riddling, contradictions, ambiguities and even typographical devices – that the feminist reader might locate resistance.

In spite of a continuing flow of biographically based studies of Plath – which read her work primarily to read her life – in recent years there have also been several valuable feminist challenges to the traditional aims and methods of Plath criticism. [. . .]

Probably the most challenging and subtle intervention in this debate is Jacqueline Rose's book, *The Haunting of Sylvia Plath*. Rose focuses on the ways in which the figure of 'Sylvia Plath' has been constructed and contested by literary criticism. [. . .] She argues that 'Plath regularly unsettles certainties of language, identity, and sexuality, troubling the forms of cohesion on which "civilized" culture systematically and often oppressively relies.'[18]

'I Am Vertical' is a poem by Plath written in 1961 which does indeed unsettle 'certainties of language, identity and sexuality' (*CP*, p. 161). This text offers a troubled and troubling construction of the subject, and explores modes and possibilities of self-representation. I want to look in detail at the ways in which the subject can be read in a text like this, and at the uncertainties and instabilities that close reading can produce. Of course, the issue of self-representation – the exploration of the instance which says 'I' – has profound implications both for the validity of author-centred reading practices and for issues of gender. Explicit treatments of the subject in extracts from three other literary texts – by Ted Hughes, Virginia Woolf and Martin Amis – help to focus the textual, cultural and historical specificity of the construction of gendered subjectivity.

'I Am Vertical' is a text which a biographically based criticism tends to interpret as articulating Plath's notorious death-wish. The figure represented in the poem (which for this type of reading is Sylvia Plath) suffers a sense of rootlessness and alienation. She lacks or has lost the ability to grow or to create, and has neither the tree's solidity and stability nor the flower's fleeting panache. Her waking and walking, 'vertical', state is unbearably lonely (I walk among them, but none of them are noticing') – and so in the second stanza the voice yearns towards sleep, unconsciousness and, ultimately, death. The pulse slows seductively in the short line: 'Thoughts gone dim.'

In death the speaker imagines herself finally released from her vertiginous individual consciousness and returned to the earth, reintegrated with her natural environment . . . For Linda W. Wagner-Martin, 'I Am Vertical' explores 'the theme of leaving the hectic world of the living for the peaceful world of the dead'.[19] Ronald Hayman discusses the poem [. . .] in a chapter entitled 'The Poetry of Death', arguing that 'the late *Ariel* poems are prefigured by the death-orientated poems of March 1961'.[20]

These represent one possible way of reading the poem – perhaps the most conspicuous one – but not, I think, the most interesting one. They contain nothing to specifically engage the feminist reader, except the simple identification of a victim on the verge of surrender. [. . .] For an alternative approach I return to the title: 'I Am Vertical'.

To dwell on these words as they stand on the page is to become aware of a kind of visual joke or pun – 'I' is literally a vertical line – 'I' *is* vertical. So, while 'I' first offers itself to be read unproblematically as referring to a human subject, on further consideration it also gains material status as a shape on a page. It is not transparent: it cannot simply be looked 'through'; it demands to be looked at. The reader becomes involved in an unstable double rapid shift of focus, between 'I' as the shape of the signifier on the page, and 'I' as the implied speaker of the poem. [. . .] Read closely, many of Plath's poems seem to deploy this type of disorientating textual and optical playfulness. That which at first glance seems obvious and natural suddenly flips over into unexpected and uncanny. These moments may cause the reader to question the ability and validity of her perceptions.

In this way, the text might be read as problematizing any reading which attempts to look 'through' the text to a biographical 'reality' beyond. The 'I' on the page gains a certain opacity which effectively prevents it from functioning as a window on to Sylvia Plath's person-ality and preoccupations. Subjectivity becomes textualized. Here it is the signifier that comes into sharp focus – and everything beyond it is a virtual image. . . . the reader is invited to look at the ways in which language works specifically at the level of the signifier to produce its meanings.

How and what does 'I' signify? As a shape on the page it seems ideally suited to stand for the bourgeois individual of liberal humanism: visually it appears as unitary, undivided, free-standing and self-con-tained. However, in relation to this text, this is an impression which conceals a range of divisions, shifts, complexities and resistances.

First, the subject is established in the poem as a position within a system of differences: it is not named and is not represented as pos-sessing an essential identity. It is defined negatively, by way of what it is not: in the body of the text it does not introduce itself by saying 'I am' – instead it appears in the structure 'I am not . . . Nor am I . . .'. Furthermore the 'I' is dispersed, shifting and in process: in spite of its visual similarity to 'I', there are no fewer than fourteen instances of 'I' throughout the text. Each 'I' is different from the previous, constituted within its own specific context.

Moreover, the speaker is represented as profoundly uncomfortable occupying the position(s) marked by the 'I' in the text – and here another important gap appears in this 'I', this time between the spoken and the speaking subject.[21] The speaker is represented straining against the vertical, the perpendicular, resisting his or her alignment with it. From the very first line he or she attempts to topple it: 'I would rather be horizontal.' As horizontal, asleep or dead, the subject would no longer speak, no longer say 'I', and so become the meaning-less ' – ' escaping the divisions and differences of the symbolic order.

This escape, however, can only ever be imaginary within the para-meters of a (symbolic) text. This can be illustrated by the discrepancy in the lines that run:

It is more natural to me, lying down.
Then the sky and I are in open conversation,

This invokes a situation in which the individual subject lies parallel to the earth and sky, rather than existing as perpendicular to them – as it were along the grain rather than against it. This would apparently enable what the text calls an 'open conversation' with nature – an imaginary, full, perfect and transparent speech without gaps or resistances in communication. Perhaps this is hinted at in the auditory affinity between 'I' and 'sky'. However, on the signifying surface of the text, the (written) 'I' remains, standing stubbornly bolt upright in the middle of the second line quoted here. In effect the 'I' resists: it will not lie down and die. The subject of the poem invokes an imaginary unity and plenitude while remaining unavoidably committed to the positions and differences of the symbolic. [. . .]

In the first stanza, the 'I' is not only marked by a split between speaking and spoken subject. It is also discussed in relation to not one, but two different types of vertical figure or mode of existence. In these ways the 'I' is divided on not just one but several different planes.

The first possible position or mode of existence is signified by the tree: powerful and robustly erect, thrusting its root into the soil. The second is signified by the flower bed or flower-head: fragile and ornamental, 'painted' in order to attract admiration. Could these alternative positions be read as polarized versions of masculinity and femininity? The first-person pronoun conceals the gender of the speaker in a way that the third-person singular does not – and I do not believe it is possible to determine in any absolute sense the gender of the speaker in this text, once the 'I' is separated from the author.

However, gender does seem to be a vital issue here: its binary, polarized configuration poses a problem for the subject and plays a critical role in generating the profound unease represented. The speaker of the poem cannot properly inhabit or 'become' the extremities of either of the two positions offered: tree or flower, masculine or feminine – and is thus left in a state of dissatisfaction and lack.

A biographically based reading of the poem would read the 'I' as feminine, reflecting the gender of the author. On the other hand, if this text was presented to a reader who did not know the identity of the author, it is possible (or even likely?) that this reader would refer to the subject of the poem as 'he'. Patriarchal culture takes masculinity as its norm, and femininity is a deviation, exception or afterthought to this. See for example an excerpt from a poem by Ted Hughes:

To the staturing 'I am',
To the upthrust affirmative head of man
Braggart-browed complacency in most calm
Collusion with his own

Dewdrop frailty . . . [22]

It is possible to argue that these lines do something similar to 'I Am Vertical', in that they identify an inherent insecurity in the act of self-definition. [. . .]

However, the 'I' of Hughes's text is unquestioningly gendered masculine. 'Man', in the second line, has a universal quality to it. While Plath's poem identifies two possible modes of (vertical) existence, here there is only one. The feminine subject is ignored and invisible within the terms of the analysis. [. . .]

The way in which the feminine subject tends to be excluded and alienated from these cultural definitions and enquiries is discussed in a famous section of Virginia Woolf's *A Room of One's Own*, likewise exploring the instance that says 'I':

> But after reading a chapter or two a shadow seemed to lie across the page. It was a straight dark bar, a shadow shaped something like the letter 'I'. One began dodging this way and that to catch a glimpse of the landscape behind it. Whether that was indeed a tree or a woman walking I was not quite sure. Back one was always hailed to the letter 'I'. One began to be tired of 'I'. Not but that this 'I' was a most respectable 'I', honest and logical; as hard as a nut and polished for centuries by good teaching and good feeding. I respect and admire that 'I' from the bottom of my heart. But . . . the worst of it is that in the shadow of the letter 'I' all is as shapeless as mist. Is that a tree? No, it is a woman.[23]

This text presents many interesting parallels with Plath's poem. Here too, the 'I' is discussed as a shape on a page, in terms of its material status [. . .] It is far from transparent: the reader must engage in ridiculous 'dodging' manoeuvres to get an impression of anything 'behind' it. And here the 'I' is explicitly masculine [. . .] It has the 'staturing . . . braggart-browed' and complacent characteristics of Hughes's 'I am' (though none of its frailty). Here, the masculinist 'I' explicitly obscures, silences or 'even obliterates' the feminine.

However, the voice that speaks on behalf of the feminine must also say 'I' in the text, in order to mark out its own position. This feminine 'I' is differentiated from the masculine 'I' in that it is used out of scare quotes – but this differentiation is a provisional measure. For an

English-speaking woman there is always a discrepancy between identification with the ungendered 'I' of the spoken subject, and
identification with the obscured and silenced position 'she'. This passage enacts a problem encountered by much feminist thought: how
can a woman speak critically within the patriarchal/symbolic order –
that is, without reproducing its patterning? The 'direct, straightforward . . . well-nourished, well-educated, free . . . and logical'
masculine subject of Woolf's text may be culturally dominant, but the
feminine subject must find ways of speaking as well, speaking differently. Perhaps denaturalizing the 'I', drawing attention to its operation
on the level of the signifier, and to the gender division which takes
place invisibly within it, is a valuable first step.

Woolf's text speaks of the masculine 'I' as 'polished *for centuries* by
good *teaching*'. Here, subjectivity is taught and learned as language and
cultural norms are taught and learned: it does not come naturally.
Furthermore the subject gains a historical dimension: different historical periods do different types of work in the construction of the
subject. The signifier 'I' may give the impression of being unique and
free-standing, but the subject is in fact produced by and anchored in
its specific historical and cultural contexts.

The subject is a position taken up within language: it is linguistically
determined and enabled. As Benveniste argues, 'the establishment of
"subjectivity" in language creates the category of person . . . '.[24] Thus
the characteristics and potentialities of 'a person' may differ from language to language. A section in *Time's Arrow* by Martin Amis plays on
this type of difference:

And take the first person singular: 'Ich'. 'Ich'. 'Ich'. Not a master-
piece of reassurance, is it? 'I' sounds nobly erect. 'Je' has a certain
strength and intimacy. 'Eo''s okay. 'Yo' I can really relate to. 'Yo'!
But 'Ich'? It's like the sound a child makes when it confronts its
own . . . Perhaps that's part of the point. No doubt all will become
clear as my German gets better.[25]

Here, the subject is denaturalized by cultural and linguistic difference,
its material status as a signifier more striking in its unfamiliar foreign
constructions. The illusion of transparency is only gained through
familiarity: 'No doubt *it will become clear* as my German gets better.' As
the subject learns a language he or she comes to 'occupy' it: as it
becomes increasingly familiar so too do its configurations of subjectivity.

In all these ways the impression of transparent, singular, free-
standing, self-containment produced by the liberal humanist 'I' of the
English language can be radically undermined. The 'I' is culturally
and historically specific rather than natural, universal and eternal, and

is divided on a number of different planes. Subjectivity is dispersed across its various utterances – and deep rifts appear between the spoken subject and the (inaccessible, partially represented) speaking subject, and between the central, dominant masculine subject and the peripheral, subordinate feminine subject.[26] □

Just as Tripp draws a comparison between 'I Am Vertical' and Hughes's 'Egg Head', much recent criticism has revived interest in the literary relationship between Plath and Hughes, a discussion that looks sure to continue following the publication of Hughes's *Birthday Letters*, a collection of poems addressed to Plath, and Hughes's recent death, which would appear to invite a major reassessment and comparison of both poets. Although their marriage arouses intense biographical interest, recent critics such as Sinfield and Rose have done much to distance the personalities from the textual discussion, concentrating instead on issues of gender, nationality, and sexuality. Part of the forthcoming *Literary Couples*,[27] Sarah Churchwell's essay 'Ted Hughes and the Corpus of Sylvia Plath' (1998), considers Hughes's critical writing on Plath, from his initial comments on *Ariel* to a 1994 interview in *Raritan*. Churchwell's article is partly a response to Rose's comments in her chapter 'The Archive', further discussing the literary battle in light of Janet Malcolm's recent 'meta-biography' *The Silent Woman*: 'In *The Haunting of Sylvia Plath*, Jacqueline Rose notes that the argument is an argument over interpretation and over reading, but, I would add, it is also an argument over who gets the right to be the author, over who has the final authority.'[28] Churchwell suggests that Hughes is not so concerned with literary ownership of Plath's work, but with authorship:

■ [. . .] Hughes's writings on Plath foreclose the possibility of rethinking Plath's words; they insist that he alone can author her accurately. To write on Sylvia Plath is, according to Ted Hughes, to join 'the wretched millions who have to find something to say in their papers,' it is to participate in the commercialistic 're-invention' of Hughes's own 'private experiences and feelings.'[29] The confusion seems to arise from Ted Hughes's refusal to be textual subject, rather than author, of writings about Sylvia Plath. Ted Hughes writes about Plath as if his readings are definitionally textual rather than biographical and others' readings are biographical rather than textual.[30] □

Churchwell supports her argument with an incisive critique of Hughes's writings on Plath. In the following analysis of Hughes's early comments, Churchwell illustrates the ways in which Hughes's privileged position has led to some problematic readings of Plath's poetry, and includes a particularly perceptive criticism of Perloff's 1984 essay on the rearrangement of *Ariel*. While it has been necessary to edit Churchwell's extract from the *Poetry Book Society Bulletin* that opens these comments, it can be found in chapter one of this Guide.

■ The clarity of Hughes's statements [in the *Poetry Book Society Bulletin*] is worth noting, as they will grow progressively more entangled as the years pass. One element that has not been subject to much change over the course of his writings on Plath is the patronizing tone Hughes's writings take toward both Plath and her poetry – which they equate. Hughes has often dissociated himself from what he terms the Plath 'Fantasia' – the myth that has grown up around her name and which he deplores. But this early comment is very much in keeping with many of the elements of the 'Fantasia,' mythologizing Plath as a mystical, fey, morbid, other-worldly 'poetess.' The implicit 'mystery' of *Ariel*, in its resistance to criticism and its 'strangeness' and 'eeri-ness,' gives way before the 'miracle' of Plath's composing poetry at all within the exigencies of being wife and mother. Plath's poetic gift may seem strange and eerie, but Hughes will solve this mystery: it was 'the birth of her first child' that enabled Plath to develop poetically, and 'her second child brought things a giant step forward.'[31] The famous rage of the *Ariel* poems is not even mentioned in a comment that emphasizes childbirth.[32] Hughes's reading of Plath's poetry as contin-gent upon maternity has presumably influenced such different readers as A. Alvarez, who declared that 'the real poems began in 1960, after the birth of her daughter Frieda,' and Helen Vendler, who wrote, 'Either marriage and childbearing alone or the encouragement and help of Ted Hughes – or, more probably, both – changed [Plath's] style.'[33] Certainly his own influence on Plath's work is an aspect of the narrative that Hughes's writing has consistently underplayed in its establishment of Plath's poetic blooming as a happy by-product of childbirth.[34] Hughes declares that the *Ariel* collection 'is her,' that the 'corpus' of her work is equivalent to the person who created it, but immediately backs away from this copula, taking refuge in similitude with a difference: 'this is just like her – but permanent.' *Ariel* in this statement is not just Plath's epitaph; it keeps her alive, giving her a textual body. This note seems to disavow Plath's mortality by equating her with her own textual productions, understanding immortality in traditional romantic terms of the transcendent literary work of art, but the result is that the work giving life to Plath is not her unmediated text, but Hughes's.

A year later, in 1966, Hughes published his 'Notes on the Chronological Order of Sylvia Plath's Poems,' the first ostensibly crit-ical piece he wrote on Plath, which establishes the main themes of all of his readings. First, 'the poems are chapters in a mythology where the plot, seen as a whole and in retrospect, is strong and clear – even if the origins of it and the dramatis personae are at bottom enigmatic.' This reading of a plot which requires retrospection in order to clarify 'enigmatic' motives and characters ('dramatis personae') implicitly invokes the mystery story, with its reliance on an apparent enigma that will give way before incontrovertible 'truth.' The 'truth' in Hughes's writings on Plath tends to be the equation of Plath's work with her self: 'in [Plath], as with perhaps few poets ever, the nature, the poetic genius and the active self were the same.' This equivalence of 'nature,' 'genius,' and 'active self,' leads to readings like this one, on the composition of 'The Stones': 'It is full of specific details of her experience in a mental hospital, and is clearly enough the first erup- tion of the voice that produced *Ariel* . . . It is the poem where the self, shattered in 1953, suddenly finds itself whole . . . dismissed every- thing prior to "The Stones" as Juvenilia, produced in the days before she became herself. . . . With the birth of her first child she received herself.'[35] Like the detective who reconstructs, *ex post facto*, the story of the murder in order to make sense of a predetermined outcome, Hughes sets up here his crucial theme, a tendentious reading of Sylvia Plath's life as a tragic narrative characterized by a struggle between destructive and nurturing impulses. Hughes's emphasis on teleology comes as no surprise to anyone who has read Marjorie Perloff's 'The Two Ariels: The (Re)making of the Sylvia Plath Canon,' in which she demonstrates how Hughes's reordering of Plath's *Ariel* collection changed the trajectory of the work from a narrative that emphasizes spring, hope, and rebirth, to one that emphasizes suicide, death, and completion. But it is important to note in this context, valuable as Perloff's research was and convincing as her arguments are, that Hughes, too, consistently emphasizes the theme of birth and rebirth in his writing on Plath. The 'whole' self for Hughes is the nurturing, maternal and fundamentally poetic self, though it is worth noting the passive construction: Plath does not create her own voice, but 'becomes' it and 'receives' it. The destructive self is consistently pro- duced in Hughes's constructions only to be disavowed, rather than emphasized (as Perloff argues). The inclusion in *Ariel* of 'Edge,' one of the last two poems Plath composed and often taken as a 'suicide note,'[36] is frequently invoked as evidence of Hughes's emphasis on suicide. But Hughes ended *Ariel*, not with the putatively 'suicidal' 'Edge,' but with 'Words,' composed four days earlier. 'Words' explores the aggressive possibilities of language; encountered 'years later,' words are '. . . dry and riderless,/. . . indefatigable hoof-taps,' or 'Axes /After whose stroke the wood rings.' Hughes's conception of Plath's 'last word' seems to be less interested in suicide than it is in combat- ing the hostile effect of her echoing language, even as he ambivalently (and thus inconsistently) attempts to protect the words she left on the page.[37] □

Much of the feminist criticism of Plath's poetry that we have seen in previous chapters remains centred around an Anglo-American approach to literature which privileges cultural and sociological considerations. While the complexities of language and sexuality have become of increasing interest to feminist critics, and the writings of Kristeva, Cixous and Irigaray are increasingly evident in discussions of Plath's poetry, a biographical/cultural perspective still dominates. Marilyn Manners's essay 'The Doxies of Daughterhood: Plath, Cixous, and The Father' attempts to redress the balance of Plath studies by proposing a comparison of Plath's poetry and Hélène Cixous's novels, which in turn raises questions of sexuality and subjectivity explored by *écriture féminine*. The following extract focuses on the similarities found in the work of these two writers.

■ As early as 1982 . . . Josette Feral called for comparative investigation of writers such as Sylvia Plath and Hélène Cixous, but until very recently neither writer has been consistently and seriously considered as a literary figure (in the United States at any rate). [. . .]

Feral based her proposal, as well as her readings of theatrical works by Plath, Cixous, and others, on the general premises of *l'écriture féminine*: a writing that 'shatter[s] traditional discourse,' or citing Irigaray, is characterized by 'excess and disruption.'[38] Although I find Feral's argument convincing I will begin at an even more preliminary, rudimentary, level. I should like to draw attention to a conjunction of interests in Plath and Cixous – by examining a few of Plath's 'father-poems,' not so much in strict comparison with, as in view of, an early Cixous novel, *Dedans*.[39] [. . .]

Both Plath and Cixous treat the father's early death as a kind of primary trauma which is re-written into the painful coming-of-age of the daughter as writer, as she who assumes language and the use of words both native and foreign – although language(s) may appear to, and even may, master her own fictional female subjects. To a certain degree, both Plath and Cixous use a 'father obsession' to overturn an old myth: 'The old myth of origins/Unimaginable . . .' (Plath, 'Full Fathom Five'). In classical tragedy Electra may be read as one stage of the historical establishment of patriarchy over matriarchy and goddess worship.[40] But Plath's and Cixous's manipulations of the 'Electra Complex' disinter the personal father – that memory of a father which becomes a fiction of the father – and at the same time attempt to bury the Father and his Law.

In both writers, the father's death leads to the daughter's physical and psychic retreat or exile into ambivalently considered 'interior' spaces. In both Plath and Cixous, the father is idealized excessively (although the self-conscious ways in which this idealization is then portrayed are much less predictable); the mother's role as wife and primary mourner is contested competitively; the mother's sexuality causes anxious concern whereas the sexuality of the father is cherished and privileged; both mothers and fathers are submitted to the rigors of love and hate. Both writers replace God/father/husband/ lover in a series of substitutions which are at times deadly serious, at other times ironic and comical. Both Plath and Cixous emphasize almost surreally the disparity in size between father and daughter. Finally, both writers identify the dead father specifically with prison. [. . .]

The questions raised by both Plath's and Cixous's father-daughter writings form one part of a discourse on female subjectivity. If Plath's lyric 'I' can be said to raise a reader's expectations for a coherent and immediate subject-speaker, the same can presumably be said about the first-person narrator of an autobiographical narrative, such as Cixous's *Dedans*. These expectations operate even though Cixous's autobiographical 'I' usually remains elusive, or solidifies momentarily only to dissolve once again. To what extent does the female 'I' in and out of itself necessarily cast doubt upon preconceptions about a unified, coherent, and, especially, masterful subjectivity? In the cases of Plath and Cixous, or at least in the works under consideration here, a number of issues are put into play which set the subject, or 'any theory of the subject' (Irigaray), a-quivering. The sheer excessiveness of attention to the father, for example, serves a number of purposes: it oversteps the boundaries of Oedipal anxiety and propriety; it furnishes a useful smokescreen for the expanding significance of the daughter's voice; it re-enacts the circuitous coming-into-being of the female subject and demonstrates that she cannot, because of her difference(s), ever be the Self-Same. She must (also) be Other, therefore at once subject and not subject; she is never entirely subject to the Father's Law, whether that father be 'her own,' Freud, Lear, Prospero, Polonius, or the Symbolic.[41] □

Although we have seen the ways in which several broadly Anglo-American critics engage with the theoretical writing of *écriture féminine*, Manners's essay is valuable for her identification of shared concerns and strategies between Plath and an essentially European tradition of women's writing and criticism, and it would seem to indicate an area of possible future investigation.

The critics in this chapter all suggest potential new directions for Plath studies; revitalised readings of the mythic and biographical strategies of the poetry are found alongside sophisticated theoretical approaches which debate the lyrical 'I' and often reinvigorate feminist readings of Plath's work. Finally, we will consider two recent articles by Tracy Brain, which intelligently intervene in Plath criticism. In the first essay we will consider, Brain reinvigorates the discussion of Plath's 'nature' poems, largely neglected since Marjorie Perloff's rejection of her own argument for Plath's affinity with nature,[42] while in a second essay concerned with the midatlantic nature of Plath's poetry, Brain contributes to the discussion of nationality following the work of Sinfield and Rose.

We will begin with a brief discussion of Brain's essay, '"Or shall I bring you the sound of poisons?": *Silent Spring* and Sylvia Plath', included in *Writing the Environment: Ecocriticism and Literature* (1998), a collection which brings together a variety of environmentalist positions, and theorises their contribution to critical theory, literature and popular culture. Brain explores the shared concerns of Plath's poetry and Rachel Carson's seminal environmentalist text, *Silent Spring,* suggesting that Plath's 'nature' poems often engage with an ecofeminist perspective. Brain suggests that 'Plath depicts an ecosystem that overwhelms any sense of an individual self and body, whatever its sex'.[43] I have chosen an extract from the beginning of this essay in which Brain outlines her argument by placing Plath within the historical context of emerging environmentalist debates and then progresses to a consideration of 'Elm':

■ There is a previously unremarked concern with pollution underlying Sylvia Plath's work. Indeed, there is a recurrent exploration of the ways that substances are exchanged between human beings and the environment. Although Plath has been a powerful writer to generations of readers, she has so far not been identified as an environmentalist. This chapter bypasses the usual biographical preoccupations and confessional readings of Plath's work, and places her as a writer who is concerned with public issues and the environment.

Much of Plath's writing draws attention to exchanges within a global ecosystem that includes the climate, the soil, the air, animal life and the individual body. Such a configuration is made more powerful by Plath's complex view of men's and women's shared places in this system, and contradicts the still prevalent view of Plath as self-obsessed. Plath's writing depicts the permeation and poisoning of the human body by toxic chemicals and pollutants; these *material* interpenetrations mirror the ideas of *cultural* movement and permeability which are also important in Plath's work. I want to situate Plath's writing in the framework of some environmental, especially ecofeminist, concerns that began to emerge in the 1950s and early 1960s.

This emergent environmentalism was most famously expressed in

Rachel Carson's *Silent Spring* (1962). Carson's exposé of the effects of pesticides on the environment was important in informing a wider public, of both scientists and non-specialists, that agricultural and industrial chemicals were having deadly and unforeseen consequences for animals, plants and human beings. *Silent Spring* is typically referred to as the 'classic environmental book of our times'.[44] That the book 'sparked off the beginnings of the North's environmental movement'[45] is common cultural currency. [. . .]

Silent Spring was published as a book in the USA in 1962, and in Britain in 1963. Before publication in book form, however, roughly one-third of the material was serialized in three issues of *The New Yorker*, in June 1962. Plath died in early 1963. My arguments about Plath's work do not depend on establishing with any certainty that she read *Silent Spring*. Nevertheless, she would almost certainly have been aware of the loud and very public controversy which followed *Silent Spring*'s appearance in *The New Yorker*. It is likely that she would have read the serialized version.[46] [. . .] there are numerous references to *The New Yorker* in Plath's letters and journals.[47] *The New Yorker* published many of her poems in a period roughly coincident with the excerpts from *Silent Spring*. [. . .]

Plath was clearly interested in Carson as a writer. There is evidence that she knew of Carson and her work as early as 1952.[48] In a letter to her mother written on 5 July 1958, Plath specifically acknowledges Carson's influence:

> I am reading . . . the delightful book *The Sea Around Us*, by Rachel Carson. Ted's reading her *Under the Sea Wind*, which he says is also fine. Do read these if you haven't already; they are poetically written and magnificently informative. I am going back to the ocean as my poetic heritage and hope to revisit all the places I remember in Winthrop with Ted this summer (*LH*, pp. 345–46).

Plath did utilize her 'poetic heritage' and, in doing so, expressed concern about the impact of technology on the ecosystem. Within days of the letter, she wrote 'Green Rock, Winthrop Bay', in which the speaker describes with regret the changes wrought on the seaside since she last visited it: 'Barge-tar clotted at the tide-line', and '. . . The cries of scavenging gulls sound thin/In the traffic of planes'. The speaker remarks on the contamination of the air by metal machinery: 'Gulls circle gray under shadow of a steelier flight'. She worries about the effects of capitalist consumerism upon the environment, rejecting 'lame excuses', and stating that 'Loss cancels profit' (*CP*, pp. 104–105).

[. . .] Plath's concern with environmental pollution can be understood best by placing it in the historical context of the environmentalist debates that were taking place during her writing career, spearheaded by Carson's book.

A similarly expressed environmentalism to that of *Silent Spring*, at the same historical moment, can be found in Plath's poem, 'Elm'. David Holbrook, in his still influential book on Plath, reads 'Elm' as evidence that Plath was 'schizoid', and as proof of her 'anguish' and 'deep lack of satisfaction'.[49] This personalist approach misses the extent of 'Elm's environmentalist preoccupations, indicated first by Plath's placing of a tree as the poem's central persona, and by the fact that the poem's 'action' consists of the Elm describing and reflecting upon its physical situation. The identity and circumstances of the tree merge with those of another of the poem's personae, a woman.

The poem was written on the 19 April 1962, two months before *Silent Spring* was serialized in *The New Yorker*. When the tree asks, 'Or shall I bring you the sound of poisons?', Plath pre-empts *Silent Spring*'s central metaphor. As for Carson, for Plath the 'sound of poisons' is silence, or 'hush' (*CP*, p.192). The water which the elm tree/woman sucks with its 'great tap root' from the soil is deadly: 'This is rain now, this big hush./And this is the fruit of it: tin-white, like arsenic'. The hush does not only evoke the paradoxically noiseless sound of rain, but also the lack of animal noises, caused by the poison that the rain carries.[50] *Silent Spring* tells us that arsenic is 'the basic ingredient in a variety of weed and insect killers'.[51]

Like the earlier 'Waking in Winter' (1960), 'Elm' plays on a common environmentalist trope of sunsets that are not quite right, that are artificial rather than natural, or over-bright and too intense. [. . .] 'Elm' describes the effects of nuclear and chemical damage upon a tree and a woman. 'I have suffered the atrocity of sunsets', the speaker explains, and further; 'My red filaments burn and stand, a hand of wires' (*CP*, p.192). At the end of 1961, Plath wrote of 'the repulsive shelter craze for fallout', and her inability to sleep because of 'all the warlike talk in the papers', and her fear of a nuclear attack.[52] 'Elm' is one of the many poems in which Plath explores the consequences of isolation, and argues against the impulse to hold oneself as separate from the rest of the world – an impulse which she deplores in the craze for fallout shelters. The poem's speaker declares, 'A wind of such violence/Will tolerate no bystanding: I must shriek'. (*CP*, 192). The poison cannot be ignored. It injures, causing pain which cannot be endured in stoical silence. It also calls for responsibility, a willingness to declare or 'shriek' protest, a refusal of complicit acceptance.[53] □

Entering into larger debates about ecocriticism and postmodernism, Brain concludes with a statement that foreshadows the final essay we will consider:

■ Transatlantic poems such as 'Cut', 'New Year on Dartmoor' and 'Stars Over the Dordogne' dramatise the hybridity of any national identity, through disorientations of place, self and language. Like other postmodern interpenetrations – for instance between genres, identities and histories – Plath's interpenetrations between body and ecosystem are often concomitant with intersections between femininity and masculinity, or between America and Europe.[54] □

Tracy Brain's essay, '"Your Puddle-jumping daughter": Sylvia Plath's Midatlanticism' (1998) is a significant consideration of nationality and language. Although Plath lived on both sides of the Atlantic, Brain argues that most critics tend either to ignore this issue of nationality or restrict Plath's cultural lineage to either American or British. Brain accuses Rose of negating Plath's Americanness, a position which fails to recognise Plath's ambivalence over nationality.[55] In contrast to Rose, Brain argues that Plath's writing explores an uncertain nationality, raising many interesting comments about ownership, hybridity and displacement. In the following extract she offers an analysis of previous critics and then develops her argument for midatlanticism, which is considered within postmodernist aesthetics.

■ Sylvia Plath's speaking voices hover at different points over the Atlantic in her recorded interviews and readings.[56] Plath's writing is arresting as a 'polyglot stew' (*JP*, p. 34) of American and English vocabularies. Her accents and lexicon are difficult to reconcile with her uncharacteristically simple description of herself as straightforwardly American: 'I think that as far as language goes I'm an American, I'm afraid, my accent is American, my way of talk is an American way of talk, I'm an old-fashioned American'.[57] Despite such a rare and disingenuous assertion, what seems to me to make Plath's work so compelling is the sense that it retains some material residue of a voice that, like her accent, moved *between* England and America.

I want to show that Plath's writing plays out a perpetual displacement, a midatlanticism that is neither American nor English. To do this will at times depend on a binary opposition between Americanness and Englishness that Plath puts into question. As the years spent living in England multiply, the tensions in Plath's work between Americanness and Englishness increasingly register as a larger crisis about what might constitute European identity. Yet Plath's midatlanticism is largely ignored by critics, who contest ownership of Plath and the 'facts' about her life and work by fighting over her nationality, making her one thing or the other, or disregarding the issue of nationality altogether.[58]

[. . .] In 'Stone Boy with Dolphin' (*JP*, pp. 297–322) we are confronted with familiar stereotypes. Americans are free and expressive to the point of vulgarity, materially over-privileged, greedily consumerist, and hedonistic. The English are uptight, repressed, ascetic. [. . .] The simplicity of such an oppositional view, we will see, could not be sustained in Plath's later work, which increasingly addresses what Homi Bhabha has described as the postmodern 'contingency and ambivalence in the positioning of cultural and political identity'.[59] [. . .]

The term transatlantic is often used to describe a hybrid *accent*, or someone who is on one side or the other, depending on where she stands. Midatlantic is a more apt description of Plath's position: a refusal to choose between two places. Such a mind set is nicely represented when Plath closes a letter with the signature, 'Your puddle-jumping daughter' (*LH*, p. 165) or entitles a 1962 poem 'Crossing the Water' while making it impossible to identify just what water is being crossed. [. . .]

In keeping with her status of not belonging and her neither entirely American nor purely English accent, Plath's feelings about both England and America were ambivalent. Not surprisingly, she oscillates between Anglophilia and Anglophobia. [. . .] While Plath is critical of American commercialism, neither is she satisfied by what she regards as English shabbiness. She moves between disassociation and identification with Americanness.[60] □

Brain proceeds to explore the ambivalence over nationality in Plath's poetry, discussing national identity in 'Daddy' as 'contingent and multiple' and offering an incisive reading of the bee sequence which concludes with the statement: 'Taken as a whole, as I think they must be, the bee poems express unease with the tendency of the English to assimilate foreigners, the ambivalence of foreigners about being assimilated, and the impulse for women to regulate those who do not belong.'[61] I have chosen, however, to end with Brain's reading of 'Cut'. Although this poem has been discussed by many feminist critics in terms of gender, the complexities of nationality are often ignored. Here, Brain raises questions of nationality and assimilation which she argues remain unresolved and uncertain:

■ I want to conclude with a reading of Plath's 1962 poem 'Cut', which systematically destroys any illusion that there can be any separate or genuine American identity or place. Like the bee poems, 'Cut' reveals the blurred edges between friend and foe, or native and alien. Alicia Ostriker argues that Plath's voice is 'distinctly American' because it 'represent[s] life without falsification'. [. . .] For Ostriker, the 'brusque, business like, and bitchy' quality of the speech of the *Ariel* poems marks them as an 'American language'.[62] She cites 'Cut' as an example. Though I feel dubious about the implication here that to be American is somehow to be authentic, Ostriker makes an important intervention in Plath criticism by identifying the American vernacular that seeps into Plath's work. Nonetheless, Ostriker ends up with a view of Plath that is culturally and nationally absolutist because it neglects the fact that this vernacular is not protected, but rather, is frequently interrupted, displaced by or forced to coexist with other languages. Such a view elides not just Plath's view of herself as hybrid, but also the thematic and linguistic cross-breeding of her poems.

If we digress for just a moment to the 1962 poem 'The Tour', which was written the day after 'Cut' during the time Plath was writing those supposedly 'distinctly American' *Ariel* poems, we find Plath deliberately parodying an overdetermined *English* voice. [. . .] The humour and satire rest not just in the exaggerated English voice, but also in the mocking of the stereotype by which the stoical English find a virtue in anything and everything.

'Cut' is also comic about such stoicism, this time of a more American version. The poem dramatises the transatlantic flux between English and Americanness. The speaker gazes at her thumb, the top of which she has sliced off while cutting an onion. In 'America! America!' Plath expresses her conviction that Americans are educated 'Invisibly', breathing in 'a world of history that more or less began and ended with the Boston Tea Party – Pilgrims and Indians being, like the eohippus, prehistoric.' (*JP*, p.35). Using the vocabulary American school children are taught when learning about the settling of America and the American Revolution, speaking as if to an injured child, 'Cut''s speaker describes and addresses the appendage:

Little pilgrim,
The Indian's axed your scalp.
Your turkey wattle
Carpet rolls

Straight from the heart. . . .

Out of a gap
A million soldiers run,
Redcoats, every one.

Whose side are they on?
CP, p.235

Certainly this poetic language defamiliarises the sliced and bleeding thumb, or even the vagina leaking menstrual fluid. Yet the bodily experience, the physical split of the skin flap, comes to represent an incorporeal division of identity itself. The thumb whose outside appearance is described through images that are American is separated into pieces. Americanness cannot be sustained by the very American treatment of the injury – suggested by the 'pink fizz'. This fizz suggests the diluted, almost carbonated blood that is the effect of pouring hydrogen peroxide on a wound, as Americans do. What emerges from inside the American shell is alien: the Redcoats who were America's opponents during the revolution. The outside layer of familiar American history contains the British enemy within, and the speaker is not sure which is which, for, 'Whose side are they on?'.

The 'other', that blameworthy signifier of difference and alienation, is always already within the self. Kristeva has argued that the abject is that which is 'opposed to I', and thus threatens our sense of self. Abjection is strongest when the self, or 'subject, weary of fruitless attempts to identify with something on the outside, finds the impossible within; when it finds that the impossible constitutes its very *being*'.[63] This seems a good description of what happens to 'Cut''s speaker, when she discovers that the Redcoats aren't coming but have been there all along, inside her very self, or finger, as it were. What better image of something that should be inside, instead outside, than the 'turkey wattle carpet' of the bird's neck – a picture of something that looks like brains or intestines. Yet at this stage, the poem also defies Kristeva's notion of abjection, which has it that abjection is 'directed against a threat that seems to emanate from an exorbitant outside or inside . . . It lies there, quite close, but it cannot be assimilated'.[64] For a brief instant, the speaker of 'Cut' does assimilate difference, can be said in fact to take pleasure in it. Yet this position is not maintained for long.

The poem shifts dramatically from the language of the nursery and the speaker's seeming acceptance and pleasure in the mixture of English and American identities to an unease and violence which explores the impact of a larger world. The poem catapults us from the speaker's loving fascination to her assertion of illness. The thumb ceases to be a signifier of distant historical events that – in contrast to its present bleeding state – have been drained of material reality by time and the infantalised rhetoric of the school room. More recent and still present history crowds out the past, and the now-bandaged thumb, wrapped in gauze, takes on a number of national identities that have threatened America from without and within. We have the Japanese 'Kamikaze man', or suicide bomber who attacked the United States during World War II and proved with deadly clarity that American borders were penetrable. Yet threat does not issue only from outside United States borders, as we see in the 'Saboteur' who causes material or political damage from within. 'The stain on your/Gauze Ku

Klux Klan/Babushka' (*CP*, pp.235–36) represents the dangers and destruction that come from inside the heartland of America itself, from a group self-appointed to police cultural purity and obliterate all infringements against that not existent entity: pure American nationality. The Russian reference to 'Babushka', or 'little grandmother', is to those dolls within a doll that provide another image of the transgression of borders, like the thumb, of something unexpected hidden within.

Kristeva argues that what causes abjection is:

> . . . what disturbs identity, system, order. What does not respect borders, positions, rules. The in-between, the ambiguous, the composite. The traitor, the liar . . . Any crime, because it draws attention to the fragility of the law, is abject, but premeditated crime, cunning murder, hypocritical outrage . . . heighten the display of such fragility.[65]

This account could double as a description of what disturbs the speaker of 'Cut'. The cut itself challenges the borders between inside and outside, self and not self. As I have said already, the blood that issues from it evokes menstrual blood, which Kristeva argues 'stands for the danger issuing from within the identity . . . it threatens . . . the identity of each sex in the face of sexual difference'.[66] The threats to identity which are played out in 'Cut', then, are not just to nationality and health, but also to sexual identity, as we see with increasing clarity by the poem's end. The thumb becomes a circus performer who jumps or performs tricks, and is, ultimately, of unresolved gender and nationality. It is both female, the 'Dirty Girl' who as Susan Van Dyne observes, symbolises 'her culture's revulsion at female blood, sexuality and domesticity',[67] and male, a 'veteran' who finalises the poem's images of recent world war participants. Male or female, in the end, the thumb is castrated, a 'stump' whose transgressions have left it, like the speaker, and, ultimately, like Sylvia Plath's reader, unsure of the borders not just of skin and gender, but also of country.[68] □

As we have seen, in the space of a few decades, Sylvia Plath has become one of the most discussed and debated poets of contemporary literature, a writer who has evoked fierce loyalties and, at times, fierce criticism. The history of Plath's critical reception can be seen to reflect, in particular, the evolving theoretical approach to women's writing, progressing from restricted biographical readings which struggled to reconcile the persona of a bright young mother with the powerful intensity of the poetry, to criticism which confronts questions of ideology, subjectivity and sexuality, increasingly theoretical readings which engage with psychoanalytic and cultural analyses. Yet Plath's critically limiting status as cultural icon, embodying our received ideas of 'woman' and 'poet', looks set to strengthen with increased speculation about her life generated by Hughes's death and the increasing likelihood of a Hollywood film. As critical discussion of Plath's poetry appears to become progressively textualised, the popular perception of the suicidal poet with an unavoidable fate seems destined to return. However, for the disciplined student of literature approaching Plath's poetry it is worth returning to one of her last poems, 'Words', for a reminder of the real legacy of Plath's name, not her marriage, nor her suicide, but her extraordinary talent as a poet, confronting words unhindered by personality:

■   Years later I
    Encounter them on the road –

    Words dry and riderless,
    The indefatigable hoof-taps. □
                                   CP, p. 270

NOTES

INTRODUCTION

1 Sylvia Plath, *The Journals of Sylvia Plath*, ed. Ted Hughes and Frances McCullough (New York: Random House (Ballantine), 1982; 1987), p.211; hereafter referred to as *Journals*.

2 Sylvia Plath, *Johnny Panic and the Bible of Dreams and other prose writings*, ed. Ted Hughes (London: Faber and Faber 1977, revised 1979), p.124; hereafter referred to as *JP*.

3 Sandra M. Gilbert, 'A Fine, White Flying Myth: The Life/Work of Sylvia Plath' in *Shakespeare's Sisters: Feminist Essays on Women Poets* (Bloomington: Indiana University Press, 1979), p.245.

4 Sylvia Plath, *The Bell Jar*, 1963 (London: Faber and Faber, 1966).

5 Edward Butscher, *Sylvia Plath: Method and Madness* (New York: Seabury Press, 1976), reproduced in photograph section.

6 Sylvia Plath, *Letters Home: Correspondence 1950–1963*, ed. Aurelia Schober Plath (London: Faber and Faber, 1975), p.466; hereafter referred to as *LH*.

7 Adrienne Rich, *Of Woman Born: Motherhood as Experience and Institution* (London: Virago, 1977).

8 C.B. Cox, 'Editorial', *Critical Quarterly*, 8, Autumn 1966, p.195; Linda Wagner-Martin, *Sylvia Plath: The Critical Heritage* (London and New York: Routledge, 1988), p.5; hereafter referred to as *Critical Heritage*.

9 See reviews of *The Bell Jar* in *Critical Heritage*, particularly Margaret L. Shook, 'Sylvia Plath: The Poet and the College', pp.114–24.

10 Tony Tanner, *City of Words: American Fiction 1950–1970* (London: Jonathan Cape, 1971).

11 Pat MacPherson, *Reflecting on The Bell Jar* (London: Routledge, 1991); see also Linda Wagner-Martin, *The Bell Jar: A Novel of the Fifties* (New York and Oxford: Maxwell, Macmillan International, 1992).

12 Linda Anderson, *Women and Auto-*

biography in the 20th Century: Remembered Futures (London: Prentice Hall, 1977).

13 See *Critical Heritage*.

14 Margaret Atwood, 'Poet's Prose', *New York Times Book Review* (28 January 1979), pp.10, 31; *Critical Heritage*, p.18.

15 Jacqueline Rose, *The Haunting of Sylvia Plath* (London: Virago, 1991).

16 Jo Brans, 'The Girl Who Wanted to be God', *Southwest Review*, 61, Summer 1976, p.325; *Critical Heritage*, p.15.

17 Marjorie Perloff, 'Sylvia Plath's "Sivvy" Poems: A Portrait of the Poet as Daughter' in Gary Lane, ed., *Sylvia Plath: New Views on the Poetry* (Baltimore: Johns Hopkins University Press, 1979), pp.155–78.

18 In a foreword to the *Journals*, Hughes explains that one of the late journals disappeared, while he destroyed the other to protect his children, p.xv.

19 Dee Horne, 'Biography in Disguise: Sylvia Plath's Journals', *Wascana Review*, 1992, 27:1, pp.90–104.

20 Nancy Hunter Steiner, *A Closer Look at Ariel: A Memory of Sylvia Plath*, 1973 (London: Faber and Faber, 1974); Janet Malcolm, *The Silent Woman* (New York: Alfred A. Knopf, 1993; London: Picador, 1994).

21 Anne Stevenson, *Bitter Fame: A Life of Sylvia Plath* (London: Viking, 1989); it is worthwhile comparing *Bitter Fame* with Linda W. Wagner-Martin's sympathetic, admittedly feminist biography of Plath, *Sylvia Plath: A Biography* (London: Chatto & Windus, 1988).

CHAPTER ONE

1 Plath and Hughes spent two months in a writers' colony at Yaddo, Saratoga Springs in the USA.

2 Plath, *Letters Home*, ed. Aurelia Schober Plath (London: Faber and Faber, 1975), p.366. Plath had been rearranging, discarding and adding poems to her first volume since the mid-1950s, frequently changing the title until she decided on *The Colossus*.

3 Hereafter referred to as *The Colossus*.

4 See *Letters Home*, p. 397: 'I am touched that my publisher got them out in my birthday week after I told him how superstitious I was.'

5 Another possible reason for this, rather than simply national pride, may be Plath's opinion that English poetry 'is in a bit of a strait-jacket', an opinion shared by Robert Lowell in an interview from 1965: '[American artists] are not burdened by this sort of baggage of life the English poet carries.' Peter Orr, ed., *The Poet Speaks* (London: Routledge, Kegan & Paul, 1966), [pp. 167–72], p. 168; Lowell interview by Alvarez, *Encounter*, February 1965, p. 43.

6 Linda W. Wagner, *Sylvia Plath: The Critical Heritage* (London and New York: Routledge, 1988); hereafter *Critical Heritage*.

7 Orr, ibid., p. 167.

8 Bernard Bergonzi, 'The Ransom Note', *Manchester Guardian*, 25 November 1960, p. 9; *Critical Heritage*, p. 32.

9 Roy Fuller, review, *London Magazine*, March 1961, pp. 69–70; *Critical Heritage*, p. 36.

10 A. E. Dyson, review, *Critical Quarterly*, Summer 1961, pp. 181–85; *Critical Heritage*, p. 40.

11 Nicholas King, 'Poetry: A Late Summer Roundup', *New York Herald-Tribune Book Review*, 26 August 1962, p. 4; *Critical Heritage*, p. 48.

12 John Wain, 'Farewell to the World', *Spectator*, 13 January 1961, p. 50; *Critical Heritage*, p. 33.

13 A. E. Dyson, review, *Critical Quarterly*, summer 1961, pp. 181–85; *Critical Heritage*, pp. 40, 38.

14 Roy Fuller, *London Magazine*, March 1961, pp. 69–70; *Critical Heritage*, p. 36.

15 Alvarez provided a memoir of Plath (although it has often been referred to as a case study) as the prologue to his 1971 book *The Savage God: A Study of Suicide* (London: Weidenfeld & Nicholson, 1971).

16 A. Alvarez, 'The Poet and the Poetess', *Observer*, 18 December 1960, p. 12; *Critical Heritage*, pp. 34–35.

17 Reed Whittemore, 'The Colossus and other Poems', *Carleton Miscellany*, 3 (Fall 1962), p. 89; *Critical Heritage*, p. 3.

18 Mark Linenthal, 'Sensibility and Reflection from the Poet's Corner', *San Francisco Sunday Chronicle, This World*, 10 March 1963, p. 33; *Critical Heritage*, p. 47.

19 Nicholas King, 'Poetry: A Late Summer Roundup', *New York Herald-Tribune Book Review*, 26 August 1962, p. 4; *Critical Heritage*, p. 48.

20 Myers must be referring to the British edition, as the American edition cut all but 'Flute Notes from a Reedy Pond' and 'The Stones' from the 'Poem for a Birthday' sequence.

21 Lucas Myers, 'The Tranquilized Fifties', *Sewanee Review*, January–March 1962, pp. 212–13, 216; *Critical Heritage*, pp. 42–44.

22 A. Alvarez, 'Sylvia Plath' in *Beyond all this Fiddle: Essays 1955–1967* (London: Allen Lane, Penguin, 1968), p. 47.

23 Mary Kinzie perceptively comments: 'It is interesting to speculate whether "the meanings" which M. L. Rosenthal subsequently found to call out from every poem, would even have been divined, had people not been motivated by her death to go back and re-read.' In Charles Newman, ed., *The Art of Sylvia Plath* (London: Faber, 1970), p. 283.

24 M. L. Rosenthal, 'Metamorphosis of a Book', *Spectator*, 21 April 1967, pp. 456–57; *Critical Heritage*, pp. 92, 93, 95; see also Richard Howard, 'And I Have No Face, I Have Wanted to Efface Myself [. . .]' in Newman, *Art of Sylvia Plath*, ibid., pp. 77–88.

25 Orr, ibid., p. 170.

26 See Derek Parker, 'Ariel, Indeed', *Poetry Review*, 56, summer 1965, pp. 118–20; Richard Tillinghurst, 'Worlds of Their Own', *Southern Review*, 5, spring 1969, pp. 582–96; Samuel F. Morse, 'Poetry 1966', *Contemporary Literature*, 9, winter 1968, pp. 112–29; *Critical Heritage*, p. 7.

27 Peter Dale, 'O Honey Bees Come Build', *Agenda*, Summer 1966, pp. 49–55; Hugh Kenner, 'Arts and the Age, On

Ariel', *Triumph*, September 1966, pp.33–34: *Critical Heritage*, pp.64, 77.

28 Irving Feldman, 'The Religion of One', *Book Week*, 19 June 1966, p.3; Stephen Spender, 'Warnings From the Grave', *New Republic*, 18 June 1966, 23, 25–6; *Critical Heritage*, pp.85, 72.

29 Alvarez, 'Sylvia Plath', in *Beyond all this Fiddle*, ibid., pp.46–57.

30 For example: '[Plath's] works do not come to us posthumously. They were written posthumously. Between suicides.' Scholes, 'The Bell Jar', *The New York Times Book Review*, 11 April 1971, p.7.

31 This is a parallel that will later be disputed by Anthony Easthope, 'Reading the Poetry of Sylvia Plath', *English*, 43:177, Autumn 1994, pp.223–35.

32 C.B. Cox and A.R. Jones, 'After the Tranquilized Fifties, Notes on Sylvia Plath and James Baldwin', *Critical Quarterly*, 6 (Summer 1964), pp.99–100; *Critical Heritage*, p.11, later rewritten and published by A.R Jones as 'On "Daddy"' in Newman, *Art of Sylvia Plath*, ibid.

33 Cited by Sarah Churchwell, 'Ted Hughes and the Corpus of Sylvia Plath', *Criticism*, Winter 1998, vol. XL, no. 1, [pp.99–132], p.111.

34 For the classic discussion of this rearrangement see Marjorie Perloff, 'The Two Ariels: The Re(making) of the Sylvia Plath Canon', *American Poetry Review* 13, no. 6, Nov/Dec 1984, pp.10–18.

35 Stephen Spender, 'Warnings From the Grave', *New Republic*, 18 June 1966, pp.23, 25–26; *Critical Heritage*, p.70.

36 Peter Davidson, 'Inhabited by a Cry: The Last Poetry of Sylvia Plath', *Atlantic Monthly*, August 1966, pp.76–77; Robin Skelton, review, *Massachusetts Review*, Autumn 1965, pp.834–35; *Critical Heritage*, pp.83, 90.

37 Peter Dale, 'O Honey Bees Come Build', *Agenda*, Summer 1966, pp.49–55; *The Critical Heritage*, pp.66, 67; see also Richard Tillinghurst, 'Worlds of Their Own', *Southern Review*, Spring 1969, pp.582–83; *Critical Heritage*, pp.79–80.

38 A. Alvarez, 'Poetry in Extremis',

Observer, 12 March 1965, p.26; *Critical Heritage*, pp.55, 57, 56, 57.

39 M.L. Rosenthal, 'Poets of the Dangerous Way', *Spectator*, 19 March 1965, p.367; *Critical Heritage*, pp.60–62.

40 M.L. Rosenthal, 'Other Confessional Poets: Sylvia Plath' in *The New Poets: American and British Poetry Since World War II* (London and New York: Oxford University Press, 1967), pp.79–80.

41 Peter Dale, 'O Honey Bees Come Build', *Agenda*, Summer 1966, pp.49–55; *Critical Heritage*, p.63.

42 Robert Lowell, Foreword to *Ariel* (New York: Harper & Row 1966), pp.vii–ix.

43 P.N. Furbank, 'New Poetry', *Listener*, 11 March 1965, p.379; *Critical Heritage*, p.74.

44 Richard Tillinghurst, 'Worlds of Their Own', *Southern Review*, Spring 1969, pp.582–83; *Critical Heritage*, p.79.

45 David Holbrook, *Sylvia Plath: Poetry and Existence* (London: Athlone Press, 1976).

46 Hugh Kenner, 'Arts and the Age, On Ariel', *Triumph*, September 1966, pp.33–34; *The Critical Heritage*, pp.75, 77–88. This argument is later extended in Kenner's essay 'Sincerity Kills' in Lane, *New Views on the Poetry*, ibid., pp.33–49.

47 John Malcolm Brinnin, 'Plath, Jarrell, Kinnell, Smith', *Partisan Review*, Winter 1967, pp.156–57; *Critical Heritage*, p.76.

48 Alicia Ostriker, 'The Americanization of Sylvia Plath', collected in Linda W. Wagner, ed., *Critical Essays on Sylvia Plath* (Boston: Hall & Company, 1984), [p.97–109], p.100; Ostriker's identification of the American vernacular is further explored in Brita Lindberg-Seyersted, '"Bad" Language Can Be Good: Slang and Other Expressions of Extreme Informality in Sylvia Plath's Poetry', *English Studies*, 1997, 78:1, pp.19–31.

49 Ostriker, ibid., pp.100, 108.

50 George Steiner, 'Dying is an Art' (1965), collected in *Language and Silence* (London: Faber and Faber, 1967), pp.327–29.

51 Steiner, ibid., pp. 329–31.

52 Mary Kinzie, 'An Informal Checklist of Criticism' in Newman, *Art of Sylvia Plath*, ibid., p. 290.

53 Mary Ellman, *Thinking About Women* (London: Macmillan, 1968), pp. 142, 34.

CHAPTER TWO

1 Margaret Dickie Uroff, *Sylvia Plath and Ted Hughes* (Urbana and Chicago: University of Illinois Press, 1979), p. 38; Marjorie Perloff, 'Angst and Animism in the Poetry of Sylvia Plath' (1970), reprinted in Wagner, *Critical Essays on Sylvia Plath*, ibid., [pp. 109–24], p. 121.

2 For an early, perceptive reading of duality see George Stade, 'Afterword' in Nancy Hunter Steiner, *A Closer Look at Ariel: A Memory of Sylvia Plath* (London: Faber and Faber, 1974).

3 Jo Brans, 'The Girl Who Wanted to be God', *Southwest Review*, Summer 1976, pp. 325–28, 330; *Critical Heritage*, p. 213.

4 Ellen Moers, *Literary Women* (New York: Doubleday, 1976), p. xv.

5 Sylvia Plath, *Crossing the Water* (London: Faber and Faber, 1971); Sylvia Plath, *Winter Trees* (London: Faber and Faber, 1971).

6 *Uncollected Poems* (London: Turret Books, 1965); 'Three Women' (London: Turret Books, 1968); *Wreath for a Bridal* (Surrey: Sceptre Press, 1970); *Fiesta Melons* (Exeter: Rougemont Press, 1971); *Child* (Exeter: Rougemont Press, 1971); *Lyonesse* (London: Rainbow Press, 1971); *Crystal Gazer* (London: Rainbow Press, 1971).

7 Robert Boyers, 'On Sylvia Plath', *Salmagundi*, Winter 1973, pp. 96–104; Raymond Smith, 'Late Harvest', *Modern Poetry Studies*, 1972, pp. 91–93; *Critical Heritage*, pp. 144, 181.

8 Linda Ray Platt, '"The Spirit of Blackness is in Us. . .,"' *Prairie Schooner*, Spring 1973, pp. 87–90; *Critical Heritage*, pp. 169–70.

9 Robin Skelton, 'Poetry', *Malahat Review*, 20, October 1971, pp. 137–38; *Critical Heritage*, p. 13.

10 Victor Howes, 'I am Silver and Exact', *Christian Science Monitor*, 30 September 1971, p. 8; *Critical Heritage*, p. 142.

11 Eileen M. Aird, review, *Critical Quarterly*, Autumn 1971, pp. 286–88; *Critical Heritage*, pp. 137–38 see also Victor Kramer, 'Life-and-Death Dialectics', *Modern Poetry Studies*, 1972, pp. 40–42; Douglas Dunn, 'Damaged Instruments', *Encounter*, August 1971, pp. 68–70; *Critical Heritage*, pp. 162, 140.

12 Helen Vendler, review, *New York Times Book Review*, 10 October 1971; collected in *Part of Nature, Part of Us: Modern American Poets* (Cambridge, Mass.: Harvard University Press, 1980), [pp. 271–76], p. 271. David Holbrook argues for Plath to be read as a schizophrenic poet in the essays 'The 200-inch Distorting Mirror', *New Society* 12 (11 July 1968), pp. 57–58; 'R.D. Laing and the Death Circuit', *Encounter*, 31 (August 1968), pp. 35–45.

13 Vendler, ibid., pp. 273–74, 276.

14 Robert Boyers, 'On Sylvia Plath', *Salmagundi*, Winter 1973, pp. 96–104; *Critical Heritage*, p. 150.

15 The sequence is 'The Bee Meeting', 'The Arrival of the Bee Box', 'Stings', 'The Swarm', and 'Wintering'.

16 See Douglas Cleverdon, introduction, 'Three Women' (London: Turret Books, 1968); reprinted in Newman, *The Art of Sylvia Plath*, ibid., pp. 228–29.

17 Barbara Hardy, 'The Poetry of Sylvia Plath: Enlargement or Derangement' in Martin Dodsworth, ed., *The Survival of Poetry: A Contemporary Survey* (London: Faber and Faber, 1970), pp. 164–87; for a comparative reading see Sally Greene, 'A Flare of Resistance in Sylvia Plath's "Nick and the Candlestick"', *Notes on Contemporary Literature*, 24:1, January 1994, pp. 4–6.

18 Raymond Smith, 'Late Harvest', *Modern Poetry Studies*, 1972, pp. 91–93; *Critical Heritage*, pp. 179–80.

19 Joyce Carol Oates, 'Winter Trees', *Library Journal*, 1 November 1972, p. 3595; *Critical Heritage*, p. 176.

20 Terry Eagleton, 'New Poetry', *Stand*,

1971–1972, p.76; *Critical Heritage*, pp.152–55, p.153, p.155.

21 Eric Homberger, 'The Uncollected Plath', *New Statesman*, 22 September 1972, pp.404–405; *Critical Heritage*, pp.187–91; see also Homberger's *A Chronological Checklist of the Periodical Publications of Sylvia Plath* (Exeter: University of Exeter Press, 1970), the first bibliography.

22 John Fredrick Nims, 'The Poetry of Sylvia Plath: A Technical Analysis'; Annette Lavers, 'The World as Icon – On Sylvia Plath's Themes'; Richard Howard, 'Sylvia Plath: "And I Have No Face, I Have Wanted to Efface Myself. . . "' in Newman, *The Art of Sylvia Plath*, ibid. For a broadly stylistic approach see Richard Allen Blessing, 'The Shape of the Psyche: Vision and Technique in the Late Poems of Sylvia Plath' in Lane, *Sylvia Plath: New Views on the Poetry*, ibid.; see also Pamela Smith, 'The Unitive Urge in the Poetry of Sylvia Plath', *New England Quarterly*, 45, September 1972, pp.323–39.

23 Ingrid Melander, *The Poetry of Sylvia Plath: A Study of Themes* (Stockholm: Almquist & Wiksell 1972), p.7; see also Leonard M. Scigaj, 'The Painterly Plath That Nobody Knows', *The Centennial Review*, 32:3, 1988, pp.220–49.

24 Melander, ibid., pp.38–39.

25 Eileen Aird, *Sylvia Plath: The Woman and Her Work* (Edinburgh: Oliver Boyd, 1973), p.7.

26 Ibid., p.14.

27 Ibid., p.62.

28 Ibid., pp.64–65.

29 For critics sympathetic to Holbrook, see Murray M. Schwartz and Christopher Bollas: 'We will follow David Holbrook's insight that an incapacity to love was at the heart of Plath's experience' in 'The Absence at the Center: Sylvia Plath and Suicide' in Lane, *New Views on the Poetry*, ibid., p.180; and Robert Philips, 'The Dark Funnel' in Butscher, ed., *The Woman and the Work* (New York: Dodd, Mead and Company, 1977). In contrast, most feminist critics have not been so kind, Carole Ferrier describing

Holbrook's argument as 'reminiscent of those of a conservative Christian social worker', 'The Beekeeper's Apprentice' in Lane, *New Views on the Poetry*, ibid., p.205.

30 David Holbrook, *Sylvia Plath: Poetry and Existence* (London: Athlone Press, 1976), p.23.

31 Ibid., p.125–26.

32 Ibid., p.1. To stress these points, Holbrook concludes with the chapter 'The Artist, Responsibility and Freedom'.

33 Judith Kroll, *Chapters in a Mythology: The Poetry of Sylvia Plath* (New York: Harper & Row, 1976), pp.4–5.

34 Cited by ibid., p.6.

35 Ibid., pp.2–3, 6.

36 Ibid., p.78; see also Louis Simpson, *Studies of Dylan Thomas, Allen Ginsberg, Sylvia Plath and Robert Lowell* (New York: Macmillan Press, 1978), who recognises Plath as 'creating a "mythology"', p.90.

37 Jon Rosenblatt, *Sylvia Plath: The Poetry of Initiation* (Chapel Hill: The University of North Carolina Press, 1979), p.ix.

38 Ibid., p.xi.

39 Ibid., p.3.

40 Ibid., p.xiv.

41 Ibid., pp.110–11.

42 Margaret Dickie Uroff, *Sylvia Plath and Ted Hughes* (Urbana: University of Illinois Press, 1979), p.8.

43 Ibid., pp.13–14.

44 Uroff identifies 'multiple cross-currents between *Lupercal* and *The Colossus*', ibid., p.88.

45 Ibid., pp.214–15.

46 Sherry Lutz Zivley's article 'Ted Hughes's Apologia Pro Matrimonio Suo', *The New England Quarterly*, 55 (2), June 1982, pp.187–200, advances Uroff's consideration of Plath's influence on Hughes's later work through close analysis of his *Moon Whales and Other Moon Poems* from 1976. See also Anthony Libby, 'God's Lioness and the Priest of Sycorax: Plath and Hughes', *Contemporary Literature*, 15 (1975), p.389; Ekbert Faas, 'Chapters in a Shared Mythology: Sylvia Plath and Ted Hughes' in Keith Sagar, ed., *The Achievement of Ted Hughes*

(Manchester: Manchester University Press, 1983), pp.107–24; and for a consideration of mutual influence in the context of Hughes's recent *Birthday Letters* see Anthony Julius, 'New Lost Land', *Poetry Review*, vol. 88, no. 1, Spring 1998, pp.80–82.

47 Calvin Bedient, 'Sylvia Plath, Romantic . . .' in Lane, *New Views on the Poetry*, ibid., [pp.3–18], pp.19, 8, 5; see also Calvin Bedient, 'Oh Plath!', *Parnassus*, 12–13: 2–1, pp.275–81.

48 Hugh Kenner, 'Sincerity Kills' in Lane, *Sylvia Plath: New Views on the Poetry*, ibid., [pp.33–44], p.44.

49 David Shapiro, 'Sylvia Plath: Drama and Melodrama' in Lane, *Sylvia Plath: New Views on the Poetry*, ibid., pp.45–53.

50 Joyce Carol Oates, 'The Death Throes of Romanticism: The Poetry of Sylvia Plath' (1972) reprinted in Paul Alexander, ed., *Ariel Ascending* (New York: Harper & Row, 1985), [pp.26–45], pp.35, 38, 30, 43–44.

51 Marjorie Perloff, 'Sylvia Plath's "Sivvy Poems": A Portrait of the Poet as Daughter' in Lane, *Sylvia Plath: New Views on the Poetry*, ibid., [pp.155–78], p.177n; Marjorie Perloff, 'Angst and Animism in the Poetry of Sylvia Plath' (1970), collected in Wagner, *Critical Essays on Sylvia Plath*, ibid., pp.109–24.

52 Perloff, 'Sivvy Poems', ibid., p.173.

53 Irving Howe, 'The Plath Celebration: A Partial Dissent' in Butscher, *Sylvia Plath: The Woman and the Work*, ibid., [pp.223–35], pp.231–33.

54 Patricia Meyer Sparks, *The Female Imagination: A Literary and Psychological Investigation of Women's Writing* (London: Allen and Unwin, 1976).

55 Sandra M. Gilbert and Susan Gubar, *The Madwoman in the Attic: The Woman Writer and the Nineteenth-Century Literary Imagination* (New Haven and London: Yale University Press, 1979), pp.45–92.

56 Elaine Showalter, *A Literature of Their Own: British Women Novelists From Brontë To Lessing* (Princeton: Princeton University Press 1977; London: Virago, 1978), p.12.

57 Elaine Showalter, 'Towards a Feminist Poetics' in Mary Jacobus, ed., *Women's Writing and Writing About Women* (London: Croom Helm, 1979), pp.22–41.

58 Douglas Dunn, 'Damaged Instruments', *Encounter*, August 1971, pp.68–70; *Critical Heritage*, pp.140–41; Holbrook, *Sylvia Plath: Poetry and Existence*, ibid., p.179.

59 Cora Kaplan, *Salt and Bitter and Good: Three Centuries of English and American Women Poets* (New York and London: Paddington Press, 1975), p.290.

60 Olsen takes issue with the lack of women writers in Tony Tanner's influential study *City of Words: American Fiction 1950–1970*: 'Plath is written off on two pages. . .', Tillie Olsen, *Silences* (London: Virago 1980, c. 1978), pp.35–37, 187.

61 Suzanne Juhasz, *Naked and Fiery Forms: Modern American Poetry by Women – A New Tradition* (New York: Harper and Row, 1976), pp.1–6; for Plath's own understanding of this dilemma see her early poem 'Female Author', collected in Juvenilia section of *Collected Poems*, p.301, where she satirises the indulgent sentimentality of the woman writer.

62 Sandra M. Gilbert and Susan Gubar, eds, *Shakespeare's Sisters: Feminist Essays on Women Poets* (Bloomington: Indiana University Press, 1979), pp.xx, xxii.

63 Barbara Charlesworth Gelpi, 'A Common Language: The American Woman Poet' in Gilbert and Gubar, *Shakespeare's Sisters*, ibid., [pp.269–279], p.276.

64 Ellen Moers, *Literary Women*, ibid.

65 Gilbert., ibid., pp.245–49.

66 Simone de Beauvoir, *The Second Sex*, (New York: Bantam, 1961), p.467.

67 Mary Shelley, *Frankenstein*, chapter 24.

68 Anne Sexton, 'Third Psalm', *Death Notebooks* (Boston: Houghton Mifflin, 1974), pp.83–84.

69 de Beauvoir, ibid., p.468.

70 Ibid., p.469.

71 Gilbert, ibid., pp.251, (252), 253, 254–57.

72 Ibid., pp.258, 260.

73 Judith Kroll, in *Chapters in a Mythology*, ibid., discusses Plath's early interest in Graves and his account of Cardea, the White Goddess (pp. 37–79, passim).

74 Carole Ferrier, 'The Beekeeper's Apprentice' in Lane, *Sylvia Plath: New Views on the Poetry*, ibid., pp. 208–11.

75 Ibid., p. 215.

76 Mary Lynn Broe, *Protean Poetic: The Poetry of Sylvia Plath* (Columbia: University of Missouri Press, 1980); see also Broe, '"Enigmatical, Shifting My Clarities"' in Alexander, ed., *Ariel Ascending*, ibid., pp. 80–94.

CHAPTER THREE

1 Stan Smith, 'Waist-Deep in History: Sylvia Plath' in *Inviolable Voice: History and Twentieth-Century Poetry* (Dublin: Gill and Macmillan, 1982), p. 219.

2 Laurence Lerner, 'Sylvia Plath', *Encounter* 1982, pp. 53–54; John Bayley, 'Games with Death and Co.', *New Statesman*, 102, 2 October 1981, p. 19; *Critical Heritage*, pp. 259, 24.

3 Laurence Lerner, 'Sylvia Plath', *Encounter*, January 1982, pp. 53–54; Michael Hulse, 'Formal Bleeding', *Spectator*, 14 November 1981, p. 20; *Critical Heritage*, pp. 259, 292.

4 Michael Kirkham, 'Sylvia Plath', *Queen's Quarterly*, Spring 1984, pp. 153–66; *Critical Heritage*, p. 291.

5 William H. Pritchard, 'An Interesting Minor Poet?' *New Republic*, 30 December 1981, pp. 32–35; *Critical Heritage*, pp. 262–63, 268.

6 Marjorie Perloff, 'Sylvia Plath's Collected Poems', *Resources for American Literary Study*, Autumn 1981, pp. 304–13; *Critical Heritage*, pp. 295, 297, 294.

7 Dave Smith, 'Sylvia Plath, the Electric Horse', *American Poetry Review*, January 1982, pp. 43–46; *Critical Heritage*, pp. 269–70.

8 Helen Vendler, 'Sylvia Plath' (1982) collected in *The Music of What Happens: Poems, Poets and Critics* (Cambridge, Mass.: Harvard University Press, 1988), [pp. 272–83], pp. 276, 283.

9 Michael Hulse, 'Formal Bleeding', *Spectator*, 14 November 1981, p. 20; *Critical Heritage*, p. 293.

10 Laurence Lerner, 'Sylvia Plath', *Encounter*, January 1982, pp. 53–54; Dave Smith, 'Sylvia Plath, the Electric Horse', *American Poetry Review*, January 1982, pp. 43–46; *Critical Heritage*, pp. 260, 275.

11 Marjorie Perloff, 'Sylvia Plath's Collected Poems', *Resources for American Literary Study*, Autumn 1981, pp. 304–13; *Critical Heritage*, p. 294.

12 Jerome Mazzaro, 'Sylvia Plath and the Cycles of History' in Lane, *Sylvia Plath: New Views on the Poetry*, ibid., p. 219.

13 Ibid., p. 238.

14 Smith, ibid., pp. 1, 9.

15 Ibid., pp. 1–2.

16 Ibid., p. 202.

17 Ibid., p. 208.

18 Ibid., pp. 208–10.

19 Ellin Sarot, '"Becoming More and More Historical": Sylvia Plath's "The Swarm"', *Concerning Poetry*, 1987, 20, [pp. 41–56], pp. 42–43, 50.

20 Smith, ibid., pp. 218–20.

21 James E. Young, *Writing and Rewriting the Holocaust: Narrative and the Consequences of Interpretation* (Bloomington: Indiana University Press, 1988), p. vii.

22 For a comparison of Plath's 'Daddy' and Anne Sexton's 'My Friend, My Friend', see Heather Cam, '"Daddy": Sylvia Plath's Debt to Anne Sexton', *American Literature*, October 1987, 59:3, pp. 429–32.

23 Young, ibid., p. 84.

24 Ibid., p. 127.

25 Alvin H. Rosenfeld, *A Double Dying: Reflections on Holocaust Literature* (Bloomington and London: Indiana University Press, 1980), p. 181.

26 Butscher, *Sylvia Plath: Method and Madness*, ibid., p. 327.

27 Alvarez, *The Savage God*, ibid., p. 17.

28 Arthur Oberg, *Modern American Lyric: Lowell, Berryman, Creely, and Plath* (New Brunswick: Rutgers University Press, 1978), p. 146.

29 Sylvia Plath, *Collected Poems* (London: Faber and Faber, 1981), p. 257; hereafter

referred to as *CP* within text.

30 From the introductory notes to 'New Poems', a reading prepared for the BBC Third Programme but never broadcast. Quoted in Newman, *The Art of Sylvia Plath*, ibid., p. 65.

31 Young, ibid., pp. 117–19, 120–24.

32 Ibid., p. 131.

33 Ibid., p. 132.

34 Harold Bloom, 'Introduction' in Harold Bloom, ed., *Modern Critical Views: Sylvia Plath* (New York: Chelsea House Publishers, 1989), pp. 3–4.

35 Seamus Heaney, 'The Indefatigable Hoof-Taps,' *The Government of the Tongue* (London: Faber, 1989), [pp.148–70].

36 Benita Eisler, *Private Lives: Men and Women of the Fifties* (New York: Franklin, 1986); Wini Breines, *Young, White and Miserable: Growing Up Female in the Fifties* (Boston: Beacon, 1992); see also Douglas Miller and Marion Novak, *The Way We Really Were* (New York: Doubleday, 1977); and Deborah Nelson, 'Penetrating Privacy: Confessional Poetry and the Surveillance Society' in *Homemaking: Women Writers and the Politics and Poetics of Home* (New York: Garland, 1996), pp. 87–114 which discusses Plath and Anne Sexton.

37 Eisler, ibid., p. 79.

38 Elaine Showalter, *The Female Malady: Women, Madness and English Culture, 1830–1980* (London: Virago, 1987, repr. 1993), p. 216; see also Susan Bassnett, *Sylvia Plath* (London: Macmillan, 1987), p. 125, and Mary Daly's radical reading of patriarchal oppression *Gyn/Ecology* (Boston: Beacon Press, 1978), especially 'American Gynecology' and 'Nazi Medicine and American Gynecology: A Torture Cross-Cultural Comparison'.

39 Margaret Dickie [Uroff], 'Sylvia Plath's Narrative Strategies' (1982), collected in Wagner, *Critical Essays on Sylvia Plath*, ibid., [pp. 170–82], p. 170.

40 For example, Paula Bennett questions the artistic value of these poems: '. . . they are so ugly and personal in their personal attack that they hardly qualify as art', *My Life a Loaded Gun:*

Dickinson, Plath, Rich and Female Creativity (Urbana: University of Illinois Press, 1986), p. 159.

41 Dickie, ibid., p. 8.

42 Ibid., pp. 12–13.

43 Linda W. Wagner, 'Plath's *Ladies' Home Journal* Syndrome', *Journal of American Culture*, Spring/Summer 1984, V, [pp. 32–8], p. 36.

44 Ibid., p. 32.

45 Ibid., p. 36.

46 Ibid., p. 37.

47 Ibid., p. 33.

48 Gary M. Leonard, '"The Woman is Perfected. Her Dead Body Wears the Smile of Accomplishment": Sylvia Plath and *Mademoiselle* Magazine', *College Literature*, 1992, 2, [pp. 60–82], p. 61.

49 Ibid., p. 73.

50 Marjorie Perloff, 'Icon of the Fifties', *Parnassus*, Spring/Winter 1985, 12–13 (2–1): [pp. 282–85], pp. 282, 284.

51 Pamela J. Annas, *A Disturbance in Mirrors: The Poetry of Sylvia Plath* (New York: Greenwood Press, 1988), p. 2.

52 Orr, *The Poet Speaks*, ibid., pp. 169–70.

53 Annas, ibid., pp. 10–12.

54 Ibid., p. 6.

55 Ibid., p. 53; for Annas's definition of transitional poetry see her chapter 3, endnote 1, p. 70.

56 Ibid., pp. 53, 54.

57 Ibid., p. 97.

58 Ibid., p. 104.

59 Ibid., p. 77.

60 Ibid., pp. 81, 82.

61 Betty Friedan, *The Feminine Mystique* (New York: Dell, 1963), p. 55.

62 Georg Lukács, 'The Ideology of Modernism' in Arpad Kadarkay, ed., *The Lukács Reader* (Oxford: Blackwell, 1995), pp. 187–209.

63 Annas, ibid., pp. 73–74, 76–77, 86, 87–91, 92.

64 Alan Sinfield, *Literature, Politics and Culture in Postwar Britain* (Oxford: Blackwell, 1989), p. 209.

65 Ibid., p. 209.

66 Ibid., p. 210.

67 Ibid., p. 227.

68 Ibid., p.206.

69 Ibid., pp.206–207.

70 Ibid., p.216.

71 Ibid., p.216.

72 Butscher, *Sylvia Plath: The Woman and the Work*, ibid., p.100.

73 Sinfield, ibid., pp.221–22.

74 Ibid., p.222.

75 Irving Howe, 'The Plath Celebration' in Butscher, *Sylvia Plath: The Woman and the Work*, ibid., pp.233–35. Arnold is quoted by Mary Jacobus, 'The Buried Letter', in Mary Jacobus, ed., *Women Writing and Writing About Women* (London: Croom Helm, 1979), p.43.

76 Mary Daly, *Beyond God the Father* (Boston: Beacon Press, 1973), pp.62–63, 114–22.

77 Rich, *Of Women Born*, ibid., pp.67, 70.

78 Rich, ibid., p.279.

79 *Editor's endnote*: Lynne Reid Banks, *The L-Shaped Room* (1960) (Harmondsworth: Penguin, 1962); Penelope Mortimer, *The Pumpkin Eater* (1962) (Harmondsworth: Penguin, 1964); J.D. Salinger, *Franny and Zooey* (1961) (Harmondsworth: Penguin, 1964).

80 Nancy K. Miller, 'Emphasis Added' in Elaine Showalter, *The New Feminist Criticism: Essays on Women, Theory and Literature* (London: Virago, 1986).

81 Ibid., p.348.

82 Ibid., p.357.

83 For similar reasons, Sandra M. Gilbert argues that women find themselves writing extravagant, mythic, gothic and fairy-tale plots; Gilbert and Gubar, *Shakespeare's Sisters*, ibid., pp.248–60. See also Alicia Ostriker, 'The Thieves of Language' in Showalter, *New Feminist Criticism*, ibid., pp.314–38.

84 Juliet Mitchell, *Women: The Longest Revolution* (London: Virago, 1984), pp.289–90; see also pp.293–94. Mitchell traces 'hysteria' back through the invalid lady of the Victorian period to medieval witchcraft (pp.117–20). See also Olsen, *Silences*, ibid., p.224 and passim; Showalter, *The Female Malady*, ibid., pp.51–73.

85 Sinfield, ibid., pp.223–26.

CHAPTER FOUR

1 Susan Bassnett, *Sylvia Plath* (London: Macmillan, 1987), pp.5, 6.

2 Bennett, *My Life a Loaded Gun*, ibid., pp.8, 10, 11, 99.

3 Ibid., pp.147–49.

4 Ibid., p.11.

5 Sandra M. Gilbert and Susan Gubar, 'In Yeats' House: The Death and Resurrection of Sylvia Plath', in *No Man's Land: The Place of the Woman Writer in the Twentieth Century*, vol. 3, *Letters From the Front* (New Haven and London: Yale University Press, 1994), p.305; they go on to discuss the maternity poetry of Plath's contemporaries, Sexton, Levertov, Wakowski, and Rich.

6 Barbara Hardy, 'The Poetry of Sylvia Plath' in Sue Roe, ed., *Women Reading Women's Writing* (Brighton: Harvester Press, 1987), pp.209–26.

7 Janice Markey, *A Journey into the Red Eye, The Poetry of Sylvia Plath – a critique* (London: The Women's Press, 1993), pp.18–30; for an excellent pedagogic approach to close readings of Plath's poetry which is aimed directly at the undergraduate see Robyn Marsack, *Sylvia Plath* (Buckingham: Open University Press, 1992).

8 Bassnett, *Sylvia Plath*, ibid., p.68; for a biochemical explanation of the menstruation imagery in Plath's poetry which offers some interesting literary insights see Catherine Thompson, ' "Dawn Poems in Blood": Sylvia Plath and PMS', *Triquarterly* 90/91, 80, pp.221–49.

9 Natalie Harris, 'New Life in American Poetry: The Child as Mother of the Poet', *The Centennial Review*, 31:3, 1987, [pp.240–54], p.242 ; see also David John Wood, *A Critical Study of the Birth Imagery of Sylvia Plath* (New York: Edwin Mellen Press, 1992), which offers a sustained, but limited, discussion of 'the influence that Plath's maternal experiences had on her creative output'; and Alicia Ostriker's valuable comments on motherhood as 'both an enlargement and a loss of identity', *Stealing the Language: The Emergence*

of *Women's Poetry in America* (Boston: Beacon Press, 1986; London: The Women's Press, 1987), p. 180–81.

10 Lynda K. Bundtzen, *Plath's Incarnations: Women and the Creative Process* (Ann Arbor: University of Michigan Press, 1983), p. 255.

11 For an excellent introduction to French feminist theory, which includes a comparison with Anglo-American criticism see Toril Moi, *Sexual/Textual Politics: Feminist Literary Theory* (London: Methuen, 1985); see also, Toril Moi, ed., *French Feminist Thought: A Reader* (Oxford: Blackwell, 1987).

12 Ostriker, *Stealing the Language*, ibid., p. 221.

13 Ibid., p. 11.

14 Ibid., pp. 82–83.

15 Ibid., p. 140.

16 Simone de Beauvoir, *The Second Sex*, trans. and ed. H. M. Parshley (London: Penguin, 1972), p. 790.

17 Julia Kristeva, 'Women can never be defined', and 'Oscillation between power and denial', trans. Marilyn A. August, in Elaine Marks and Isabelle de Courtivron, eds, *New French Feminisms* (Manchester: Harvester Press, 1981), pp. 137, 166.

18 Hélène Cixous, 'The Laugh of the Medusa', trans. Keith Cohen and Paul Cohen, *New French Feminisms*, ibid., pp. 256–59.

19 Luce Irigaray, 'This sex which is not one', trans. Claudia Reeder, *New French Feminisms*, ibid., p. 103.

20 Rich, *Of Women Born*, ibid., p. 62.

21 [. . .] Discussions and critiques of *l'écriture féminine* and feminist 'biocriticism' include Showalter, *The New Feminist Criticism*, ibid., pp. 250–56, and Ann Rosalind Jones, 'Writing the Body: Toward an Understanding of *l'écriture féminine*' in Showalter, ibid., pp. 361–77.

22 Alvarez, *The Savage God*, ibid., p. 25.

23 Ostriker, *Stealing the Language*, ibid., pp. 94–96, 99–103.

24 Liz Yorke, *Impertinent Voices: Subversive Strategies in Contemporary Women's Poetry* (London: Routledge, 1991), p. 3.

25 Luce Irigaray, 'Any Theory of the "Subject" Has Always Been Appropriated by the "Masculine"', trans. Gillian C. Gill, in *Speculum of the Other Woman* (Ithaca, New York: Cornell University Press, 1985), p. 140; Yorke, ibid., p. 51.

26 Stephen Gould Axelrod, *Sylvia Plath: The Wound and the Cure of Words* (Baltimore: Johns Hopkins University Press, 1990); Toni Saldivar, *Sylvia Plath: Confessing the Fictive Self* (New York: Peter Lang, 1992).

27 Yorke, ibid., p. 74.

28 Ibid., p. 70.

29 Hélène Cixous and Catherine Clement, 'The Guilty One', in *The Newly Born Woman*, trans. Betsy Wing (Manchester: Manchester University Press, 1986), p. 5.

30 Jean-Paul Sartre, *Anti-Semite and Jew*, trans. George Becker (New York: Schocken Books, 1970), pp. 48–49.

31 Cixous and Clement, 'The Guilty One', ibid., p. 5.

32 Yorke, ibid., pp. 85–88.

33 Susan Van Dyne, *Revising Life: Sylvia Plath's Ariel Poems* (Chapel Hill and London: University of North Carolina Press, 1993), p. 34.

34 '"More Terrible Than She Ever Was": The Manuscripts of Sylvia Plath's Bee Poems' in Wagner, *Critical Essays on Sylvia Plath*, ibid., pp. 154–70; Van Dyne offers a perceptive reading of the manuscripts for 'Wintering', qualifying the often accepted affirmation of Plath's closing lines by highlighting her hesitancy over such a positive ending, moving from the tentative options of 'What sort of spring?' and 'O God, let them taste of spring' to the eventual 'The bees are flying. They taste the spring.'

35 Van Dyne, *Revising Life*, ibid., p. 41.

36 Ibid., p. 76.

37 Ibid., pp. 119–23, 126.

38 Gilbert and Gubar, *No Man's Land, Volume 3, Letters From The Front*, ibid., p. xi; for an analysis of the creative relationship of Plath and Hughes, see *No Man's Land, Volume 1, The War of the Words* (New Haven and London: Yale University Press, 1988).

39 Gilbert and Gubar, *Letters From The Front*, ibid., p.268.

40 Ibid., p.319.

41 Hélène Cixous, 'Sorties' in Cixous and Catherine Clement, *The Newly Born Woman*, trans. Betsy Wing (Minneapolis: University of Minnesota Press, 1986), p.95.

42 See Otto Plath as 'scapegoat' and consider biology of bees as well as 'dead man' in first draft.

43 Gilbert and Gubar, *Letters From the Front*, ibid., pp.298–300.

44 Kathleen Margaret Lant, 'The Big Strip Tease: Female Bodies and Male Power in the Poetry of Sylvia Plath', *Contemporary Literature*, 34:4, [pp.620–69], p.640.

45 Ibid., p.666.

46 Lant quotes from Allen Ginsberg's 'On Burroughs' Work' (1954); Ginsberg, 'Fragment 1956' (1956); Robert Lowell, 'Plane-Ticket' (1973).

47 [. . .] Frances McCullough [in editing the *Journals* with Hughes] inadvertently foregrounds Plath's sexuality rather than downplaying it when she writes, 'there are a few other cuts – of intimacies – that have the effect of diminishing Plath's eroticism, which was quite strong' (*Journals*, p.x).

48 Stephen Gould Axelrod, *Sylvia Plath: The Wound and the Cure of Words* (Baltimore: Johns Hopkins University Press, 1990), pp.9–10.

49 Joanne Feit Diehl, *Women Poets and the American Sublime* (Bloomington: Indiana University Press, 1990), p.136.

50 Anne Sexton, 'You, Dr. Martin', *To Bedlam and Part Way Back* (Boston: Houghton, 1960), p.4.

51 Lant, ibid., pp.624–25, 630, 637–38; see also Susan Bohandy, 'Defining the Self Through the Body in Four Poems by Katerina Anghelaki-Rooke and Sylvia Plath', *Journal of Modern Greek Studies*, vol. 12, no. 1, May 1994, [pp.1–36] which considers 'Edge' and 'Lady Lazarus'.

52 Axelrod, *The Wound and the Cure of Words*, ibid., p.13.

53 Ibid., p.189.

54 Freud, 'Female Sexuality', 1931, trans. James Strachey, *Collected Papers*, vol. 5 (London: Hogarth, 1950), [pp.252–72], p.259.

55 Freud, 'Some Psychic Consequences of the Anatomical Distinction Between the Sexes', 1925, trans. James Strachey, *Collected Papers*, vol. 5 (London: Hogarth, 1953), [pp.186–97], p.192.

56 Ibid., p.195.

57 Jacques Lacan, *Ecrits: A Selection*, 1966, trans. Alan Sheridan (New York: Norton, 1977), pp.285–90; Lacan, 'Desire and the Interpretation of Desire in *Hamlet*', 1959, trans. James Hulbert, ed. Shoshana Felman, *Literature and Psychoanalysis* (Baltimore: Johns Hopkins University Press, 1982), [pp.11–52], p.23.

58 Freud, 'Anatomical Distinction', ibid., p.191.

59 Nancy Chodorow, *The Reproduction of Mothering* (Berkeley: University of California Press, 1978), p.201.

60 Margaret Homans, *Bearing the Word: Language and Female Experience in Nineteenth Century Women's Writing* (Chicago: University of Chicago, Press, 1986), pp.2–6, 41–52.

61 Axelrod, ibid., pp.164–65.

62 Ibid., pp.173, 174.

63 Ibid., pp.175–77.

64 Gilbert, 'A Fine White Flying Myth' in Bloom, *Modern Critical Views*, ibid., pp.49–65.

65 Axelrod, *The Wound and the Cure of Words*, ibid.

66 Toni Saldivar, *Sylvia Plath: Confessing the Fictive Self* (New York: Peter Lang, 1992), p.xi.

67 Gilbert and Gubar, *No Man's Land, volume 1, War of the Words*, ibid.

68 Saldivar, ibid., p.154.

69 Jacqueline Rose, *The Haunting of Sylvia Plath* (London: Virago, 1991, 1992), p.69.

70 Linda Anderson, *Women and Autobiography*, ibid., p.102.

71 Rose, ibid., p.173.

72 Ibid., p.198.

73 Gilbert and Gubar, *The Madwoman in the Attic*, ibid.

74 Hélène Cixous, 'The Laugh of the Medusa' in Elaine Marks and Isabelle de Courtivron, eds, *New French Feminisms* (Brighton: Harvester, 1981), pp. 245–65.

75 Interestingly, Oates's reading of Plath sits right in the centre of the two.

76 See Toril Moi, *Sexual/Textual Politics*, ibid.

77 Gilbert and Gubar, *No Man's Land, volume 1, The War of the Words*, ibid.

78 Rose, ibid., p. 26–27.

79 Uroff: 'The lioness unloosed in "Purdah" is the identity for which Plath searched in her bee poems', *Sylvia Plath and Ted Hughes*, ibid., p. 144. Van Dyne: 'I read the entire bee sequence as Plath's struggle to bring forth an articulate, intelligible self from the death-box of the hive', '"More Terrible Than She Ever Was": The Manuscripts of Sylvia Plath's Bee Poems' in Wagner, *Critical Essays on Sylvia Plath*, ibid., p. 165. Gilbert: '[she became] most triumphantly, the fierce virgin whose fallen selves peel away from her as she ascends to a heaven of her own invention, shivering all creation with her purified "I am I, I am I"', 'In Yeats' House: The Death and Resurrection of Sylvia Plath' in Wagner, ibid., p. 220.

80 See Cora Kaplan, 'Language and Gender' in *Sea Changes: Culture and Feminism* (London: Verso, 1986); and John Barrell, *Poetry, Language and Politics* (Manchester: Manchester University Press, 1988), Introduction, pp. 1–17.

81 Uroff, ibid., p. 154.

82 See Toril Moi's discussion of these issues in relation to feminist literary criticism, *Sexual/Textual Politics*, ibid.

83 Mary Lynn Broe discusses Plath's work in these terms in her book *Protean Poetic: The Poetry of Sylvia Plath*, ibid. It is interesting to see the extent to which the fundamental aesthetic here is still ultimately one of encompassment or control: 'And indeed Plath is in control . . . she has found both a critical and emotional vocabulary for *encompassing*'; Broe, '"Enigmatical, Shifting My Clarities"' in Alexander, *Ariel Ascending*, ibid.,

[pp. 80–94], pp. 91, 93.

84 Kristeva, 'From One Identity to Another' in *Desire in Language* (Oxford: Blackwell, 1980), pp. 124–47.

85 Rose, pp. 144–45, 148–50.

86 Leon Wieseltier, 'In a Universe of Ghosts', *New York Review of Books*, 25 November 1976, [pp. 20–23], p. 20.

87 Joyce Carol Oates, 'The Death Throes of Romanticism' in Alexander, *Ariel Ascending*, ibid., p. 39; Seamus Heaney, 'The Indefatigable Hoof-Taps', ibid., p. 144; Irving Howe, 'The Plath Celebration: A Partial Dissent' in Butscher, *Sylvia Plath: The Woman and the Work*, ibid., [pp. 224–35], p. 233; Marjorie Perloff, 'The Two Ariels', *The American Poetry Review*, November–December, 1984, pp. 14–15.

88 'The sense of history, both personal and social, found in a poem like "For the Union Dead" is conspicuously absent from the *Ariel* poems. This is not mere coincidence: for the oracular poet, past and future are meaningless abstractions . . . For Sylvia Plath, there is only the given moment, only now.' Marjorie Perloff, 'Angst and Animism in the Poetry of Sylvia Plath' in Wagner, ibid., p. 121. For a much more positive assessment of Plath's relation to history, see Stan Smith, *Inviolable Voices*, ibid.

89 The conference took place in Hamburg in 1985. The papers were published in a special issue of the *International Journal of Psycho-Analysis*, vol. 67, 1986.

90 Cited by Janine Chasseguet-Smirgel, opening comments, *International Journal*, ibid., p. 7. [. . .]

91 Eickhoff, 'Identification and its Vicissitudes in the Context of the Nazi Phenomenon', *International Journal*, ibid., p. 34.

92 Ibid.

93 The reference here is to an earlier paper by Anita Eckstaedt, one of the contributors to the Hamburg Conference, cited by Henry Krystal in a review of Martin S. Bergmann and Milton N. Jucovy, *Generations of the Holocaust* (New

York: Basic Books, 1982), in the *Psycho-Analytic Quarterly*, 53, [pp. 466–73], p. 469.

94 Anita Eckstaedt, 'Two Complementary Cases of Identification Involving Third Reich Fathers', *International Journal*, ibid., p. 326.

95 Eickhoff (citing L. Wurmser), ibid., p. 37.

96 I am aware of the danger of reducing the complexities of these individual case-histories to a formula. Each of them showed a particular set of vicissitudes, not only in relation to the historical position of the patient's parents and their own history in relation to Nazism, but also as regards other details of the patient's personal history [. . .] Readers are encouraged to refer to these papers, which make an extraordinary historical document in themselves.

97 Jean François Lyotard, *The Differend: Phrases in Dispute* (Manchester: Manchester University Press, 1988), p. 27. Lyotard is discussing the issues of Holocaust denial or the Faurisson debate, see p. 3 ff.

98 The concept comes from Freud, *The Ego and the Id*, 1923, James Strachey, ed., *The Standard Edition of the Complete Psychological Works of Sigmund Freud*, 24 vols. (London: Hogarth, 1953–73) vol. XIX, pp. 31–2; Pelican Freud, 11, pp. 370–71, and *Group Psychology and the Analysis of the Ego*, 1921, *Standard Edition*, vol. XVIII, pp. 105–106; Pelican Freud, 12, pp. 134–35. It has been most fully theorised by Julia Kristeva in *Tales of Love* (New York: Columbia University Press, 1987), pp. 24–29.

99 For Kristeva this father founds the possibility of identification for the subject and is critically linked to – enables the subject to symbolise – the orality, and hence the abjection, which was the focus of discussion of 'Poem for a Birthday', in Chapter 2.

100 'Sylvia Plath' in Orr, *The Poet Speaks*, ibid., p. 169.

101 Eickhoff, ibid., p. 38.

102 'On one side I am a first generation American, on one side I'm a second generation American, and so my concern with concentration camps and so on is uniquely intense', Orr, ibid., p. 169.

103 Virginia Woolf, *Three Guineas* (London: Hogarth, 1938; Harmondsworth: Penguin, 1977), p. 162.

104 Elizabeth Wilson, 'Coming out for a brand new age', *Guardian*, 14 March 1989. The same line has also been taken as a slogan to explain German women's involvement in Nazism; see Murray Sayle, 'Adolf and the Women', *The Independent Magazine*, 9 November 1988: '"Every woman adores a Fascist," wrote Sylvia Plath. Is this why so many German women voted for Hitler, despite the male emphasis of the Nazi regime?' (caption under title).

105 For a study of this difficult question, see Claudia Koonz, *Mothers in the Fatherland: Women, the Family, and Nazi Politics* (London: Jonathan Cape, 1987).

106 Thanks to Natasha Korda for pointing this out to me.

107 Rose, ibid., pp. 205–208, 209–10, 212–14, 222–30, 232–34, 237–38.

CHAPTER FIVE

1 Al Strangeways, '"The Boot in the Face": The Problem of the Holocaust in the Poetry of Sylvia Plath', *Contemporary Literature*, 37:3, [pp. 370–90], p. 371.

2 Ibid., p. 375.

3 More recently, critics such as Christopher Norris and Ian Whitehouse have explored in depth the particular rhetoric associated with the Cold War; Christopher Norris and Ian Whitehouse, 'The Rhetoric of Deterrence', *Styles of Discourse*, ed. Nikolas Coupland (London: Croom Helm, 1988), pp. 293–322.

4 Strangeways, ibid., pp. 374, 375.

5 Ibid., p. 376.

6 Seamus Heaney, 'The Indefatigable Hoof-Taps,' *The Government of the Tongue* (London: Faber, 1989), [pp. 148–70], p. 168.

7 Robert Graves, *The White Goddess*, 1948 (London: Faber, 1961), pp. 101, 443.

8 Plath, 'Context', *Johnny Panic and the Bible of Dreams and other prose writings*, ed. Ted Hughes (London: Faber and Faber 1977, rev. ed., 1979), p.92.

9 Richard Gray notes this general movement in American poetry, away from the idea of poetry as (to quote Richard Wilbur, a strong influence on Plath's early poetry) 'a conflict with disorder, not a message from one person to another' and toward 'more occasional subjects, whether political or private'. Richard Gray, *American Poetry of the Twentieth Century* (New York and London: Longman, 1990), pp.221, 223.

10 Teresa De Lauretis, *Alice Doesn't: Feminism, Semiotics, Cinema* (London: Macmillan, 1984), p.206.

11 Judith Butler, *Gender Trouble: Feminism and the Subversion of Identity* (London: Routledge, 1990), p.139.

12 At the beginning of the article, Strangeways compares Steiner's comments on 'Daddy' as 'the "Guernica" of modern poetry' with his slightly later comments from 1969: 'Does any writer, does any human being other than an actual survivor, have the right to put on this death-rig?'; George Steiner, 'In Extremis' (1969), collected in *The Cambridge Mind: Ninety Years of the 'Cambridge Review': 1879–1969*, ed. Eric Homberger, et al. (London: Cape, 1970), [pp.303–307], p.305.

13 Kroll, *Chapters in a Mythology*, ibid., pp.160–61.

14 Uroff, *Sylvia Plath and Ted Hughes*, ibid., p.54

15 Strangeways, ibid., pp.378, 379–82, 385–88.

16 Anthony Easthope, 'Reading the Poetry of Sylvia Plath', *English*, vol. 43, no. 177, Autumn 1994, [pp.223–35], p.229.

17 Moi, *Sexual/Textual Politics*, ibid., p.8; Easthope, ibid., pp.231–35; for a further reply to Rose see H.C. Phelps, 'Sylvia Plath's "Polack Friend": The Ambiguous Geography, History, and Ethnic Hierarchies of 'Daddy'', *Notes on Contemporary Literature*, vol. 26, no. 1,

1996, pp.7–8.

18 Rose, ibid., p.xiv.

19 Wagner-Martin, *Sylvia Plath: A Biography*, ibid., p.183.

20 Ronald Hayman, *The Death and Life of Sylvia Plath* (London: Heinemann, 1991), p.121.

21 Although perhaps the speaking subject can only ever be a virtual image in this text?

22 Ted Hughes, 'Egg Head', in *Selected Poems 1957–1981* (London: Faber and Faber, 1982), pp.23–24.

23 Virginia Woolf, *A Room of One's Own* (London: Grafton, 1977), p.95.

24 Benveniste, *Problems in General Linguistics*, trans. Mary Elizabeth Meek (Miami: University of Miami Press, 1971), p.227.

25 Martin Amis, *Time's Arrow* (London: QPD, 1992,) p.134.

26 Anna Tripp, 'Saying "I": Sylvia Plath as Tragic Author or Feminist Text', *Women: A Cultural Review*, vol. 5, no. 3, 1994, [pp.253–63], pp.254–60.

27 Marjorie Stone and Judith Thompson, eds, *Literary Couples*, forthcoming.

28 Sarah Churchwell, 'Ted Hughes and the Corpus of Sylvia Plath' in *Criticism*, Winter 1998, vol. XL, no. 1, [pp.99–132], p.104.

29 Malcolm, *The Silent Woman*, ibid., pp.128, 125.

30 Churchwell, ibid., p.100.

31 Later, in his introduction to Plath's *Journals*, Hughes makes this equation in an even more astonishing manner: 'In that first month [of 1961] her collection of poems, *The Colossus*, was taken for publication in England by Heinemann. With that out of the way, in April she produced a daughter' (Hughes, 'Sylvia Plath and Her Journals', p.160).

32 Certainly many of Plath's late poems focus on pregnancy, childbirth, and maternity. The point here is the reductiveness of Hughes's reading, as if tacitly to abnegate the equally unbalanced readings of Plath as vengeful 'bitch-goddess'.

33 Alvarez, 'Sylvia Plath' in Newman,

The Art of Sylvia Plath, ibid., p. 58, his emphasis; Helen Vendler, 'An Intractable Metal', in Alexander, *Ariel Ascending,* ibid., p. 5.

34 In 'The Art of Poetry', Hughes disingenuously addresses the question as follows: 'I don't know whether our verse exchanged much, if we influenced each other that way – not in the early days. Maybe others see that differently' in *The Poetry Review,* 134, Spring 1995, p. 77. Compare this to his statements thirty years earlier on the composition of 'Flute Notes From a Reedy Pond': 'At this time she was concentratedly trying to break down the tyranny, the fixed focus and public persona which descriptive or discursive poems take as a norm. *We* devised exercises of meditation and invocation.' (Ted Hughes, 'Notes on the Chronological Order of Sylvia Plath's Poems' in Newman, ibid., p. 191; emphasis added).

35 Hughes, 'Notes on the Chronological Order', ibid., pp. 187–93.

36 See, for instance, Alvarez: '"Edge" . . . is specifically about the act she was about to perform', 'Prologue: Sylvia Plath' in *The Savage God,* ibid., p. 51.

37 Churchwell, ibid., pp. 111–14.

38 Josette Feral, 'Writing and Displacement: Women in Theatre', trans. Barbara Kerslake, *Modern Drama,* 27, 1987, pp. 549, 550.

39 The numerous thematic, narrative, and structural similarities that mark Plath's poems and *Dedans* are not to be found in a recent Cixous novel which also deals with the death of the father, *Jours de l'an.* Hélène Cixous, *Dedans* (Paris: Grasset, 1969); Hélène Cixous, *Jours de l'an* (Paris: des femmes, 1990).

40 Robert Graves, *The Greek Myths,* vol. 2 (Harmondsworth: Penguin, 1960), pp. 62–64; Hélène Cixous and Catherine Clement, *La jeune née* (Paris: Union Générale D-Editions, Collection 10/18, 1975), pp. 186–208.

41 Marilyn Manners, 'The Doxies of Daughterhood: Plath, Cixous, and The Father', *Comparative Literature,* 48:2, Spring 1996, [pp. 150–71], pp. 150, 151, 152–53, 165.

42 Marjorie Perloff, 'Sylvia Plath's "Sivvy Poems": A Portrait of the Poet as Daughter' in Lane, *Sylvia Plath: New Views on the Poetry,* ibid., [pp. 155–78]; Marjorie Perloff, 'Angst and Animism in the Poetry of Sylvia Plath' (1970), collected in Wagner, *Critical Essays on Sylvia Plath,* ibid., pp. 109–24.

43 Tracy Brain, '"Or shall I bring you the sounds of poisons?": *Silent Spring* and Sylvia Plath' in *Writing the Environment: Ecocriticism and Literature* (London and New York: Zed Books, 1998), [pp. 146–64], p. 161.

44 Gino J. Marco et al., eds, *Silent Spring Revisited* (Washington, DC: *American Chemical Society,* 1987), p. xv.

45 Rosi Braidotti et al., eds, *Women, the Environment and Sustainable Development: Towards a Theoretical Synthesis* (London and New Jersey: Zed Books, 1994), p. 173.

46 Because of this likelihood, throughout this chapter any quotation from *Silent Spring* will be from *The New Yorker* version.

47 After Plath's move to England, her mother sent copies on a weekly basis.

48 See Plath, *Letters Home,* p. 92; and *Journals,* p. 55.

49 David Holbrook, *Sylvia Plath: Poetry and Existence* (London: Athlone Press, 1976), p. 121.

50 Plath uses the 'silent spring' image again one month later, in 'Apprehensions' (*CP,* pp. 195–96).

51 *The New Yorker,* 16 June 1962, p. 35.

52 *Letters Home,* p. 438.

53 Ibid., pp. 146–50.

54 Ibid., pp. 159–60.

55 Tracy Brain, '"Your Puddle-jumping daughter": Sylvia Plath's Midatlanticism', *English,* 47:187, Spring 1988, [pp. 17–39], p. 23.

56 Elizabeth Hardwick has also taken note of Plath's speaking voice, though she regards its sound as primarily English: 'these bitter poems were "beautifully" read, projected in full-throated, plump, diction-perfect, Englishy, mes-

merizing cadences . . . Poor recessive Massachusetts had been erased'; 'On Sylvia Plath', in Alexander, *Ariel Ascending*, ibid., [pp. 100–115], p. 115.

57 Orr, *The Poet Speaks*, ibid., p. 168.

58 Brain argues that Jeni Couzyn appropriates Plath as English, while Anne Stevenson's unsympathetic portrayal convicts her of being American; Jeni Couzyn, ed., *The Bloodaxe Book of Contemporary Women Poets: Eleven British Writers* (Newcastle upon Tyne: Bloodaxe, 1985); Stevenson, *Bitter Fame*, ibid.

59 Homi K. Bhabha, 'Postcolonial Authority and Postmodern Guilt' in Lawrence Grossberg et al., eds, *Cultural Studies* (New York: Routledge, 1992), [pp. 56–68], p. 59.

60 Brain, ibid., pp. 17–19, 22.

61 Brain, ibid., pp. 24, 32.

62 Alicia Ostriker, 'The Americanization of Sylvia' in Wagner, *Critical Essays on Sylvia Plath*, ibid., pp. 99, 100, 103.

63 Julia Kristeva, *Powers of Horror: an Essay on Abjection* (1980) (New York: Columbia University Press, 1982), pp. 5, 1.

64 Ibid., p. 235–36.

65 Ibid., p. 4.

66 Ibid., p. 71.

67 Van Dyne, *Revising Life*, ibid., p. 148.

68 Brain, ibid., pp. 33–35.

BIBLIOGRAPHY

Sylvia Plath, *Ariel* (London: Faber and Faber, 1965).

Sylvia Plath, *The Bell Jar*, 1963 (London: Faber and Faber, 1966).

Sylvia Plath, *Collected Poems* (London: Faber and Faber, 1981).

Sylvia Plath, *The Colossus and Other Poems* (London: Heinemann, 1960).

Sylvia Plath, *Crossing the Water* (London: Faber and Faber, 1971).

Sylvia Plath, *Johnny Panic and the Bible of Dreams and other prose writings*, ed. Ted Hughes (London: Faber and Faber, 1977, rev. ed., 1979).

Sylvia Plath, *The Journals of Sylvia Plath*, ed. Ted Hughes and Frances McCullough (New York: Random House (Ballantine), 1982; 1987).

Sylvia Plath, *Letters Home: Correspondence 1950–1963*, ed. Aurelia Schober Plath (London: Faber and Faber, 1975).

Sylvia Plath, *Winter Trees* (London: Faber and Faber, 1971).

Secondary sources

Eileen M. Aird, *Sylvia Plath: The Woman and Her Work* (Edinburgh: Oliver Boyd, 1973).

Paul Alexander, ed., *Ariel Ascending* (New York: Harper & Row, 1985).

A. Alvarez, 'Sylvia Plath' in *Beyond all this Fiddle: Essays 1955–1967* (London: Allen Lane; Penguin, 1968).

A. Alvarez, *The Savage God: A Study of Suicide* (London: Weidenfeld & Nicholson, 1971).

Linda Anderson, *Women and Autobiography in the 20th Century: Remembered Futures* (London: Prentice Hall, 1977).

Pamela J. Annas, *A Disturbance in Mirrors: The Poetry of Sylvia Plath* (New York: Greenwood Press, 1988).

Steven Gould Axelrod, *Sylvia Plath: The Wound and the Cure of Words* (Baltimore: Johns Hopkins University Press, 1990).

Susan Bassnett, *Sylvia Plath* (London: Macmillan, 1987).

Paula Bennett, *My Life a Loaded Gun: Dickinson, Plath, Rich and Female Creativity* (Urbana: University of Illinois Press, 1986).

Harold Bloom, ed., *Modern Critical Views: Sylvia Plath* (New York: Chelsea House Publishers, 1989).

Tracy Brain, '"Or shall I bring you the sounds of poisons?": *Silent Spring* and Sylvia Plath' in *Writing the Environment: Ecocriticism and Literature* (London and New York: Zed Books, 1998), pp. 146–64.

Tracy Brain, '"Your Puddle-jumping daughter": Sylvia Plath's Midatlanticism', *English*, 47:187, Spring 1988, pp. 17–39.

Wini Breines, *Young, White and Miserable: Growing Up Female in the Fifties* (Boston: Beacon, 1992).

Mary Lynn Broe, *Protean Poetic: The Poetry of Sylvia Plath* (Columbia: University of Missouri, 1980).

Lynda K. Bundtzen, *Plath's Incarnations: Women and the Creative Process*

(Ann Arbor: University of Michigan Press, 1983).

Edward Butscher, *Sylvia Plath: Method and Madness* (New York: Seabury Press, 1976).

Edward Butscher, *Sylvia Plath: The Woman and the Work* (New York: Dodd, Mead and Company, 1977).

Sarah Churchwell, 'Ted Hughes and the Corpus of Sylvia Plath' in *Criticism*, vol. XL, no. 1, Winter 1998, pp. 99–132.

Anthony Easthope, 'Reading the Poetry of Sylvia Plath', *English*, vol. 43, no. 177, Autumn 1994, pp. 223–35.

Benita Eisler, *Private Lives: Men and Women of the Fifties* (New York: Franklin, 1986).

Mary Ellman, *Thinking About Women* (London: Macmillan, 1968).

Sandra M. Gilbert and Susan Gubar, *The Madwoman in the Attic: The Woman Writer and the Nineteenth-Century Literary Imagination* (New Haven and London: Yale University Press, 1979).

Sandra M. Gilbert and Susan Gubar, *No Man's Land, Volume 3, Letters From The Front* (New Haven and London: Yale University Press, 1994).

Sandra M. Gilbert and Susan Gubar, eds, *Shakespeare's Sisters: Feminist Essays on Women Poets* (Bloomington: Indiana University Press, 1979).

Barbara Hardy, 'The Poetry of Sylvia Plath' in Sue Roe, ed., *Women Reading Women's Writing* (Brighton: Harvester Press, 1987), pp. 209–26.

Barbara Hardy, 'The Poetry of Sylvia Plath: Enlargement or Derangement' in Martin Dodsworth, ed., *The Survival of Poetry: A Contemporary Survey* (London: Faber and Faber, 1970), pp. 164–87.

Natalie Harris, 'New Life in American Poetry: The Child as Mother of the Poet', *The Centennial Review*, 31:3, 1987, pp. 240–54.

Seamus Heaney, 'The Indefatigable Hoof-Taps', *Times Literary Supplement*, 5–11 February 1988, pp. 134, 143–44.

David Holbrook, *Sylvia Plath: Poetry and Existence* (London: Athlone Press, 1976).

Suzanne Juhasz, *Naked and Fiery Forms: Modern American Poetry by Women – A New Tradition* (New York: Harper and Row, 1976).

Cora Kaplan, *Salt and Bitter and Good: Three Centuries of English and American Women Poets* (New York and London: Paddington Press, 1975).

Judith Kroll, *Chapters in a Mythology: The Poetry of Sylvia Plath* (New York: Harper & Row, 1976).

Gary Lane, ed., *Sylvia Plath: New Views on the Poetry* (Baltimore: Johns Hopkins University Press, 1979).

Kathleen Margaret Lant, 'The Big Strip Tease: Female Bodies and Male Power in the Poetry of Sylvia Plath', *Contemporary Literature*, 1993, 34:4, pp. 620–69.

Gary M. Leonard, '"The Woman is Perfected. Her Dead Body Wears the Smile of Accomplishment": Sylvia Plath and *Mademoiselle* Magazine', *College Literature*, 1992, 2, pp. 60–82.

Robert Lowell, Foreword to *Ariel* (New York: Harper & Row, 1966).

Janet Malcolm, *The Silent Woman: Sylvia Plath and Ted Hughes* (New York:

Knopf, 1993; London: Picador, 1994).

Marilyn Manners, 'The Doxies of Daughterhood: Plath, Cixous, and The Father', *Comparative Literature*, 48:2, Spring 1996, pp.150–71.

Janice Markey, *A Journey into the Red Eye, The Poetry of Sylvia Plath – a critique* (London: The Women's Press, 1993).

Ingrid Melander, *The Poetry of Sylvia Plath: A Study of Themes* (Stockholm: Almquist & Wiksell, 1972).

Ellen Moers, *Literary Women* (New York: Doubleday, 1976).

Charles Newman, ed., *The Art of Sylvia Plath* (London: Faber, 1970).

Tillie Olsen, *Silences* (1978). (London: Virago, 1980).

Peter Orr, ed. *The Poet Speaks* (London: Routledge, Kegan & Paul, 1966).

Alicia Suskin Ostriker, *Stealing the Language: The Emergence of Women's Poetry in America* (Boston: Beacon Press, 1986; London: The Women's Press, 1987).

Marjorie Perloff, 'Icon of the Fifties', *Parnassus*, Spring/Winter 1985, 12–13: 1–2, pp.282–85.

Adrienne Rich, *Of Woman Born: Motherhood as Experience and Institution* (London: Virago, 1977).

Jacqueline Rose, *The Haunting of Sylvia Plath* (London: Virago, 1991).

Jon Rosenblatt, *Sylvia Plath: The Poetry of Initiation* (Chapel Hill: The University of North Carolina Press, 1979).

M. L. Rosenthal, 'Other Confessional Poets: Sylvia Plath' in *The New Poets: American and British Poetry Since World War II* (London and New York: Oxford University Press, 1967).

Toni Saldivar, *Sylvia Plath: Confessing the Fictive Self* (New York: Peter Lang, 1992).

Ellin Sarot, '"Becoming More and More Historical": Sylvia Plath's "The Swarm"', *Concerning Poetry*, 20, 1987, pp.41–56.

Elaine Showalter, *The Female Malady: Women, Madness and English Culture, 1830–1980* (London: Virago 1987, repr. 1993).

Elaine Showalter, *A Literature of Their Own: British Women Novelists From Brontë to Lessing* (Princeton University Press, 1977; London: Virago, 1978).

Alan Sinfield, *Literature, Politics and Culture in Postwar Britain* (Oxford: Blackwell, 1989).

Stan Smith, *Inviolable Voice: History and Twentieth-Century Poetry* (Dublin: Gill and Macmillan, 1982).

George Steiner, 'Dying is an Art' (1965), collected in *Language and Silence* (London: Faber and Faber, 1967), pp.327–29.

Nancy Hunter Steiner, *A Closer Look at Ariel: a memory of Sylvia Plath* (London: Faber and Faber, 1974).

Al Strangeways, '"The Boot in the Face": The Problem of the Holocaust in the Poetry of Sylvia Plath', *Contemporary Literature*, 37:3, Fall 1996, pp.370–90.

Anna Tripp, 'Saying "I": Sylvia Plath as Tragic Author or Feminist Text', *Women: A Cultural Review*, vol. 5, no. 3, 1994, pp.253–63.

Margaret Dickie Uroff, *Sylvia Plath and Ted Hughes* (Urbana and Chicago:

University of Illinois Press, 1979).

Susan Van Dyne, *Revising Life: Sylvia Plath's Ariel Poems* (Chapel Hill and London: University of North Carolina Press, 1993).

Helen Vendler, *Part of Nature, Part of Us: Modern American Poets* (Cambridge, Mass.: Harvard University Press, 1980).

Helen Vendler, *The Music of What Happens: Poems, Poets and Critics* (Cambridge, Mass.: Harvard University Press, 1988).

Linda W. Wagner, 'Plath's *Ladies' Home Journal* Syndrome', *Journal of American Culture*, Spring/Summer 1984, pp.32–38.

Linda W. Wagner, ed., *Sylvia Plath: The Critical Heritage* (London: Routledge, 1988).

Linda W. Wagner, ed., *Critical Essays on Sylvia Plath* (Boston: Hall & Company, 1984).

Liz Yorke, *Impertinent Voices: Subversive Strategies in Contemporary Women's Poetry* (London: Routledge, 1991).

James E. Young, *Writing and Rewriting the Holocaust: Narrative and the Consequences of Interpretation* (Bloomington: Indiana University Press, 1988).

SUGGESTED FURTHER READING

Paul Alexander, *Rough Magic: A Biography of Sylvia Plath* (New York: Viking Penguin, 1991).

Calvin Bedient, 'Oh Plath!', *Parnassus*, 12–13: 1–2, pp. 275–81.

Mutlu Konuk Blasing, 'Sylvia Plath's Black Car of Lethe' in *American Poetry: The Rhetoric of its Forms* (New Haven: Yale University Press, 1987), pp. 50–63.

Susan Bohandy, 'Defining the Self Through the Body in Four Poems by Katerina Anghelaki-Rooke and Sylvia Plath', *Journal of Modern Greek Studies*, vol. 12, no. 1, May 1994, pp. 1–36.

Elizabeth Bronfen, *Sylvia Plath* (Plymouth: Northcote House Publishers, 1998).

Heather Cam, '"Daddy": Sylvia Plath's Debt to Anne Sexton', *American Literature*, October 1987, 59:3, pp. 429–32.

Jeni Couzyn, ed., *The Bloodaxe Book of Contemporary Women Poets: Eleven British Writers* (Newcastle upon Tyne: Bloodaxe, 1985).

Charlotte Croft, '"The Peanut-Crunching Crowd" in the Work of Sylvia Plath: Holocaust as Spectacle', Manuscript: *Graduate Journal in English*, 1:1, Autumn 1995, pp. 49–61.

Mary Daly, *Gyn/Ecology* (Boston: Beacon Press, 1978; London: Women's Press, 1979).

Ekbert Faas, 'Chapters in a Shared Mythology: Sylvia Plath and Ted Hughes' in Keith Sagar, ed., *The Achievement of Ted Hughes* (Manchester: Manchester University Press, 1983).

Sandra M. Gilbert, 'My Name is Darkness' in Donald Hall, ed., *Claims for Poetry* (Ann Arbor: University of Michigan Press, 1983).

Sandra M. Gilbert and Susan Gubar, *No Man's Land, Volume 1, War of the Words* (New Haven and London: Yale University Press, 1988).

Richard Gray, *American Poetry of the Twentieth Century* (New York and London: Longman, 1990).

Sally Greene, 'A Flare of Resistance in Sylvia Plath's "Nick and the Candlestick"', *Notes on Contemporary Literature*, 24:1, January 1994, pp. 4–6.

Caroline King Barnard Hall, *Sylvia Plath*, revised edn (New York: Twayne Publishers; London: Prentice Hall, 1998).

Barbara Hardy, 'The Poetry of Sylvia Plath' in Sue Roe, ed., *Women Reading Women's Writing* (Brighton: Harvester Press, 1987).

Ronald Hayman, *The Death and Life of Sylvia Plath* (London: William Heinemann, 1991).

Philip Hobsbaum, 'The Temptation of Giant Despair', *Hudson Review* 25, Winter 1972–1973, pp. 597–612.

David Holbrook, 'The 200-inch Distorting Mirror', *New Society* 12 (11 July 1968), pp. 57–58.

David Holbrook, 'R.D. Laing and the Death Circuit', *Encounter* 31 (August

1968), pp. 35–45.

Eric Homberger, *A Chronological Checklist of the Periodical Publications of Sylvia Plath* (Exeter: University of Exeter Press, 1970).

Dee Horne, 'Biography in Disguise: Sylvia Plath's Journals', *Wascana Review*, 1992, 27:1, pp. 90–104.

Anthony Julius, 'New Lost Land', *Poetry Review*, vol. 88, no. 1, Spring 1998, pp. 80–82.

Anthony Libby, 'God's Lioness and the Priest of Sycorax: Plath and Hughes', *Contemporary Review* 15, Summer 1974, pp. 386–405.

Brita Lindberg-Seyersted, '"Bad" Language Can Be Good: Slang and Other Expressions of Extreme Informality in Sylvia Plath's Poetry', *English Studies*, 78:1, 1997, pp. 19–31.

Sherry Lutz Zivley, 'Ted Hughes's Apologia Pro Matrimonio Suo', *The New England Quarterly*, 55:2, June 1982, pp. 187–200.

Pat MacPherson, *Reflecting on The Bell Jar* (London: Routledge, 1991).

Robyn Marsack, *Sylvia Plath* (Buckingham: Open University Press, 1992).

Patricia Meyer Sparks, *The Female Imagination: A Literary and Psychological Investigation of Women's Writing* (London: Allen and Unwin, 1976).

Sheryl L. Meyering, *Sylvia Plath: A Reference Guide 1973–88* (Boston: G. K. Hall, 1990).

Douglas Miller and Marion Novak, *The Way We Really Were* (New York: Doubleday, 1977).

Toril Moi, *Sexual/Textual Politics: Feminist Literary Theory* (London: Methuen, 1985).

Toril Moi, ed., *French Feminist Thought: A Reader* (Oxford: Blackwell, 1987).

Deborah Nelson, 'Penetrating Privacy: Confessional Poetry and the Surveillance Society' in *Homemaking: Women Writers and the Politics and Poetics of Home* (New York: Garland, 1996).

Arthur Oberg, *Modern American Lyric: Lowell, Berryman, Creely, and Plath* (New Brunswick: Rutgers University Press, 1978).

Marjorie Perloff, 'The Two Ariels: The Re(making) of the Sylvia Plath Canon', *American Poetry Review* 13, no. 6, November/December 1984, pp. 10–18.

H. C. Phelps, 'Sylvia Plath's "Polack Friend": The Ambiguous Geography, History, and Ethnic Hierarchies of "Daddy"', *Notes on Contemporary Literature*, vol. 26, no. 1, 1996, pp. 7–8.

M. L. Rosenthal and Sally M. Gall, 'The Confessional Mode: Lowell and Others' in *The Modern Poetic Sequence: The Genius of Modern Poetry* (New York: Oxford University Press, 1983).

Leonard M. Scigaj, 'The Painterly Plath That Nobody Knows', *The Centennial Review* 32:3, 1988, pp. 220–49.

Elaine Showalter, *The New Feminist Criticism: Essays on Women, Theory and Literature* (London: Virago, 1986).

Elaine Showalter, 'Towards a Feminist Poetics' in Mary Jacobus, ed., *Women's Writing and Writing About Women* (London: Croom Helm, 1979), pp. 22–41.

Louis Simpson, *Studies of Dylan Thomas, Allen Ginsberg, Sylvia Plath and Robert Lowell* (New York: Macmillan, 1978).

Pamela Smith, 'The Unitive Urge in the Poetry of Sylvia Plath', *New England Quarterly* 45, September 1972, pp. 323–39.

Al Strangeways, *Sylvia Plath: The Shaping of Shadows* (Madison and London: Fairleigh Dickinson University Press, 1998).

Stephen Tabor, *Sylvia Plath: An Analytical Bibliography* (London: Mansell, 1987).

Tony Tanner, *City of Words: American Fiction 1950–1970* (London: Jonathan Cape, 1971).

Catherine Thompson, '"Dawn Poems in Blood": Sylvia Plath and PMS', *Triquarterly* 80, 1990–1991, pp. 221–49.

Margaret Dickie Uroff, 'Sylvia Plath on Motherhood', *Midwest Quarterly*, 15, October 1973, pp. 70–90.

Linda Wagner-Martin, *The Bell Jar: A Novel of the Fifties* (New York and Oxford: Maxwell, Macmillan International, 1992).

Linda W. Wagner-Martin, *Sylvia Plath: A Biography* (London: Chatto & Windus, 1988).

David John Wood, *A Critical Study of the Birth Imagery of Sylvia Plath* (New York: Edwin Mellen Press, 1992).

ACKNOWLEDGEMENTS

The editor and publisher wish to thank the following for their permission to reprint copyright material: Faber and Faber (for material from *Letters Home, Johnny Panic and the Bible of Dreams and other prose writings* and *Language and Silence*); Routledge (for material from *Sylvia Plath: The Critical Heritage*); Penguin (for material from *Beyond all this Fiddle: Essays 1955–1967*); *Criticism* (for material from 'Ted Hughes and the Corpus of Sylvia Plath'); Hall & Co. (for material from *Critical Essays on Sylvia Plath*); Harper & Row (for material from *Chapters in a Mythology: The Poetry of Sylvia Plath*); The University of North Carolina Press (for material from *Sylvia Plath: The Poetry of Initiation* and *Revising Life: Sylvia Plath's Ariel Poems*); University of Illinois Press (for material from *Sylvia Plath and Ted Hughes*); Johns Hopkins University Press (for material from *Sylvia Plath: New Views on the Poetry* and *Sylvia Plath: The Wound and the Cure of Words*); Dodd, Mead & Co. (for material from *Sylvia Plath: The Woman and the Work*); Indiana University Press (for material from *Shakespeare's Sisters: Feminist Essays on Women Poets* and *Writing and Rewriting the Holocaust: Narrative and the Consequences of Interpretation*); Gill & Macmillan (for material from *Inviolable Voice: History and Twentieth-Century Poetry*); Greenwood Press (for material from *A Disturbance in Mirrors: The Poetry of Sylvia Plath*); Blackwell (for material from *Literature, Politics and Culture in Postwar Britain*); Yale University Press (for material from *No Man's Land, Volume 3, Letters From the Front*); Beacon Press and The Women's Press (for material from *Stealing the Language: The Emergence of Women's Poetry in America*); Routledge (for material from *Impertinent Voices: Subversive Strategies in Contemporary Women's Poetry*); *Contemporary Literature* (for material from 'The Big Strip Tease: Female Bodies and Male Power in the Poetry of Sylvia Plath' and '"The Boot in the Face": The Problem of the Holocaust in the Poetry of Sylvia Plath'); Peter Lang (for material from *Sylvia Plath: Confessing the Fictive Self*); Virago (for material from *The Haunting of Sylvia Plath*); *English* (for material from 'Reading the Poetry of Sylvia Plath' and '"Your Puddle-jumping daughter"': Sylvia Plath's Mid-atlanticism'); *Women: A Cultural Review* (for material from 'Saying "I": Sylvia Plath as Tragic Author or Feminist Text'); *Comparative Literature* (for material from 'The Doxies of Daughterhood: Plath, Cixous, and The Father'); Zed Books (for material from *Writing the Environment: Ecocriticism and Literature*).

There are instances where we have been unable to trace or contact copyright holders before our printing deadline. If notified, the publisher will be pleased to acknowledge the use of copyright material.

Claire Brennan lectures in English at the University of Dundee. A recent graduate of the University of Glasgow, she is currently preparing her thesis on Sylvia Plath for publication.

INDEX

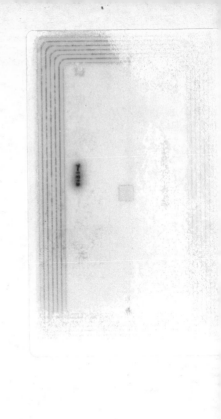